RETHINKING THE FUTURE

RETHINKING THE FUTURE

The Correspondence between Geoffrey Vickers and Adolph Lowe

Edited by
JEANNE VICKERS

With a Foreword by
Robert Heilbroner

Transaction Publishers
New Brunswick (U.S.A.) and London (U.K.)

H
59
V43
A4
1991

Library of Congress Catalog Number: 90-22226
ISBN: 0-88738-412-9
Printed in the United States of America

Library of Congress Cataloging-in-Publication Data

Rethinking the future: the Correspondence between Geoffrey Vickers and Adolph Lowe/edited by Jeanne Vickers; and with a foreword by Robert Heilbroner.
       p.   cm.
    Includes bibliographical references (p.   ) and index.
    ISBN: 0-88738-412-9 (C)
    1. Vickers, Geoffrey, Sir, 1894–   —Correspondence. 2. Lowe, Adolf, 1983–   —Correspondence. 3. Social scientists—Correspondence. I. Vickers, Jeanne.
H59.V43A4   1991   90–22226
300-dc20   CIP

Contents

Foreword

In the fall of 1946, newly out of the Army, not yet clear as to what I wished to do but impelled by a vague wish to continue my undergraduate education in economics, I signed up at the New School for Social Research in New York for a course on Keynesian and post-Keynesian economics. It was taught by Prof. A. Lowe, of whom I had never heard. On the first day of class, fifteen or twenty students, some like myself in their mid-twenties, others considerably older, looked with varying degrees of nervousness or composure on our instructor, who looked back at us with equal curiosity as he examined the registration cards that described our previous academic attainments. I remember, although it is probably a composite memory formed of many such first days, his mouth and eyebrows registering surprise, anticipation, or dismay as the cards gave him a foretaste of what he could expect.

The appointed hour having struck, he began to talk, and I was acutely conscious that my graduate education had commenced. In my earlier schooling at Harvard I had heard many famous lecturers, but never anyone like Adolph Lowe. He lectured with the vitality of an animated conversation, as if the thoughts had just struck him, but the conversation concealed—or rather, soon displayed—the structure of a powerfully constructed argument. The subject was the economy as Keynes perceived it—its structure, motivations, institutions, interconnections. We became as intently involved in this exercise of social deconstruction and reconstruction as the medical students in Rembrandt's 'Anatomy Lesson'.

From the same composite photograph I recall the atmosphere of a hundred such classes—Lowe's face expressing amazement one moment, disbelief the next; wicked conspiratorial smiles followed by innocent consternation; the suspense of cumulative argument punctuated by irritated snorts when a blackboard demonstration failed to come off. It was magic. Better, it was the very embodiment of teaching, for the virtuoso exposition, which evoked feelings of respect verging on awe, never prevented—indeed, seemed to encourage—the most timid student from raising a hand when there was something to be further explained, or a point to be made, or an objection lodged.

ix

Before I was done I had taken every course that Lowe offered, and had sat in on countless seminars. I began to realize, after a while, that I was seeing a mixture of teaching styles—a breadth of culture and learning that was very German, an English clarity of expression, and—already!—an American 'openness' to students. Perhaps most important, he was utterly engaged with whatever he was teaching, endowing it with life and with importance. It *mattered* how Ricardo or Smith or Marx or Keynes thought; it mattered how we thought about how they thought. He was the greatest and most inspiring teacher I have ever known, a judgment I have heard echoed many times.

From student I progressed by degrees to protégé. By the end of my second year, excited by his seminar on the economics of Ricardo, I determined to make the history of economic thought my own domain in economics, and in 1952 I wrote *The Worldly Philosophers*, my first venture into my chosen domain. Professor Lowe (I did not yet dare to call him by his first name) read every word of it, to my immense benefit. Soon thereafter I was asked to read drafts of his work—more to advise on matters of syntax than substance—and ten years after TWP we began a lengthy correspondence on the slowly emerging work that was to become the signature opus of his career.

On Economic Knowledge was published in 1965 and republished in 1977. Its theme has been repeated in other essays of Lowe, and lies beneath his 'magisterial' *The Path of Economic Growth* published some years later (the complimentary adjective comes from Professor E.J. Nell in the highly prestigious *Journal of Economic Literature*, June 1989). Lowe's seminal book occupies a unique place in the literature of economics. Its basic argument is that the tacit premise of conventional economic analysis is no longer tenable. That premise consists in the belief that the behavior of economic agents—workers, employers, consumers—is sufficiently subject to economic necessity to enable us to treat it as a constant, described by economists as 'short-run maximizing'. In ordinary terms, this means that behavior is constantly under such economic pressure, whether from need or competition, that it drives all economic actors at all times to take their immediate penny of advantage. On this assumption Marx as well as Smith erected their majestic models of capitalist development, while conventional economics builds its less ambitious predictions based on the 'laws' of supply and demand.

An immense admirer of the classical economists, Lowe's intention was not to controvert their analytical genius but to demonstrate that changes in the institutional setting of modern capitalism no longer allowed the behavior premise to be uncritically accepted. In modern capitalism, Lowe declared, the pressures that enforced short-run maximizing in the late 18th and early to mid-19th centuries were abating. Supported by modern entitlements, workers no longer found themselves compelled to maximize wages at every moment. Enjoying middle-class comforts, the average consumer was not driven to make price the overriding consideration. And the capitalist, forced by the sheer scale of modern technology to make long-term investment plans, similarly found his behavioral horizon much further extended than in earlier days.

Hence as the economic milieu changed, economics itself changed. The 'law-like' fixity of behavior eroded before the loosening of the constraints of the social environment. From this diagnosis, Lowe's conclusion follows with incontrovertible force. In a world where behavior cannot be reliably projected into the future, the course of the economy becomes increasingly beyond the reach of prediction. Thus, to remain an effective tool of social policy, economics must radically refashion its self-conception. It must surrender its vaunted claim to predictive ability founded on law-like behavior, and take on another role—to be the hand-maiden of social policy, using economic knowledge to bring about the kind of behavior required to reach the goals that citizens have chosen for themselves. Economics thus becomes, in Lowe's words, 'Political Economics', not economic 'science'; and the basis for its social usefulness changes from 'prediction' to 'instrumentalism'—that is, from detached observation that deduces the movement of the system, to an engaged effort to find incentives and constraints that will move the economy where we want to go.

This is the barest sketch of the message of *On Economic Knowledge*. It pays no heed to Lowe's earlier or later books, or to his increasing concern with the consequences of technology, particularly with respect to technological unemployment. But it will serve to illustrate the difference between Lowe's approach to economics and that of the profession, and allows me to add that it is hardly surprising that someone who has urged such a chastening diminution in the pretensions of his discipline should have met initially with little more than polite indifference from his fellow economists. Happily, there are now many signs that his importance is being recognized, the aforementioned review in the *Journal of Economic Literature* being a clear case in point.

*****

From protégé I became colleague. In 1963 I joined the Graduate Faculty of the New School, where I watched Lowe at work in his other natural calling—that of academic politician. The Faculty had been born as the University in Exile during the late 1930s and early 1940s, when Lowe was still at Manchester. Domesticated to American institutional procedures, the Faculty had lost none of the intensity one would expect from a small number of remarkable individuals who were quite aware of their remarkableness. It was a perfect setting for Adolph (by now I called him that), who watched in attentive silence as opinions clashed and tempers flared—for once, the mouth and eyebrows not registering their visible appraisals. Only at the end would the politician speak, summing up both sides in the best possible light, before putting forward his own view. Almost invariably that view prevailed. I presume that he learned these skills while working for the Weimar Government, or in his subsequent direction of the famous research center at Kiel. At any rate, he was a shrewd and effective influence in university affairs, a role he thoroughly enjoyed.

In the course of my apprenticeship we became friendly, then close friends. We talked by 'phone several times a week, and during summers corresponded endlessly, an exchange that still goes on—letters of praise and criticism mixed in with personal and school gossip, philosophical and technical problems with family news and occasional soul searching. Over forty years we have encouraged, prodded, cautioned, and on occasion scolded one another. We have read nearly every word the other has produced—passing it, as Adolph said in a letter written on my retirement from the Faculty in 1989, 'through the crucible of the other's judgment'.

The unknown Prof. A. Lowe of forty-odd years ago has bestowed on me the honor of being the dedicatee of his latest book, *Has Freedom a Future?* He was, of course, on the original dedication page of *The Worldly Philosophers*, and in its latest edition is in the text, where he belongs.

ROBERT HEILBRONER
New York, September 1990

Preface

When in 1947, aged 23 and soon to marry his son Burnell, I first met Sir Geoffrey Vickers, he scared me to death. He was thirty years older than I, a formidable figure, a man with an overwhelmingly powerful intellect to which I felt sure I could never measure up. But it did not take me long to realize that behind his natural reserve and dignified demeanor was a very modest, kind and warm human being.

He was a man of great charm and considerable wit, an indefatigable correspondent with an insatiable curiosity about one's thought processes and attitudes towards life and its vicissitudes. One felt that one's reactions were of great interest to him—they really mattered. It was perhaps this genuine desire for contact which so appealed to those much younger than he, making him a sort of intellectual guru to whom they could turn for enlightenment.

As the years went by we became close friends, and our conversations on international affairs were of considerable benefit to me in my development education work with the United Nations. He cared, not only about the world's problems but also about those with whom he exchanged ideas, thoughts and feelings. He was a man of great integrity and wisdom.

Sir Geoffrey's work on social roles, the place of authority and personal responsibility, and his concept of the 'appreciative system', were of considerable significance on both sides of the Atlantic during his lifetime, and continue to be influential since his death in 1982. Indeed, there is growing interest in his books and in the incredibly broad range of his contributions to learned journals, from articles in *The Lancet* and other medical publications to papers in journals of professional psychology or psychiatry, management, policy sciences, ecology, education, communication, as well as in systems-thinking—a rapidly growing, complex field in which he became a recognized expert.

Dr. C. West Churchman of the University of California, in his preface to *The Vickers Papers*, published posthumously in 1984, considered Sir Geoffrey to have been an important contributor to systems theory through his emphasis on the ethical implication of legal processes and on the 'appreciative system'. He was profoundly influenced by Sir Geoffrey's concept of responsibility and his emphasis on the fact that freedom implies not only the ability to make choices but also to assume the ethical responsibility of the choice one makes. For Dr. Churchman, this further implied that "most political leaders, educators, workers, even 'concerned citizens', are irresponsible. Perhaps the most tragic implication to people like Vickers and myself who are lovers of science is that most of today's so-called scientists are irresponsible."

Like Dr. Churchman, Sir Geoffrey often wondered whether the message was getting through to those to whom it was addressed and, if not, whether the way in which it was being communicated made it difficult to understand. Silvia B. Sutton, in the 'affectionate portrait' which prefaced *Human Systems are Different* (1983), quotes a humorous letter written by Geoffrey at the age of 84:

> I once said to someone that I felt like a very minor prophet who arose and said, 'The Lord gave me a most important message for you, but I couldn't quite hear what he said'. I have now almost abandoned hope of discovering what the message was. On the other hand, people keep on coming and talking and asking me to utter; and I still occasionally do. Some message must be getting out.

The message, it seems, was so much ahead of its time that it rang bells primarily with young people whose minds were more open to the broader, more complex horizons of a systemic future. Five years after his death his continuing impact upon later generations was evidenced by the publication of a selection of his papers by three young American university professors under the title *Policymaking, Communication and Social Learning* (1987).

The following quotation, from his *Freedom in a Rocking Boat* (1970), illustrates Sir Geoffrey's often wry approach to humankind's ability to see and evaluate its problems:

> Lobster pots are designed to catch lobsters. A man entering a man-sized lobster pot would become suspicious of the narrowing tunnel, he would shrink from the drop at the end; and if he fell in, he would recognize the entrance as a possible exit and climb out again—even if he were the shape of a lobster.

> A trap is a trap only for creatures which cannot solve the problems that it sets. Man-traps are dangerous only in relation to the limitations on what men can see and value and do. The nature of the trap is a function of the nature of the trapped. To describe either is to imply the other.

> I start with the trap, because it is more consciously familiar; we the trapped tend to take our own state of mind for granted—which is partly why we are trapped. With the shape of the trap in our minds, we shall be better able to see the relevance of our limitations and to question those assumptions about ourselves which are most inept to the activity and the experience of being human now.

"Wisdom is easier to recognize than to define", noted Dr. Kenneth E. Boulding in his foreword to what is perhaps Sir Geoffrey's best-known book, *The Art of Judgment: a Study of Policy Making*, when it was reprinted by Harper & Row in 1983. "One recognizes it in every chapter of this classic volume, which is just as wise today as when it was published in 1965. It comes from a rich and complex life experience coupled with the ability to generalize, plus the rarer ability to see all generalizations and descriptions as only shadows of the complex truth.

"Sir Geoffrey Vickers combined a very productive and varied experience in the 'real world' of legal, political and economic life with a wide knowledge of academic thought and writings about it ... (his) experience taught him that the real world is an endless dynamic flux, that all goals are transient, that equilibrium is a figment of the human imagination, even though a useful one, and that our images of facts and of evaluations are inextricably mixed and are formed mainly in an interactive learning process which he calls 'appreciation'... Certainly if the powerful figures of this world whose decisions may affect the lives of all of us could catch the lessons of this volume, our chances of survival could be much enhanced."

In his foreword to *Human Systems are Different* Sir Geoffrey called the book "an attempt to apply systems thinking to human history, to the extent needed to understand the present predicament of Britain in particular, and more generally of the industrial Western countries which share the cultural inheritance of the Enlightenment, a phase of history which I believe to be abruptly ending now. In what new form can its inherent nobility of aspiration be realized in an over-crowded world, filled with confident, cultural competitors? Has it a future? If so, what and at what cost? And if not, what?"

The shape of this future world was also a question of major importance to Dr. Adolph Lowe, whose *Has Freedom a Future?* was published in 1988. (Now 98, he remains intellectually active and a vital, involved, and thoroughly delightful human being.) His exposition of the 'New Economics' and of the problems of inflation, employment and distribution in this correspondence with Sir Geoffrey are both lucid and enlightening for those who, like myself, are neophytes in these subjects. The knowledge, experience and wisdom of the two men provide a solid background for thought on the part of those who are concerned about the future which awaits us as the twentieth century comes to an end.

I am particularly grateful to Dr. Lowe for providing his side of this correspondence. While originally conceived as a tribute to the memory of my father-in-law, this book is clearly also a tribute to Dr. Lowe, who was in a very real sense Sir Geoffrey's teacher and mentor while himself benefiting greatly from the latter's insights and capacity for in-depth analysis of public policies.

I am also very much indebted to Dr. Robert Heilbroner, probably the most famous of Dr. Lowe's erstwhile students at the New School for Social Research in New York, for providing a few reminiscences in the form of a Foreword to this volume. His relationship with Dr. Lowe remains a very close one, and there are few economists so capable of commenting upon the immediate relevance today of the economic theories advanced by Dr. Lowe during the course of his long and very active life.

Finally, I should like to thank Dr. Margaret Blunden, Dr. Margaret Vickers, and Sir Geoffrey's daughter, Pamela Miller, for their valuable advice and support. Much of the information contained in the Introduction with regard to Geoffrey's 'intellectual journey' has been gleaned from Dr. Blunden's percep-tive introduction to the Open University's *The Vickers Papers*; from S.B. Sutton's fine introductory chapter to Geoffrey's last book, *Human Systems are Different*; and from the Foreword to *Policymaking, Communication and Social Learning* and its Preface by editors Guy Adams, John Forester and Bayard Catron, who were responsible for much of the stimulus and pleasure Geoffrey found in the American academic world.

JEANNE VICKERS
Geneva, September 1990

AN INTRODUCTION TO
SIR GEOFFREY VICKERS AND
DR. ADOLPH LOWE

An Introduction to Sir Geoffrey Vickers and Dr. Adolph Lowe

The Correspondents

This is the story of a relationship between two remarkable men who achieved great distinction in their chosen fields and in their respective countries. It was a relationship which took shape mainly through a prolific correspondence and occasional visits to one side or the other of the Atlantic, and it lasted some 40 years. The letters in this volume illustrate the extraordinarily wide-ranging nature of the correspondence and its importance with regard to the still ongoing discussion of what it means to be human as the end of the 20th century draws near. They also provide a personal commentary on some of the major events of this century, and show how these events contributed to the development of the central ideas of the two men.

Geoffrey Vickers was born in Nottingham, England, in 1894, was awarded the Victoria Cross in World War I, became a lawyer with a prestigious London law firm, served the UK government in a number of capacities, and was knighted for his services to his country. Prolific author and writer of articles for a wide variety of publications, he became an authority on 'systems thinking' and on what he called the 'appreciative system'. His scholarly output after his formal retirement in March 1955, at the age of 61—some 87 papers, nine books, and an energetic lecturing schedule in two continents—exceeded that of most professional academics. The quality of the output was also highly distinctive. His concerns and his methodological approach, focused on high-level public issues in a broad context of time and space, cut right across prevailing academic and professional specializations. His writing commands attention not only in the established disciplines of government, politics, public administration, planning, ecology, management and epistemology, but in the newly emerging fields of futures research and systems thinking. He died in 1982 at the age of 87.

Adolph Lowe was born in Stuttgart in 1893, studied law but became a 'political economist' and philosopher, and achieved renown internationally as a teacher and guide. He had to leave Germany after the rise of the Nazis, and settled first in England and then in the United States. He is the author of a number

3

of seminal works on political economy, and on the subject of freedom. He now lives in Germany and, at age 98, remains intellectually active and in touch with both the people and the literature concerned with his subject.

Only a year apart in age, these two men grew up in the twenty years before World War I. It was a world, in Geoffrey's words, in which frontiers in Europe still required no passports and the golden sovereign was exchangeable at a fixed rate for any currency from Antwerp to Athens:

> Freedom and order, security and stability, progress and unity seemed to my young eyes to be operative standards, enjoyable realities, even natural assumptions. I grew to manhood in an England that took stability for granted, and regarded order— national and international—both as a self-regulating process of betterment called *progress* and also as a field for human design directed to the same end. These two not wholly consistent ideas applied in the political-social, financial-economic and scientific-technological fields; all regarded as benign partners.[1]

> In those days *belonging* was good, and all its related words resonated with approval—loyalty, commitment, responsibility. It was good socially because by it alone human institutions hung together. It was good in each personal context, not only because it guaranteed to each the social structure on which he depended, but also because it humanized and ennobled him as a person. Conflicts of loyalty could, of course, occur and could be agonizing. But their resolution was also ennobling, the primary task of creatures ethical by nature. Life was not less meaningful because it was also often tragic.

But it was a world undergoing rapid change. During the fifty years following the birth of these two men in 1893 and 1894, ten were spent in intensive warfare and the rest in a vain search for both national and international stability. All of Geoffrey's early assumptions were shaken, if not destroyed. "Stability could not be taken for granted, could not necessarily be assured by even the greatest conscious effort. Still, neither automatic regulation nor human design could be trusted to achieve 'betterment' by any of the diverse criteria that had emerged."[2]

What was it that brought these two men together in what was to be a lifelong friendship? They could not have had more different backgrounds, although Geoffrey's stable family background in England was to some extent matched by Adolph's in Germany, at least until World War I. Educated almost wholly in the humanities, "that is to say in the study of human experience", Geoffrey considered mathematics and logic important intellectual tools in the ordering of experience. "But the Word was paramount". He became a lawyer, an analyst and architect of legal relations. He was intensely interested in poetry, and was fully aware of the range of language between the never quite complete precision of legal expression and the richness of connotation accessible through poetic form.

Adolph was born into a liberal, middle-class German-Jewish family with a business background. His studies began in Munich, Berlin and Tubingen in the years just before World War I. His chosen field was the law, one of the few careers open to talents that happened to be Jewish, although even at that time it was practically impossible for a Jew to become a judge. At Munich, however, he studied under Lujo Brentano, the great economic historian, and changed his mind about his intended profession. Under the guise of being a law student he studied economics and philosophy, but passed his law finals in 1916 and became a doctor of law in 1918. He never took an exam in economics. He became first a bureaucrat and then an academic, and his experience of World War I was diametrically opposed to that of Geoffrey.

Going to war

In 1914, Geoffrey Vickers and Adolph Lowe were 20 and 21 years of age. Each was to find the war a turning point in his life. Geoffrey had spent a few months in Germany in 1913 in an interval between Oundle School and Oxford University, where he studied 'Greats'—classical languages and civilization. While at Oundle he joined the Officers' Training Corps but, like most of his contemporaries, remained unaware of the dangerous political developments in Europe. When Britain declared war against Germany on 4 August 1914 he immediately enlisted. In the spring of 1915 his battalion was involved in heavy fighting in France, and on his 21st birthday he was seriously wounded in a single-handed defence against enemy attack. For this he was awarded the Victoria Cross, England's most prestigious war medal.

During the twelve months which it took Geoffrey to recover from his wounds, his elder brother Burnell was killed at Ypres. In October 1916 he returned to France, and was awarded the French *Croix de Guerre* for further bravery. In 1918 he returned to Oxford and married Helen Newton, with whom he had first a daughter and then a son then, in 1926, became one of the four partners in the prestigious London law firm of Slaughter and May at the age of 32. In 1928 he was divorced, and married Ellen Tweed, with whom he had a son.

Like Geoffrey, Adolph responded to the war with enthusiasm—a response which he finds very difficult to understand in hindsight. He was reading law and looking forward to "a boring future"; the general feeling was: "Thank God, this is action—now anything is possible". Although he managed to get to Verdun, a military doctor there tested his heart and found him unfit for military service and he was sent home. Of his company, among the first to attack the French at Verdun, only three returned alive. Unwilling to accept the verdict, Adolph saw a heart specialist in Berlin, who told him that he suffered from pre-sclerosis of the heart muscle, and must not overstrain himself.

At the age of 45, Adolph's father had been told the same thing, and that he had only another five years to live. He died at the age of 97. Meanwhile, doctors have learned that certain heart murmurs are meaningless, but for Adolph it seemed that he owed his life to a diagnostic error. From 1918 to 1926 he found himself in government service, dealing first with demobilization, then with socialization, and finally in charge of reparations. During that period his work was almost entirely concerned with the harsh realities of German economic life, such as nationalization and the stabilization of the mark. He was still mainly an economic negotiator, dealing with labor unions, business groups and government officials at the national level and at international conferences, which he attended as a German delegate.

The rise of the Nazis

It was in 1924 that the Nazis achieved a sizeable party breakthrough. "They suddenly had 45 representatives in parliament, which terrified the government" says Adolph. "As a Jew, I was moved from the Ministry of Economics to the Central Office of Statistics—which I found truly boring—and in 1926 I left government to become Professor of Economic Theory and Sociology at the University of Kiel. At the same time I took on the directorship of the research activities of the Kiel Institute of World Economics, where my associates included Gerhard Colm, Hans Neisser, Jakob Marschak and Wassily Leontief, the first three of whom were again to be my associates at the New School a quarter century later."

In 1931 Adolph accepted an invitation from the Vice-Chancellor of Frankfurt University, who wished to make it the cultural academic center of Germany, to join Tillich, Mannheim, Wertheimer and others on the staff. He was an active member of the Social Democratic Party and, with Tillich and others, very active in domestic policy. "But Nazism was gaining ground and on 7 May 1933— Hitler having come to power 31 January 1933—I received notification that I must vacate my chair; not, it seemed, because I was a Jew but because I refused to guarantee that I would, at any time and without any regard, support the national government."

He received that notification in Switzerland. "On April 1, 1933, the first day of the boycott against the Jews, our children were sent home from school, Jewish shops were guarded by security men who prevented customers from entering, and the government's intentions became quite clear. Sensing that something was afoot, I went out to get the Saturday edition of the *Frankfurter Zeitung* on Friday evening at midnight, and read on page 5 that on Monday morning all Jews would have to deliver their passports."

At 7 am the next day, Saturday April 2 1933, Adolph, his wife Bea and their two daughters boarded the train to Zurich with two suitcases containing the things they felt were most important to save. "Counting upon German bureaucracy not to withdraw passports before the announced time on Monday, we passed easily through the frontier and found ourselves on safe territory (although, hearing the next day that the synagogue in Winterthur had been burned down, we wondered if that were true!) After trying unsuccessfully to find a job, first in

Switzerland and then in France, we went to England where I was appointed visiting lecturer at Manchester University."[3]

Law and politics

During these years Geoffrey, at Slaughter and May, was involved with the legal aspects of large financial operations, often with an international dimension. In 1930 he was among the first to take the new five-day commercial flight from Britain to India. He continued to accept current thinking on imperial questions although he was sensitive to the psychological costs to the Indians. He had, indeed, little political awareness until well into the Thirties.

Geoffrey's most demanding legal work during the 1930s involved negotiating the extension of the German debt, a task which took him to Berlin many times as part of an international team of bankers and lawyers. Because of runaway inflation in Germany, the future stability of Western and world economies depended in effect upon their collaboration with their German counterparts. (Although he remained in close contact with some of the German lawyers he met during these negotiations, he did not at that time meet Adolph.)

What Geoffrey later called "my extraordinary lack of political awareness until middle age" meant that the dimensions and international implications of the Nazi movement at that time totally escaped his attention. He became politically conscious only when Prime Minister Nevile Chamberlain returned from Munich in September 1938, having agreed to Hitler's demands for the cession of the Sudetenland to Germany.

Suddenly he perceived a threat—a national threat. What was at issue was a national decision about the legitimacy of force, about national unity and national purpose. Within a month of Munich he had started a political movement in the City of London which he called 'The Association for Service and Reconstruction'. Unconnected with any political party, it proclaimed a belief that Britain was in danger from without and within:

> The danger from without lies in the policies of those nations whose governments accept war as an instrument of policy and approve it as a stimulus to virility. The danger from within lies in the confusion both in our moral and in our material resources; in the sluggishness of our overburdened government; in our acceptance of fear as a dictator of policy; and in our smugness. The whole of our national life suffers from an incoherence of which the government's policy is necessarily an expression.

The Association received so much support that he did not know what to do with it; through it, however, he met the man who, apart from Adolph, was to have perhaps the greatest influence on his life, Dr. Joseph H. Oldham, Secretary of the International Missionary Council, and through him a number of distinguished men who met regularly in a discussion group which they called The Moot.

The Moot

The Moot had grown out of a Conference on Church, Community and State, an oecumenical meeting of all Protestant churches and the Russian Orthodox church in exile, held at Oxford in the summer of 1937. Its members, in addition to Joe Oldham, included Karl Mannheim, Reinhard Niebuhr, Paul Tillich, Middleton Murray, T.S. Eliot, Michael Polanyi, Sir Walter Moberly, Geoffrey Vickers and Adolph Lowe. All were to remain lifelong friends.

What did Adolph Lowe, an economist and a Jew, have to do with the oecumenical conference, and with what followed from it? "It was Paul Tillich, a close friend since the early post-war days in Germany, who established the connection. He was an American delegate to the Conference, assigned to the section that dealt with Christianity and the Economic Order, and had been asked to draft a summary statement of the proceedings to be included in the final report. Then at Manchester University, I received an urgent call from my old friend Tillich asking me to help draft the summary statement. (Tillich had once said that he would not really feel that he had fulfilled his life's mission if he did not succeed in baptizing me—a mission that remained unfulfilled.)"

What Tillich and Lowe produced was probably the most radical, though not Marxian, critique of late capitalism ever promulgated by an ecclesiastical body. The statement was supported by Dr. Oldham, the organizer and chairman of the conference, and strongly opposed by the American delegation as an unjustified attack on business; but time did not permit any alternative and they succeeded in incorporating it into the overall report.

When Dr. Oldham realized that the Conference had come up with tangible results of practical importance, covering not only economics but politics, education and international relations, he concluded that the work should be continued with a view to producing a concrete action program for the reform of the prevailing social order in Britain. For this purpose he called together experts from various fields to meet three or four times a year for intense discussion. On the recommendation of Tillich, and partly also as a response to Adolph's pamphlet *The Price of Liberty*, which had made a considerable stir and was greatly admired—especially by Geoffrey Vickers—Adolph was asked to join the group. "The fact that Mannheim and I were Jews was regarded as an asset by the other members of the group, and at no time did either of us feel that he did not 'belong'."

The ambiguity of freedom

Oldham himself was both the challenging and the balancing voice, enhancing the public influence of the group when, early in the war, he started publishing *The Christian Newsletter*. While the lasting effect of the Moot is difficult to evaluate, its deliberations certainly affected the views of one of the leading political theologians of the time, Dr. Temple, then Archbishop of York and later of Canterbury. And it provided Geoffrey with intellectual stimulus and opportunities for political debate. In the spring of 1939 he wrote a long open letter to *The Christian Newsletter* in which he condemned the "hateful gangster rule" of the Hitler regime in revolutionary Germany and its idolatrous worship of the state, but argued that there were other aspects of National Socialism which Britain and the Western world could well learn from, particularly the "state-socializing element" based on conceptions of social responsibility and common will. Fundamental concepts and traditional values needed rethinking, he felt:

> Freedom is ambiguous ... to some it means freedom from interference, to others 'opportunity'. The negative concept of freedom which expresses itself by 'let me alone' is characteristic of the comfortably situated. The others express their demand for freedom by 'give me a chance'. The comfortable take opportunity for granted, but their illusion only reflects their good fortune. Between these conceptions of freedom there is a great gulf.[4]

In Manchester, Adolph had been having a difficult time. Diametrically opposed to the ruling opinion on economic matters—the extreme free trade position maintained by the Manchester School—he moved to the philosophy department for two years. In *The Price of Liberty*, published in London in 1937, he had given his view as a German on contemporary Britain. He had been impressed by what appeared to be the state of general contentment of a population characterized by considerable inequality, and came to the conclusion that "England's social conformity is the spontaneous achievement of individuals. Neither a central political body nor a representative social group enforces its constant realization." It seemed to him that the thought and emotion of the average Englishman was ruled by a social code whose standards of fairness and common decency had become indisputable axioms for all classes. (Spontaneous conformity—'spon.con.'—and how to achieve it was to be one of the major topics of discussion between Adolph and Geoffrey during the years that followed.)

World War II

After World War II broke out, Geoffrey argued that the defence of 'freedom' was often a cloak for self-interest:

> The extreme aversion from allowing the central Government to use certain sorts of power has in the past been due not so much to a passion for freedom as to the natural and often unconscious desire of the ruling industrial class to keep the prerogative for themselves.[5]

It was an early indication that, himself the product of a privileged background, he was to be critical of many aspects of privilege and the 'liberal' political philosophies which protected it. By spring 1940 he had substantially broken with liberalism he had come to reject the 'free' market as a distributive mechanism, and supported a great measure of state control, seeing increasing state regulation as part of a continuing historical process.

At the age of 46 he re-enlisted in his old regiment as an infantry lieutenant, but was instead made a 'bogus Colonel' and sent on an Intelligence mission to South America. From 1941 to 1945 he was seconded to the Ministry of Economic Warfare as Deputy Director-General in charge of economic intelligence, and was also a member of the Joint Intelligence Committee of the Chiefs of Staff. As the war came to an end he was involved in meetings about Britain's role in peacetime Europe. There was, he recollected later in a letter to Adolph, "no doubt anywhere that the only unoccupied West European belligerent would have a leading part to play".

Wartime regulations prevented foreigners from engaging actively in the war effort, otherwise Adolph would probably have pursued his career in England. But, after seven years in Manchester his frustration was sufficiently great to induce him to accept an invitation from Alvin Johnson to join the Graduate Faculty of the New School for Social Research in New York, and he moved with his family to the United States in 1940. "Having missed one Atlantic crossing because of delayed passports, we took the next available boat and learned upon arrival that the vessel upon which we had originally been booked, the 'City of Benares', had been torpedoed and sunk with 200 English children and many others aboard." Once again they had had a narrow escape, and grieved for those who had not.

The post-war world

In 1947, although his law firm had treated him generously during the war, and fully expected him to remain with them until his retirement, Geoffrey left the private sector and joined the National Coal Board. His decision to undertake a much more onerous, and much less well-paid, job in what was a new, untried, controversial nationalized industry faced with a mammoth and daunting task was because he foresaw, quite rightly, that the public sector was bound to become much more important in the future, and that no-one yet knew how to make these public monopolies work. He wanted to help map out this important and uncharted territory.

In 1950 he voted Labour for the first time, but he had reservations about the welfare state:

I am not a socialist, in that I have a liberal's strong dislike of the state as an agent of positive social action. I suspect that in the set-up of the welfare state as now conceived there is a psychological flaw, not yet clearly seen, which will frustrate to some extent the dividend in human happiness and in human efficiency which its sponsors reasonably expect. Our fundamental liberties are no doubt in some danger, but it will be our fault if we cannot find a way to preserve them in the radically new and uncomfortable world into which we are moving.[6]

In 1951 he became Chairman of the Research Committee of the Mental Health Research Fund (of which he was a founder member), and from 1952-1957 served on Britain's Medical Research Council. He sat on many other public and professional bodies, including the London Passenger Transport Board and the Council of the Law Society, and was an honorary fellow of the Royal College of Psychiatrists. After retirement from the National Coal Board in 1955 he was invited to a Roundtable at the University of Toronto where he led three colloquia on values and decision-taking, lectured on control, stability and choice and gave a public lecture on the impact of industrialization on human wellbeing. For his audience of graduate social workers he adopted a broad, systemic approach:

> Thus we can sense, though we cannot yet explain or understand, a circular causal process, by which the goals of a society are set. They are continually under revision; factors which make for constancy are overcome by new demands, resulting from new experiences. This process cannot be explained without taking into account the verdict of the individual conscious mind. 'I like it', 'I hate it', 'I want it', 'I fear it'. These dynamic value judgments are both a product and a cause of the ceaseless process of goal-formulation.

Thus began his third and, in his view, most interesting career, for which his first as a lawyer, and his second in government service, had well prepared him. In 1959 the University of Toronto published a compilation of his Roundtable papers under the title *The Undirected Society*. Between then and 1980 he published eight books and a vast number of essays on a variety of subjects concerned with judgment, management, governance, liberty, responsibility and the role of institutions.[7] He lectured at institutes and summer schools and spent several periods as visiting lecturer at the Massachussetts Institute of Technology and the University of California at Berkeley. He made a great many visits to the United States, where his advice on planning was sought by both government and the academic world, and received at home a stream of students and others, of many nationalities, who wished to discuss his work.

Formulating the appreciative system

By the early 1960s Geoffrey's ideas were exciting interest in a number of North American scholars, many of whom were less locked into their disciplinary specializations than their British counterparts, more familiar with systems concepts, and more responsive to his focus on interpretation and values. It was this focus which led to his formulation of the concept of the 'appreciative system'. At a time when most literature on policy-making assumed that rational analysis of a problem should lead to agreements among the agents involved as to the appropriate course of action, Geoffrey's development of this concept was radical indeed. In his view personal, professional and cultural differences inevitably lead people to perceive situations differently, to notice and ignore different factors, to construct different meanings on the basis of what they have seen, and to place different values on the possible outcomes. These differences in the ways people appreciate situations mean that rational consensus on policy decisions is much more difficult than most writers at the time were prepared to admit.

In a contribution to an American publication on *The Urban Condition*[8], he succinctly outlines the concept of the appreciative system which had been evolving in his mind over the previous eight years:

> (We must ask) what causes an individual or a society to see and value and respond to its situation in ways which are characteristic and enduring, yet capable of growth and change? A rational ideology, a professional ethic, an individual personality, resides not in a particular set of images but in a set of *readinesses* to see and value and respond to its situation in particular ways. I call this an appreciative system.

> We know something of the ways in which these readinesses are built up. Even our eyes tell us nothing until we have learned to recognize and classify objects in particular ways; and there is little doubt that our conceptual classifications are built up in the same way. So, equally, are our values and our patterns of action. Our appreciative system grows and changes with every exercise of image formation, a process normally gradual and unconscious, and like all systems it is resistant to changes of a kind or at a rate which might endanger its coherence ... The last two hundred years have left us with an appreciative system peculiarly ill-suited to our needs.

He believed that psychology had done a disservice to the study of higher mental function by making goal-seeking the paradigm of rational behavior. "I do not accept the view that all norm-holding can be reduced to the pursuit of an endless succession of goals." And yet: "Where the norm can be taken as given, much important work has been done both by psychologists and by systems engineers in exploring the mechanisms of problem solving and learning. I, on the other hand, am concerned with ... the setting of norms to be followed, and hence of the problems to be solved."

In 1965 he published *The Art of Judgment*, the culmination of ten years of intellectual advance. William Robson, editor of *The Political Quarterly*, described it as subtle, original and profound, and called it "the most important contribution to administrative theory which has been made by a British thinker during the past twenty-five years." Yet, sixteen years later, Geoffrey was to say that "ever since I published *The Art of Judgment* in 1965 I have not read a practical book about administration which took seriously the primacy of human motivation, still less one which questioned the rational model of action which insisted that no action at human level was possible unless it was explicable as the pursuit of a purpose. The attack on rationality and purpose, or rather the effort to place these in relation to more subtle forms of human regulations, is a mammoth task."[9]

The revolutionary Sixties

Geoffrey felt increasingly alienated from the political and social world of the 1960s, with its rejection of responsibility and insistence on protest and individualism:

> There has never been a time in my lifetime when obedience, discipline and responsibility have been such dirty words. Paranoic alarm about individual rights has everyone screaming against being planned for or regulated in any way. Not only participation by everyone in everything, but almost a right of veto for everyone on anything, seem to be the standard pattern of expectation. Yet whatever else may be inherent in any solution of our governmental problem, the one thing certain, it seems to me, is that any workable solution will make much greater demands on everyone for mutual support and mutual trust.
>
> I have a theory that all this shrill screaming is not so much a protest against a new despotism as an unconscious protest against the absence of guidelines, standards of mutual expectation without which neither individual nor collective life is livable. If nothing else provides these standards, they will emerge from the disasters into which their absence will precipitate us.[10]

He predicted that, by 1984—then still nearly a quarter-century away—"the age-old stabilizers of pestilence and famine, if not also war, will be too manifest for anyone to ignore." The position required that prevailing conceptual frameworks should be rethought: "It invites us to accept a new model of our situation, a systemic model, self-limited in ways never before experienced and thus questions the validity of familiar experience as a guide to the future." It demanded a new scale of redistribution: "It threatens us ... with the need to make changes in our ways of distributing wealth and power which, though only vaguely foreseeable, are frightening and unwelcome, especially to the most favored beneficiaries of our present system."[11]

These were subjects which were exhaustively discussed over the years in the letters which form the bulk of this volume. Geoffrey's expectation of disaster was echoed by Adolph, who felt that it was only through a 'minor catastrophe' that people would learn that these changes had to be made, whereas Geoffrey considered it possible to teach people to avoid such disasters. Adolph's sober prediction was sadly borne out when the nuclear power station at Chernobyl erupted, its fallout polluting most of Europe, and thus brought humanity face to face with the catastrophic effects of pollution of all kinds about which thinkers and scientists had been warning for the past decade.

For Adolph too the years brought fame and, given the iconoclastic nature of his work, the inevitable controversy. His reputation, already well established in England with *The Price of Liberty*, which earned him praise as a perceptive sociological observer—as well as a more ambitious work, *Economics and Sociology*, which brought international recognition—grew rapidly in the United States during the '50s and '60s. He had already written a number of books in German, as well as a great many essays and articles, and so was well known as an economic theorist. His teaching at the New School for Social Research became legendary, and books such as *On Economic Knowledge*, published in 1965, broke new ground in economic thinking and in philosophy. His reputation was enhanced even further with the publication in 1976 of *The Path of Economic Growth.*[12]

The onset of ill-health

During the '60s and '70s, both families were dogged by ill-health. The condition of Adolph's wife Bea, who suffered from Parkinson's disease, a heart condition and diabetes, and of Geoffrey's wife Ellen, who was badly affected by a depressive condition, gave rise to considerable concern. Adolph became afflicted with angina pectoris, and Geoffrey began to suffer from a blood condition, myelo-fibrosis, which gradually weakened him and seems to have been accentuated by the great personal anguish caused by Ellen's death in 1972.

Although Adolph managed to continue to write in spite of these adverse conditions, Geoffrey's output was reduced by bouts of serious illness. He maintained his academic life, but after constant rejection of a manuscript first called 'Western Culture and Systems Thinking', then 'Autonomy and Responsibility', based upon a successful series of lectures at the University of Berkeley in California, he wrote to Adolph (14 January 1977) that "since I seem to be better at cooking than writing, I propose to do more of the first and less of the second".

He wrote of "the corrosive loneliness of Ellen's absence, which other presences and absences leave quite untouched, though a few of them comfort", and confided: "I have less vitality now, less mental nerve and spring, a doubt whether I have any more to say, a greater concern for personal relations and individual lives as against the socio-cultural background in which they grow, a sense of biological and psychological withdrawal from a scene in which I have almost finished playing a part of which I am not proud."[13]

Unable any longer to cope on his own, he moved in 1977 into a retirement home in his village of Goring-on-Thames, in Berkshire. He gave away most of his library and, alas, discarded quantities of personal and professional papers, but continued an intense correspondence with scholars and friends. Young people who had read his work or heard him lecture came to visit him, and came again.

In some autobiographical notes found after his death he wrote that nothing surprised and delighted him more than that he should have made more friends in the twenty-five years since he was sixty than at any other time in his life. "Nearly all those who befriend and accompany me now are in the generations of my children and grandchildren. Many are abroad, largely in North America. I owe largely to them what insight I have into the huge cultural changes of which my own life has been a tiny ingredient of both cause and effect."

He continued to undertake summer seminars at the Open University, and to work on a course book for his friends in the Systems Department there. It was unfinished at his death in 1982, but was edited by the university and published posthumously by Harper & Row in 1983 under the title *Human Systems are Different*. It was followed in 1984 by an Open University selection of his essays, published by Harper & Row as *The Vickers Papers*.

Ethics as focal point

As the 1970s came to an end Geoffrey turned his attention to ethics and morality. "To restore ethics to the center of the human stage and to explain the ethical imperatives is probably the main focus of all my interests", he wrote to Guy Adams, director of the Graduate Program in Public Administration at the Evergreen State University, in September 1979. He considered the criteria of success of human societies to be ethical standards. In 1980 he embarked upon an attempt to apply systems thinking to human history "to the extent needed to understand the present predicament of Britain in particular, and more generally of the industrial Western countries". The ideology deriving from the Enlightenment which had dominated the West for two hundred years had, he felt, aspired to realize both liberty and equality, at first for the 'greatest number' and later for each and all:

And it had hoped to do so by a self-regulating and self-exciting or self-stimulating process, powered by technology and directed by human 'reason'. In its pursuit of the doubtfully compatible goals of liberty and equality, this ideology has produced much that we should be sorry to forgo; but the contemporary outcome is the reverse of what the nineteenth century expected. An ever more scientific world was never less predictable. An ever more technological world was never less controllable. A world dedicated to majority rule is increasingly run by militant minorities.

'Free' individuals, increasingly dependent on each other, are subject to increasing demands to share the commitments, accept the constraints and accord the trust required by the multiplying systems and sub-systems to which they belong and on which they wholly depend. And these distribute their favors and, still more, their responsibilities with the equality of a battlefield. For good or ill the ideology of the Enlightenment has worked itself out, paid its dividends and revealed its shortcomings.[14]

He was, indeed, particularly concerned—one might almost say obsessed—with the problem of regulation. What he and Adolph Lowe were always searching for were the sources of spontaneous consensus as a means of agreed, non-coercive regulation. Geoffrey on the one hand abhorred the idea of 'thought control' as a means of regulation, and on the other thought that the idea of using the market as a regulator had been shown to be inadequate: "You cannot use the market to decide the allocation of places in a lifeboat". He did not live to see the large-scale adoption of the market as regulator which became prevalent in Britain and elsewhere in Europe and in the United States and is now even sweeping the former planned economies. What he did see very clearly was the inadequacy of market mechanisms as regulators in the face of the kind of major ecological problems and global challenges to which he was already drawing attention in the 1960s, the seriousness of which many people are only now beginning to understand.

Clinging to the web

Among those upon whom Geoffrey's ideas had considerable influence were three young American professors who would publish a selection of Geoffrey's writing in the United States after his death. Guy Adams, together with John Forester, Associate Professor of City and Regional Planning at Cornell University, and Bayard Catron, Professor of Public Administration at George Washington University, presented these as a collection of "seminal essays on policymaking and related issues facing modern Western culture (in which Sir Geoffrey) portrays a unique view of policymaking, building on his notion of 'appreciation' and focusing on the processes of reflection and communication in setting and changing the tacit norms which govern our conduct."

In their preface the editors point out that Geoffrey's concept of the 'responsible person', in contrast to that of the 'autonomous individual', had helped them to forge a new understanding of the relationship between the individual and society, and quote the following passage to illustrate the central human importance of his concept of the 'appreciative system':

> The sanest like the maddest of us cling like spiders to a self-spun web, obscurely moored in vacancy and fiercely shaken by the winds of change. Yet this frail web, through which many see only the void, is the one enduring artifact, the one authentic signature of humankind, and its weaving is our prime responsibility.[15]

It was not Geoffrey's ideas alone which prompted these three academics to edit a collection of his essays; it was also, they said, their admiration for the ways in which his ideas were manifested in his life, "the integrity and the wisdom of the man, his warm and gentle manner coupled with tough-minded acuity and boundless curiosity. He was unusually sensitive and open to the breadth and diversity of the human experience ... This was a man who cared—he cared about the concrete events and circumstances of the lived-in world of daily life, as well as the larger questions of the human enterprise. And he cared with a depth and exuberance and authenticity which was apparent, no doubt, to virtually everyone who spent any time in his presence ... His own 'appreciative system' was one of the keenest, most refined, and most thoroughly integrated of any human being we have had the pleasure to know".[16]

Mutual appreciation

Over the decades Geoffrey and Adolph regularly sent each other the drafts of their books and papers, upon which each would comment in depth and with total honesty. Their appreciation of each other's intellectual power and integrity was such that it would not have countenanced any blurring of criticism. Their opinions weighed heavily upon each other, and each was aware of how much he owed the other in the improvement of his work.

They often disagreed. Geoffrey, deeply steeped in the English Victorian tradition, shared also some of its prejudices, although this distance from the Victorian era enabled him to see more sharply the defects, institutional and behavioral, that create present instability at every level of present-day society. Coming from a very different tradition, a German Jew cut off from his native soil, Adolph's views on some fundamental matters were bound to contrast with those of Geoffrey—a contrast which shows clearly in some of the letters in this volume, especially when the progress of egalitarianism is at stake.

This was particularly so in the case of 'emancipation', a word carrying very different meanings for each of them, due, Adolph felt, to their inevitably different perspectives. "Certainly our respective life histories ... enter into the shaping of our perspectives and the underlying valuations", Adolph writes in December 1976. "In my case I must stress again the Jewishness—not only in view of the actual troubles which this has created during most of my life, but even more because of a 'prophetic' tradition which has only been confirmed by those experiences."

"The thing I am saying", replies Geoffrey, "is that ... life is commitment, that we are scarcely free even to choose our commitments, and that any concept of emancipation which ignores these basic facts is a delusion ... I think my message is the more topical today, though it wasn't when I was born. But this may be wrong. Mine is what my experience has fitted me to see and say."

But such differences did not affect the value each attached to their exchange of views, or the deep affection they felt for each other. They shared not only their ideas and their dreams, but their personal concern with regard to the health of their much beloved wives. Adolph was essentially a city dweller, Geoffrey a country lover whose poems reveal his deep communion with nature[17]—essentially an Englishman who, though widely travelled, had never actually lived outside his own country, a fact which made it difficult for him to understand alien cultures. Adolph, uprooted both from his home country and yet again from England, settled into an environment in the United States which he found congenial and in which he felt at home, although—in spite of 43 years in that country and naturalization—he remained essentially cosmopolitan, an 'internationalist' rather than an 'American'.

For Geoffrey, being English was a supreme privilege. In a March 1980 paper he expresses deep distress at the changes which had taken place in Britain since World War I. "The outstanding cultural change in Britain since that time seems to me to have been the almost total withdrawal of trust from every center of power and authority and from every power holder—even from all its traditional loci of loyalty: country, service, *métier*, class and family":

> This change is abnormal and, I think, cannot fail to be lethal unless it is reversed, and reversed soon, for mutual trust and trustworthiness are necessary both for the working of a society and for the human development of its individual members. A society is an ethical structure, and cannot long survive the time when its members lose sight of the ethical dimension and can no longer distinguish between an ethical judgment and a cost-benefit analysis, still less recognize the relation between them.[18]

Geoffrey believed that society had a responsibility to 'culture' if not to history. "I am not particularly attracted by the Luthers of this or any other generation. In the world into which I was born, 'God, King and Country' seemed an adequate and harmonious focus for Everyman's loyalty. God was of special importance as being the most personal and the most comprehensive. But that was a culture in the heyday of its self-confidence. There comes a time when its self-confidence needs to be challenged. And if the challenge is 'successful', what then? An immediate, desperate need to recreate the 'spontaneous conformity' which has been deliberately destroyed and which cannot be recreated spontaneously, since its spontaneity was the fruit of its self-confidence."[19]

On October 3 1981 Geoffrey wrote to his friend Nancy Milio, a professor at the Chapel Hill School of Nursing in North Carolina who, like many others, had suggested that he write his autobiography:

> When I did try to plan an autobiography I had no difficulty in deciding that it should be called 'A Kind World'. The world has been remarkably kind to me. But it would need a subtitle: Memoirs of a Clumsy Man? Not strong enough. A Blind Man? Too escapist. I could find no way of expressing the confusion with which I regard myself.

> Then, as I got older I became more burdened by a sense of cultural change for the worse and an awareness that I hated it, I had contributed to it. I have seldom known what I was doing or what I was supposed to be doing, or least of all what I was capable of doing. And yet at almost any moment in my varied life I would have been found confidently and delightedly doing it.

Two months later Geoffrey went into hospital for the routine blood transfusions which had made possible his 'medicated survival' for so long, but
internal bleeding had begun. Unable to read or write, he reflected on his past life
and realized that, aged 87, his life seemed more coherent than he had realized.
In his last, remarkable, letter to Adolph in January 1982 (quoted in full in the last
chapter of this book), he looks back on his life and divides it into eight phases,
each of which had had an indelible effect upon his approach to the issues which
preoccupied the two men during their long lives:

(My life) divides sharply at Munich when for the first time I became politically
conscious—of a domestic rather than a foreign threat; Joe ... you and the Moot ...
Phase 2, the phony war and *The Christian Newsletter* ... Phase 3, the war ... Phase
4, a civil servant ... Phase 5, the Attlee government, the Beveridge social legislation
... Phase 6, the Coal Board ... Phase 7, retirement and unexpected immersion as para-
academic ... Phase 8, 1970 onwards, sense of collapse of coherence in UK, sense of
being in a country of strangers about whom no assumptions whatever can be made.

Asking himself what has happened, why it has happened and what, if
anything, can be done about it, he comes up with answers which show a deep
degree of pessimism about this reversal of all his hopes. "I do not know what can
be done about it, but I expect that what will be done about it is social engineering
and thought control on a very large scale".

In a preface to his posthumously published *Human Systems are Different*, his
American friend Silvia Sutton says that she writes "with respect for privacy,
warmth, and admiration for a man of many parts: soldier, lawyer, administrator,
public servant, poet, friend, humanist, sage ... Any picture of him must include
his 'back room boys'—his metaphor for mental activity which seemed to him
a dialogue between his 'back room' and his 'front parlor'. He was a superb
listener, and an embarrassingly faithful correspondent. He had a particularly fine
rapport with young people, both small children and young adults, whose ideas
he entertained with utmost seriousness. He had a delicious, often mischievous
wit, usually at his own expense. Through his writings he recalled the real
meaning of words devalued by usage: love, knowledge, responsibility, morality,
appreciation; he offered tools for understanding and action in a world which, he
reckoned, sorely required attention."

The end of a partnership

Much of what Silvia Sutton says about Geoffrey can be said about Adolph.
A wonderful listener, ready to enter into discussion with all who beat a path to
his door, a faithful correspondent, and endowed with splendid wit and humor,
he too has brought light and understanding into the world. Geoffrey's death in
March 1982 was a great blow; Adolph considers him to have been one of the
most original and practically relevant thinkers in the post-war world:

I had always prided myself on having overcome the narrow specialization which is so typical of contemporary social science, and also on the fact that my views had been formed largely by the practical experiences I had had in semi-journalistic and administrative work. All of this pales when I compare it with the breadth of Geoffrey's investigations, ranging from social and economic planning and ecology to human relations and mental health, culminating in philosophical enquiries into value systems and scientific methodology.

Geoffrey's status as a non-professional outsider in some of his fields of study opened his eyes to problems the specialist fails to perceive. There is of course another side to this: such non-attachment makes it difficult for one's ideas to penetrate professional barriers, and it must be admitted that Geoffrey's work has not yet received the full response it deserves. One can only hope that the pitfalls and dangers of our era will draw full attention to an achievement that shows ways of overcoming them.[20]

Adolph retired from the New School for Social Research in 1975, aged 82, the last of the original Germans on its faculty. During his thirty-five years of teaching there many students passed through his classes, including such luminaries as Robert Heilbroner, his star student, and he remembers them all with great affection. That they remember him with equal affection is clear from the preface which Dr. Heilbroner has contributed to this volume.

Soon after the death of his wife in the United States in 1982, Adolph returned to Germany to live near his daughter in the northern city of Wolfenbüttel. Now 98, he retains a zest for life and a sense of humor in no way impaired by time and his relative immobility. He remains in contact with many of the students and lecturers he has known during his long life, with his friends (including the editor of this volume), and continues actively to write and to publish.

The letters presented in this volume are all that remain of the correspondence between the two men; some of the earliest are missing, presumably lost during their moves into retirement homes. Chapter 1 includes two "Dear Lowe" letters written by Geoffrey at an early stage of their acquaintance in the 1940s, and a long letter from Adolph to Dr. Oldham in connection with the Moot, which is included not only because it sheds a great deal of light on the discussions which took place among intellectuals in the Western world prior to and during World War II, but provides a basis for the correspondence which follows.

But most of the letters cover the three decades from the 1950s to the beginning of the 1980s. They give a vivid picture of a fascinating relationship between two exceptional men who have spent most of their lives reflecting on the huge problems facing both governments and individuals today, and testing out on each other ideas and ways in which they could be resolved. Men of vision, and ahead of their time, the importance of their work is now being increasingly recognized.

The correspondence also illuminates the extent to which each became dependent upon the other for friendship, honesty, and intellectual stimulus during the latter years of their lives. Their closeness achieved a rare intensity. The letters speak for themselves.

Notes

1. Introduction to G. Vickers, *Freedom in a Rocking Boat*, Allan Lane/Penguin Press, 1970.
2. Foreword to *Policymaking, Communications and Social Learning*, published posthumously by Transaction Books, 1987.
3. Interviewed by Jeanne Vickers, August 1987: for biographical material on Dr. Lowe I am also indebted to Dr. Robert Heilbroner's 'Portrait' in the Sept./Oct. issue of *Challenge*.
4. "A Bill of Duties for Men in England", typescript dated April 1940, Vickers papers.
5. "Purpose and Force : The Bases of Order", *op. cit.* p. 164.
6. 'Why Vote Labour?', undated typescript, Vickers papers.
7. See Bibliography.
8. G. Vickers, 'Ecology, Planning and the American Dream', in *The Urban Condition*. ed. L. Duhl, New York, 1963.
9. Letter to Guy Adams, Director of the Graduate Program in Public Administration, Evergreen State College, Washington.
10. Letter to Professor Melvin Webber of the University of California.
11. G. Vickers, 'Projections, Predictions, Models and Policies', *The Planner*, Vol. 60, No. 4, April 1974.
12. See Bibliography.
13. Letter to Adolph Lowe, September 14 1978.
14. Foreword by Sir Geoffrey to *Human Systems are Different*, Harper & Row, 1983.
15. G. Vickers, "The Psychology of Policymaking and Social Change", in *Policymaking, Communication, and Social Learning*, (eds: Adams, Forester and Catron), Transaction Publishers, 1987. Originally delivered as the Thirty-Eighth Maudsley Lecture to the Royal Medico-Psychological Association, November 15 1963, and published in the *British Journal of Psychiatry*, No. 110, July 1964.
16. Editorial preface to *Policymaking, Communication and Social Learning*, *op. cit.*
17. Geoffrey Vickers, *Moods and Tenses : Occasional Poems of an Old Man*. Published by Pamela Miller and Jeanne Vickers, 1983.
18. G. Vickers, draft of a paper on 'Current Value Changes', March 19 1980.
19. Letter to Adolph Lowe, August 31/September 1, 1977.
20. Interviewed by Jeanne Vickers, August 1987.

THE LETTERS

1

War and its Aftermath

During World War II there was a great deal of discussion with regard to the kind of Europe which should be rebuilt from the ashes of that major conflagration. One of the subjects discussed at the Moot[1] was that of the preparation of young people for the post-war world. A paper by Adolph made some far-reaching suggestions for an experimental college and a New Humanities course. In a letter dated May 13 1940 Geoffrey indicates that he is deeply interested, very much in agreement, and ready to do all he can to help:

"The problem seems to be this. Given a world in which conformity of basic assumptions has broken down and traditional teaching, both cultural and moral, is out of harmony with experience, how can university teaching (a) accommodate itself to such a situation and (b) contribute to a new synthesis. Is that at all a fair summary? And your answer, equally potted, seems to be: 'It should concentrate (a) on understanding the structure and dynamics of the world it lives in and (b) on asking the right questions about it'. Again, is that at all a fair summary? If so I feel that the next step is to become more concrete. Think of your experimental college and say more exactly what it would teach and how and to whom.

"But first perhaps another need. To say more exactly what is this change which has produced the loss of conformity, the disharmony and so on ... suppose we were presenting this to Harold Butler?[2] I believe it would be useful to distil into its simplest elements our view of the change which has happened—the 'Embarrassing Enlargement of the Area of the Controllable.' We know, of course, exactly what we mean. It is a question of seeing in how few and how forcible words it can be said.

"I was very interested in what you say about keeping in touch with practical life, letting the students work in the vacation and so on. This is difficult to make effective except in connection with real vocational training, e.g. lawyers, doctors. There is however the counterpart. What contribution can people like me, for instance, make to a university course? As a Visiting Fellow of Nuffield

25

I sit on the Finance Sub-Committee! Can you think of any more constructive way in which I could contribute to a course in the New Humanities? I'm quite willing to try experiments.

"You say they must be graduates because your new humanities are not yet a degree course; but you refer approvingly to the London School of Economics. Could anything be done to make B.Sc.Econ.-with-Sociology-as-special-subject into something like what you want? Failing this—or as well as this—Nuffield seems indicated; but I do think L.S.E. has possibilities.

"I daren't go too far along any of the roads which your paper opens up. The following suggestion is the only one in which I think you may find something of value. You criticize the study of history here for concentrating too much (a) on political history and (b) on English history. I agree (a) but wonder about (b) for the following reason.

"One of the most significant effects of 'The Change' is to stress the significance of the State. This is because the State, as the administrative and fiscal unit, is the *only* unit which is anywhere near having even potentially the techniques and the criteria for planning social life. Hence State worship isn't just any old idolatry for a godless age. It is the ideological expression of an age which is going to be concerned not with creating economic mechanisms but with creating social patterns; hence an age which *rightly* attaches importance to frontiers.

"This idea, which has only emerged clearly as I wrote it, seems to me of considerable importance. The whole Nazi business, racialism and all, becomes full of meaning if I am right in this hypothesis that we now enter for the first time on an age in which the administrative and fiscal unit—today the State—becomes the most important of all social groupings and must therefore be made into a social group. If this is right the whole teaching of history may have to be reconsidered and the chief emphasis may fall on 'state' or 'national' history, considered as the explanation of the prime social phenomenon.

"Do tell me what you think of this. I hoped to talk over some of this with Harold Butler at a Nuffield College meeting this weekend, but it was cancelled owing to the new invasions."

Adolph's reply is lost to history, but the subject was to recur on many occasions within the context of the Moot. Adolph, having been naturalized in the UK at the beginning of the war, found that his unorthodox views were not shared at the University of Manchester. In 1940 he accepted a post at the 'University in Exile', the New School for Social Research in New York, becoming Director of Research at its Institute of World Affairs in 1943. He could now only contribute to the Moot by correspondence, and the following letter, written towards the end of the war to Dr. Joe Oldham, who copied it to all members of the Moot, including Geoffrey, helps to shed light on many of the preoccupations of the participants. Adolph apologizes for the fact that it has been long delayed by complicated negotiations with the Rockefeller Foundation concerning a big research project on 'Social and Economic Control in Germany and Russia'. It is fascinating to read in the light of the developments which have taken place in the fifty years since it was written:

"In a way, this long postponement of my reply has also its good side. I am sure had I answered two months ago I should have written a good many things which the recent course of world history utterly disproved in the meantime. I certainly do not belong to those who anticipated the Russo-German war. I was convinced up to the last moment, and so was everybody here, that by one method or other Russia would be drawn into the German orbit. You may remember that I always regarded an effective alliance between Germany and Russia as the greatest possible danger, especially in view of its ideological possibilities. In the moment of utter emergency it would have given Hitler the chance of playing out the card of National Bolshevism in Germany and an ideological attack against the West in the name of the 'real social revolution'. Whatever the outcome of the Russian campaign may be, this danger appears to be over for good. Communism may well triumph in Germany in the end—I shall come back to this in a moment—but it can no longer be Hitler who appeals to it. He now must stand and fall as a reviver of some dark past.

"I do not dare to make a prediction as to the military results of the Russian campaign. Again I have to admit that, like almost everybody here, I had not expected that the Russians would resist to the degree they have so far done. Still, we are in the middle of the battle and have to be careful in our conclusions.

"Now this leads me to your request in your last letter that I should take up my old idea to write a paper on Germany and its post-war problems. It was of course impossible for me to concentrate on anything outside my immediate duties during the last months. But I am not sure whether I should have been able to get something on paper even under more favorable conditions. And now the Russian development has made things even more complicated.

"The existence of Russia was always an unknown factor in any post-war speculation. It was to be expected that Russia and Communism would draw ample benefit from the accumulated dynamite in Central Europe as soon as the iron fetters of Nazi domination were broken. Now Russia will have a legitimate claim to an equal part in the reshaping of Europe, providing that she herself can resist indefinitely. In a way this has also cleared the air by dispelling all superficial ideas that the reorganization of Europe is primarily a problem of foreign policy. With Britain and Russia trying to find a solution, the *social* reorganization of Europe has obviously become the dominant question.

"Each of these two Allies has proved its capacity for the building up of a supranational structure. The integration of the participating national units is, of coure, much stricter in the Soviet system. I am inclined to regard the Soviet system for this reason as a less advanced form of integration than is repesented by the British Commonwealth. But this very fact makes the Russian mode more appropriate for a group of 'learners', as are the Central European nations, with the possible inclusion of France, Italy, Switzerland and the Low Countries.

"Listening to the current discussion among the exiled representatives of the Central European parties, I cannot help feeling that any attempt at a Central European Federation is futile if it is to be based on the pre-war social structure of these countries. I know that public discussion of these issues is very delicate, and that the British Government is well advised to keep a benevolent silence even when the Grand Duchess of Luxemburg demands that full sovereignty be returned to her. If I was only certain that the British leaders knew for themselves that this won't do! But I am afraid that, even when they play with the ideas of a European Federation, they lose themselves in legal speculations about the relative competence of the federal organization and its component parts, and on such tedious issues as free trade, monetary organization, etc.

"The simple fact is that without a radical change in the social structure by transferring political and economic power to new and homogeneous groups, you cannot even federate Austria and Hungary and certainly not the Slavonic countries with Germany. The large remainders of feudalism, monopoly business, reactionary clericalism, the leading groups of military and civil bureaucracy, will all have to be replaced by the rule of farmers, workers and the progressive intelligentsia, both in business and administration.

"Even this alliance will not be very stable in the beginning, as was shown by the history of Czecho-Slovakia. However, Czecho-Slovakia was in 1938 the only country between the Channel and the Black Sea which was at least on the way to a regime based on a democratic social stratification. One might include Sweden, disregarding the other Scandinavian countries, and Switzerland, because these had not to tackle the really difficult problems of modern industrialism.

"If it is true that the reorganization of Europe will, first of all, be a problem of social reconstruction, all will depend on the social principles of the peacemakers. I cannot quite see the line of compromise on which Churchill and Stalin could agree. Matters are certainly not simplified by the fact that Roosevelt might try to act as umpire. All we can hope for is that the course of the war will assimilate the social structure and ideals of the 'Allies' to an increasing degree.

"This should be obvious of Britain, though I am still puzzled by what happens behind the scenes. I well understand that, as in its declaration on foreign policy, the British Government must be very careful in its utterances on the social future of Britain. I constantly try to tell my American friends that they themselves will first have to make up their minds what they want before they can blame Britain for not stating her "internal war aims". With half of American public opinion demanding a Socialist Britain while the other half wants to stop deliveries unless the future of British Capitalism is assured, the Government had indeed better be silent.

"But again, I wonder what real secrets are hidden behind the screen of silence. I have studied very carefully the minutes of the Moot to find some enlightenment on what is really happening. To tell the truth I could not find much ... do tell me a little about what is going on in this respect. To my mind the internal reconstruction of Britain is still the most important preparation for the solution of the international problems of the peace.

"But the 'assimilation' of the Allies refers, of course, equally to Russia. One fact, I think, has been brought out clearly by the military events of the last six weeks. The repression of majority will must have been far less strong than we all had assumed. This is not the way in which slaves fight. This is particularly significant with regard to the collectivization of the farms. I had always my doubts whether repression and persecution really extend to the ordinary worker and farmer. The reality comes pretty near to what we know of the conditions in Rome under the Julian Emperors. Conditions at the Court, in the Senate, etc. were intolerable, but the masses of the subjects lived, for the first time, in peace.

"This by no means justifies tyranny in the upper ranks. But it makes the problem of social reconstruction much simpler, and partly a question of the exchange of personnel. While in Britain the organization of the war will enhance centralization, the same necessities in Russia will foster regional self-government and spontaneity. Finally, we must not forget that the war spirit will create a new kind of conformity, both national and social (since the fight corresponds now after all to the original ideology). This should make it possible for the Central Government to relax part of its rigid control after the war, especially if no other state in the old world then stands for capitalist principles. In other words, the war can be a very efficient force in the direction of democratizing Communism, and every step on the side of Britain in the direction of Socialism is a support for 'Soviet reformation'.

"All this is highly speculative, but I cannot see any solution for Europe at large unless the victorious powers have a more or less common social idea, and one that gives a chance to new strata in the rest of Europe. There is no other way of 'preventing Germany from threatening again the peace of the world' than the fostering and stabilization of a regime in Germany which fulfils two conditions: satisfying the demands of a productive majority and being itself interested, materially and ideologically, in the preservation of peace.

"But you cannot maintain such a regime in Germany unless the victorious powers have the same sort of regime. A democratic republic in Germany, established by a capitalist-imperialist Britain and a communist-imperialist Russia, will have the same fate as the Weimar Republic, and the ensuing third World War will be well deserved by the victors of the second. Therefore don't let us waste time in speculations about 'what to do with Germany'. Whatever you do, she will always be formed in the victors' image. Therefore what matters is clarity and resolution in creating this image.

"All I have said is based on the silent assumption that Hitler will not succeed in really crushing Russia. By crushing I mean more than military defeat. Neither Norway nor Holland is crushed, while France is, to a large extent. If, however, he should succeed in not only occupying large stretches of the country but in uprooting the present regime in the minds of the people, he will have achieved such a victory that we had better postpone the discussion as to what 'we' should do with Germany and Europe generally.

"I know this is no substitute for the article you want me to write. But you will perhaps understand some of the reasons why I feel unable to write it. Please feel quite free to communicate my views to the other friends. I should be very much interested to have their reaction. I now should follow up this disquisition on Europe with another on America. But if I wanted to do so you would have to wait even longer for this letter.

"Superficially everything (in America) is all right, and so far as immediate help for Britain is concerned, the development goes in the right direction with increasing momentum. But the underlying problems, both in foreign and home policy, are tremendous. Our circle of friends is convinced that not only the national but also the social future of the USA depends on the outcome of the war, and even on the degree of participation of America. Yet the responsibility which history has suddenly laid on the USA goes much beyond both the understanding and the responsibility of the average American, including the educated classes. Any sort of 'new élite' is entirely lacking, and the new wine is not only filled into old bottles but, which is worse, the wine pressers are from yesterday. It might be quite possible, if everything goes well, that the participation of Russia in the final settlement will prove a necessary balance against the obvious influence of America on Britain.

"But when all this is said I must add, on the other hand, that only since I have come to this country (America) do I know what social equality is. There is, of course, another side to this, and no one who is primarily interested in 'history' can be happy here. But that there should be a society which is not hampered by the burden of feudalism and class rigidity is still one of the great hopes of mankind. Only the interdependence of the members of the human race has become so intimate that Britain will have to win this war if America is to develop her potentialities."

Adolph's reputation at the New School was growing fast. For a student who became one of America's most illustrious economists, Robert Heilbroner, Adolph was 'the greatest and most inspiring teacher I have ever known'. After the war, Adolph suggests that Geoffrey write a book about what is happening in England after the election of the post-war Labour government. Geoffrey replies that he has no time to write it, far less to make good all the gaps in his knowledge and thought and experience which would be revealed in the attempt:

"But a letter, even a long one, is less pretentious than the shortest book. Let me first try to tell you in a letter what I sense of the forces moving here and why they fill me on the whole with confidence and even with elation.

"When I try to explain something of the nature of a change, what am I trying to do? Change as such needs no explanation. Life is process and change is not merely its concomitant but its essence. But it is legitimate to seek the factors which determine the rate and direction of current developments, and from them partially to forecast the future. These factors seem to be of three kinds, and everyone will agree about two of them.

"What we do is in part at least a reaction to the situation. Facts challenge and we respond. A war, a slump, a famine create a situation about which something has got to be done. But the nature of our response is conditioned by much more complex forces, sometimes stretching back into the remote past, often quite inappropriate today. For some people—and peoples—the normal way of dealing with an obstacle may be to smash through it; for others, to evade it; for others, to halt before it. They may all be right in the light of past experience and yet all wrong today.

"These attitudes are emotional and very persistent. Both industrial and political relations in England today are affected by mutual attitudes formed between workers and employers over the last century and more, and persisting long after the circumstances which gave rise to them have passed away.

"Thus I distinguish between those factors of the situation which present an inescapable challenge and those which determine the nature of the response. My third category is the element of human initiative which in my belief occasionally breaks through and saves us from a wholly predetermined world. This, though vastly important, operates only weakly and intermittently in the field of collective relationships, and it is no part of this letter to consider how large is its part in our present struggle.

"One bewildering thing about these factors is that they are all wholly subjective. The situation to which we react is not the situation which is but the situation as we believe it to be. The forces which condition us are not our whole history, but those parts of it which have entered into us or which we have made our own. The future affects us only insofar as it is present in our hopes and fears. Thus these factors operate with an immense and varying time lag. Some of us are still reacting to the 1930s whilst others are dominated by anticipations of the 1960s. This no doubt explains why so often in history a country's deliberate actions appear in retrospect to be grotesquely inappropriate to its actual situation.

"You will see that I do not expect to find the explanation of our present courses in any tidily reasoned deduction from current facts. In fact, the task of explaining social happenings seems to me to be far more difficult than would appear from what I have already written; for I have kept the greatest difficulty until the last. Thus far I have drawn no clear distinction between the actions of an individual and a people. In fact, these collective personifications are allegories for something which we have as yet no proper means of describing.

"The 'we' which I shall use when speaking of England now stands for a multitude of people related to each other and to their past in ways of which we still have virtually no understanding at all. For instance, it makes an important difference politically that Labour in England is today top dog; yet it does not break the continuity of political history. The infinite variety of opinions and attitudes among living English men and women somehow results in political action which threatens neither our coherence in the present nor our continuity with the past. How this happens we do not know and few people even wonder.

"One advantage of a letter is that I can get this burden of abstract thinking off my chest and in doing so can give you some idea of how the world looks to me. If it seems monstrous to you, my explanation, given in these terms, will seem monstrous also. I see in England millions of people, each separated from all the others by the immense gulf which appears to isolate each of us, and yet capable of effective common action because their minds, conscious and subconscious, are tenanted by common ideas, attitudes, intuitions. Of what does this heritage consist? How does it bridge the apparent diversity of interests and aspirations between man and man, class and class, the different worlds, the different epochs in which these seemingly diverse creatures live? I don't know and my sense of this as a mystery makes me reluctant to begin what I set out to do.

"The immediate situation which demands response is, of course, the cataclysmic decline both absolute and relative in our political and economic power consequent on two world wars. And yet this seems to me to have had as yet little effect on what is happening, in that even without it the current phase of the English social revolution would probably have happened about now and would probably have taken very much the course which it has taken. Our changed circumstances have speeded it; they have made it more difficult of accomplishment; they may have compensated for this by stiffening our will to achieve it. But they have not in my view caused it or given it as yet any characteristic which it would not otherwise have had."

In 1946, Geoffrey writes a short piece for Dr. Oldham's *Christian Newsletter* in which he speaks of the 'sensitivity' which marks relationships between individuals in varying degrees:

> The individual's moral initiative can mould the social heritage, affect social and political institutions and so take root in time; and conversely, the social habits and institutions thus moulded create a more favourable climate in which future moral initiatives may germinate.

In 1947, he became Legal Adviser to Britain's newly-created National Coal Board, and the following year became Board Member in charge of manpower, training, education, health and welfare, a position he held until 1955. He confesses in a letter to Adolph to feeling more at home with the national executive of the miners' union than with his fellow Board members. In an article in *TheQuarterly Review* he questioned how personal incentive and public service, self-fulfilment and national needs, could be harmonized. How could states best combat bureaucratic inefficiency, "a problem of life and death for socialists and the communities which they govern?" In 1950, in spite of reservations about the welfare state, he voted Labour for the first time.

Notes

1. See Introduction.
2. Warden of Nuffield College, Oxford, 1939-1943. Director of the International Labour Office 1932-1938, Deputy Director 1920-32, and Secretary-General of the first International Labour Conference in Geneva, 1919.

2

The Fifties

Although they had met through the Moot in 1938, and talked and corresponded during the '40s, the relationship between Geoffrey and Adolph did not mature until after the war. Their private talks during Moot sessions revealed that their visions of the future were not at that time on the same wavelength: for Adolph the problem was to discover a new balance between the market and planning, whereas Geoffrey rejected the market altogether as an instrument of distribution and was even doubtful about individual freedom, which he conceived mainly as an ideology in favor of the privileged classes.

The breakthrough in mutual understanding occurred long after the Lowes had moved to the United States. In the course of Geoffrey's frequent visits to that country in the '50s and '60s their views on planning and freedom grew closer. Adolph's concept of 'spontaneous conformity' as the foundation of both personal liberty and social stability was subsequently formulated by Geoffrey as 'common assumptions about the world in which we live, and common standards by which we judge our own and each others' action in that world.' The institutional changes required to foster such basic conformity have been a major topic in Adolph's writings.

His wife's poor health having brought Geoffrey into contact with a number of psychiatrists and mental health specialists and increased his interest in such questions, he was invited in 1951 to become Chairman of the Research Committee of the Mental Health Research Fund, a voluntary position he held for sixteen years. The Research Committee brought together a more comprehensive gathering of medical and social scientists than met regularly in any other forum, and its members spoke on subjects outside their own specialties.

The exchange of ideas and resultant wide range of reading gave Geoffrey an exceptionally broad interdisciplinary background. In addition to his experience in the humanities, law, management and government he now acquired a new competence in psychology and a new interest in the organization and promotion of health at both macro and micro levels. From 1952-1957 he served on Britain's Medical Research Council and for ten years was a frequent contributor to the British medical journal, *The Lancet*. His knowledge of cognitive psychology was fundamental to his development of the concept of the 'appreciative system'.

Geoffrey's last years with the National Coal Board were not very happy and he retired with relief in 1955. He was now free to continue other activities and to accept invitations to lecture or be a panelist in Canada and the United States. He became more and more interested in the concept of 'systems thinking', and accepted an invitation from the School of Social Work at the University of Toronto to face a range of challenging assignments: three colloquia on 'values and decision-taking', a lecture to the Faculty of Applied Science and Engineering on 'control, stability and choice'; and a public address entitled 'The Needs of Men', on the impact of industrialization on human well-being.

Geoffrey's approach to these questions was a systemic one; in his view a system was "a regulated set of relationships, and the key to its understanding is the way in which it is regulated". Like other animals man was a goal-seeking animal, he concluded, but the new distinctive attribute apparent at the human level was that man was also a goal-setting animal; and human cultures were also goal-setting. At both the individual and the social levels goals were set by a circular causal process, operating over time:

> Thus we can sense, though we cannot yet explain or understand, a circular causal process by which the goals of a society are set. They are continually under revision; factors which make for constancy are overcome by new demands, resulting from new experiences ... This process cannot be explained without taking into account the verdict of the individual conscious mind ... dynamic value judgments (which) are both a product and a cause of the ceaseless process of goal-formulation.[1]

The appreciative system

This was an early formulation of what was later refined as the 'appreciative system', the development of which was to dominate the remaining quarter century of Geoffrey's life. He also became increasingly involved in the concept of 'systems thinking'. He writes to Adolph subsequent to a visit to the United States, just after his 63rd birthday, October 13 1957, on the question of 'relationship':

"It will clear my mind to express in a letter to you the ideas which formed in my mind after our talk. (You always have the best possible effect on my thinking apparatus!)

"1. I start from the proposition that, in the dynamic, space-time world of which we are part, all activity, including our own, must be ultimately explicable as the effort to maintain or re-establish a relationship or to escape a threshold beyond which such relationship is in danger of straying. The relationship concerned may be either between the forces which compose the system under observation, or between that system and its environment.

"2.   Such behavior is almost always directional, though its direction may be misguided. The only possible exceptions are those explosive or 'displaced' behaviours which occur when some urge to act is overwhelming but has no cue or only completely ambivalent cues which might give it a direction.

"3.   Apart from 2, the formula in 1 covers every kind of human behavior. Food-seeking behavior is directed to maintain the appropriate metabolic relationship. At the other extreme, the behavior of the saint is described theologically as the active and unceasing maintenance of a relationship with God, a 'search' which is not unsuccessful because it is ever renewed but which is sharply distinguished by the theologian from the 'state' which he conceives to be attainable in 'eternity', i.e. outside space-time. Between these remote poles, every activity falls within the category of para. 1.

"4.   Biological evolution has endowed us with an unknown set of such relationships which are necessary to our life as human beings. To them, the interplay of social and individual development adds a hierarchy of others, more or less conscious, more or less inconsistent, mediating more or less indirectly the underlying 'needs' of the system, i.e. the relationships which define it. Thus, I suspect that 'human nature' has a basic need corresponding to what we know as security. But what inner and outer relations we seek in our search for security—this is given by the diversity of individual and social interaction through time, and admits of many 'right' solutions as well as of many 'wrong' ones, of which the most glaring are anatomized by the psychiatrists.

"5.   Our 'nature', then, consists of a most complex net of relationships, inner and outer, which determine our seekings and shunnings. The ever-changing architecture of these relationships is the product of that process of interaction which at one level we call 'history' and at another 'adaptation'. If we knew enough, we could compare and evaluate different architectures, judging one to be (i) more self-consistent, (ii) more comprehensive, (iii) better adapted for further growth, and perhaps (iv) more in accordance with our 'real' underlying but unknown nature than others. I therefore reject the common idea that there is a necessary gulf between 'what is' and 'what ought to be', though I agree that we have at present inadequate guides in relating the two.

"6.   The word 'value' thus has a multiple meaning. Every seeking and shunning is an effort to realize value, and may claim to be successful insofar as it succeeds in approaching the 'norm' or moving away from the 'limit' which it attempts to achieve or elude. But these criteria can themselves be criticized at several levels of generality. The fact that many concepts of value recur at different times and places in forms sufficiently similar to make discussion of them possible reflects the fact that the kinds of system which we know respectively as 'human being' and 'society' have some common and abiding characteristics.

"7. Biological evolution widens the scope of organic systems in various dimensions; notably they become capable of pursuing a greater number of relationships with a larger repertory of responses. At the human level this widening is sharply increased by the emergence of symbolic thought, which makes it possible for the creature to represent to itself hypothetical—and hence future—relationships and to include itself in its representations. Hence choice and conflict emerge increasingly as endemic conditions of life, and at the human level become the dominant feature of the predicament.

"8. Conflict may be intrinsic or extrinsic. It is intrinsic when the relationships which I pursue are inconsistent in their nature, as for instance in my desire to be both leisured and rich. It is extrinsic when the relationships, though not inconsistent in themselves, compete for resources, time or attention, as for instance when 'more schools' and 'more atom bombs' compete for the marginal millions of a national budget.

"9. Conflict in one or both senses is a feature of *every* human decision. When we do not recognize this, it is because we have failed to notice what the chosen course excludes. It is thus misleading to say that the economic calculus arises only in conditions of scarcity. For the condition of scarcity is endemic and ubiquitous and, paradoxically, arises from the abundance of our potentialities. It must therefore grow more, not less, intense as the total of our potentialities exceeds ever further the total that we can actualize.

"10. The true cost of any activity is to be calculated in terms of what it excludes; in attending to one relationship we prejudice others with which our activity is intrinsically or extrinsically in conflict. Economics aids this calculus within the field where costs can be reduced to money, but through dangerous simplification of the distinction between means and ends.

"11. When I work for my living I (i) secure an outlet for my activities, (ii) secure a place in society, (iii) establish a specific set of relationships with my fellow workers, and (iv) earn money with which I can satisfy other needs. Of these, items (i), (ii) and (iii) are activities which satisfy desired relationships, in that the absence of them would be a deprivation which I could scarcely bear. To this extent my efforts are not a 'quid' to be set against the rewarding 'quo'. They are immediate, as distinct from mediate rewards.

"12. Even if the way I earn my living is not the way I would choose, it is not a 'quid' if the preferred alternative is not open to me.

"13. If, however, it is open to me either to follow path A and earn X or to follow path B and earn 2X, then I have a real choice, in which I must weigh the greater satisfactions which path A offers in terms of relationships directly held or avoided, against the greater satisfactions which path B indirectly offers, in terms of increased ability to hold or avoid *other* relationships, which more money will confer.

"14. Superficially, the currency of satisfaction is the same; it is the satisfaction of effectively seeking and avoiding those relationships which govern our activities. But on closer examination these appear disparate. How do we weigh against each other satisfactions so disparate as 'security' and 'success'? Despite the much talked-of hierarchy of our wants, it is applicable only in the limiting case. If I am starving in a hot climate I shall prefer food to clothes, because without the food I shall die and shall be unable to wear the clothes for which I mistakenly opted. The choice is unreal. Except in this limiting case, I shall be unable to explain why I opt for more of this and less of that or to convince you that your different preferences are less sound—except, perhaps, by appeal to the criteria referred to in para. 5.

"15. Here we must, I think, introduce the concept of pattern. The architecture of our expectations, the relationships which we are set to seek or to shun are, in greater or less degree, an interrelated whole, as the common law—evolved, I believe, in an identical way—is an inter-related whole. We do not start from a blank sheet. Every decision—itself an act of adaptation—is governed no less by the needs of inner coherence than by the needs of external adjustment. This, however, merely underlines how complex is the process of choosing. It does not explain how we choose.

"16. At this point a new question enters in. Whence comes this short-list of alternatives between which we choose? They were selected from the repertory of possible responses by reference to 'the situation'. But this situation is not directly given. It is a construct of our own minds.

"17. Conceiving myself to be threatened, I short-list possible responses which experience (my own or others) suggests as suitable. I choose between them. I reflect how best to carry out the selected response. At every stage there is room for error. I may do it badly. I may choose the wrong one. I may never consider the best one because it does not occur to me. But equally I may be wrong in my initial recognition of the situation. I was never threatened at all.

"18. Sequences equally prone to error at several stages are intimately combined in my behavior. The redressing of a relationship which I call 'reacting to a threat' is not my only operating governor, and the steps to which it moves me serve to maintain or jeopardize other relationships to which I attach importance.

"19. If, now, I try to state the nature of a decision, I say with confidence that it is always the expression of what seems to me to matter most at the time, an optimum combination of all the seekings and shunnings to which I am moved by the manifold divergences between what seems to be the state of my inner and outer relationships and what I should like them to be. But if I try to represent to myself how this calculus works, I find my conceptual analysis to be defective in two respects.

"20. First, I have no dynamic model to represent the resolution of these manifold pushes and pulls. It is obviously far more complex than the resolution of physical forces within the laws of mechanics, yet this is the only model I have.

"21. Secondly, I have no structural model to represent that inner world which I build up and to which alone I respond. This inner model of reality is constrained by three conditions, not necessarily or easily compatible. It must be sufficiently coherent for my own inner needs. It must be sufficiently like those of my neighbours to make communication possible. And it must bear such a relation to what is happening 'out there' as to make my conduct adaptive enough to be viable.

"22. Moreover, these two problems are connected; they may be parts of the same problem. Throughout the phenomenal world, structure is dynamic, a configuration of forces in time, a 'doing'. Even an animal's anatomy is something which it 'does'. There is not an 'animal' which is active. An animal *is* an activity. Conversely, all activity is structured. The dynamic and the structural models are inseparable.

"23. But the categories of our language and thought were not built that way. They were developed when matter, energy and form were sharply different concepts, half-antagonistic. They assume a world of 'particulars' anterior to and separate from the 'relations' through which the particulars affect each other. They identify 'wholeness' with 'independence', despite the fact, which all biology acclaims, that every increase in individuation is won by a further advance into interdependence. As ideas they are manifestly inadequate and inept; but the new ones, which will make them superfluous, have not yet broken through.

"Does all this seem to you to express a real problem in a significant way? Would it open a useful discussion?"

Maximization

No doubt it did, and it certainly fuelled many of the thoughts expressed in later publications. But the next letter extant is one from Geoffrey to Adolph dated January 22 1959, in which the subject is 'maximization':

"Let it be agreed that economists still need the idea of maximization. Let it be further agreed that both producers and consumers are trying to maximize something. I suggest that the change in the basis of economics has come about through a change in the object of maximization of both parties and therefore a change in their mutual relationships, i.e. an increase in the power of the producers to decide what the consumers shall effectively want to maximize.

"Consider the producers whose basis of behavior has in the past been even more simplified than that of the consumers. We must distinguish between the behavior pattern of individual producers and the behavior pattern of the societies in which they are organized, i.e. in business organizations, and we must have a working understanding of the relation between these two.

"It is because of this relation that top executives are able to seek to maximize power. They also seek to maximize personal satisfaction. They also seek to maximize the use of techniques with which they are familiar, or which for some reason they like. They also seek to maximize their own personal security and their own personal incomes; and since these are related with those of the organization (perhaps in subtle ways) they are also motivated by the wish to conserve and increase the capital assets of the undertaking and to increase its size. An increase of its undistributed profits helps to increase its size. An increase of its distributed profits increases its prestige and helps it to get more capital. In this complex of individual-social motives two things seem to be particularly important; first, the small and indirect part played by maximizing profits, and secondly the very important part played by maximizing favored techniques.

"If, for many reasons, including the last-mentioned, industry likes to reduce more and more processes to the conditions in which they can be organized on mass production lines, there will be a steady increase in all activities which can be so organized, and a decrease in all activities which even with the greatest ingenuity cannot be put on this basis.

"In such a situation there will be a continual reduction in all satisfaction which cannot be supplied on this basis. According to classical theory this would be countered in due course by the mounting demand for the services which were being denied. As these become more scarce they would command higher and higher prices until it again paid to supply them. This self-correcting mechanism does not work because: (a) the producers have a mounting control directly over the effective wants of the consumers, and (b) the culture itself indirectly discourages any expression of deviant wants.

"If this at all represents what happens, we have a typical example of a system which is not inherently unstable, but which tends to reach stability at a point at which all wants which can be satisfied by mass production means—and the means of their satisfaction—have been maximized and all other wants have been minimized or eliminated.

"I have heard informed Americans say in descriptive terms that this is what is happening in America; but it seems to me that for the purpose of your instrumental approach it needs to be and can be given greater precision. Mathematicians can do a great deal with transformations of this kind. I would have thought that a mathematician, given an instrumental problem, might have found a formula to account for the increase in mass-produced satisfactions and the relative diminutions in other sorts of satisfaction which might serve as part of the basis which you are seeking.

"I hope this is sufficiently lucid to convey my meaning. My only knowledge of this sort of mathematics is derived from Ross Ashby's *Introduction to Cy-*

bernetics, which is a wonderful bit of exposition for people like me, but probably deals only with things with which you are already familiar."

During the long years of steady contact, through Geoffrey's visits to the United States and through correspondence, the friendship became one of the greatest importance to both men and more and more fruitful in terms of the exchange of ideas and experience.

Notes

1 . 'Values and Decision-taking', paper for circulation before three colloquia held at the University of Toronto, November 1956. Vickers papers.

3

The Sixties

The beginning of revolt

In the 1960s, both in the United States and in Europe, there was considerable student unrest, especially with regard to university reform and the Vietnam War. It was the time of peace demonstrations, of violence on campus, of the 'flower children' and the 'generation gap'; of drugs and the exhortations of Timothy Leary, a university 'guru', and of an acceleration of family breakdown. These evidences of societal disintegration were of particular concern to Geoffrey, and he became increasingly alarmed by many features of Western society.

He saw these disturbances as evidence of fundamental problems: modern Western societies seemed no longer able to generate what he called 'the commitment and constraints of membership'. People did not, for instance, notice that increased power to alter the environment meant reduced power to predict or control it, because every intervention produced a host of unintended consequences. He set himself the mammoth task of directing the energy of scholars in relevant fields to the elucidation of the processes of regulation, in an attempt to alter the appreciative setting of contemporary Western society.

His two BBC radio talks in 1965, entitled 'The End of Free Fall' (and reprinted in *The Listener),* presented to the general public what he considered to be the most urgent issues of the day.[1] He began his first talk with an anecdote about the man who fell from the top of the Empire State Building and was heard to say to himself, as he whistled past the second floor, 'Well, I'm all right so far.' He described present conditions in the UK as in the last stage in a free fall—"the fall from the agricultural into the industrial epoch; from a natural into a man-made world; and so into an increasingly political world, a world so unpredictable that it demands to be regulated, nationally and internationally, by political decisions of increasing scope." He pointed out that political change is limited by the speed at which people can change their ideas of the world they live in, their expectations

43

of it, and their willingness to accept its expectations of them. "All of these I regard as *cultural changes*."

Geoffrey's *The Art of Judgment,* the culmination of the most creative and fruitful period of his life, was published in 1965, in the same year as Adolph's *On Economic Knowledge* (see Preface), and was considered by many to be a seminal work of great importance. His *Towards a Sociology of Management* was published in 1967, and his *Value Systems and Social Process* in 1968. He was concerned that Western culture was becoming dangerously destabilized, due in large part to the internal dynamics of the culture itself. Political questions became increasingly prominent in his writings in the early Seventies, at a time of frequent visits to North America. The difficulty of thinking about the future had, he argued, increased proportionately with power to change it. A century or so of growth in the West meant that "human expectations have escalated at a rate and in a direction for which the past has no parallel and the future (I think) no hope of fulfilment".

The position required that prevailing conceptual frameworks should be rethought, together with a new scale of redistribution. "It threatens us ... with the need to make changes in our ways of distributing wealth and power which, though only vaguely foreseeable, are frightening and unwelcome, especially to the most favored beneficiaries of our present system."[2] Geoffrey's thinking on political questions cut right across the conventional 'left-right' divide. In some respects, for example here on the need for redistribution of wealth, he is very radical; in others his emphasis on stability and responsibility (rather than personal autonomy) seem to many to strike a conservative note.

There are no letters from the early Sixties on file; they begin with one from Adolph of May 20 1965 in which he comments on a manuscript which Geoffrey has sent him:

"My tonsilitis has been good for something—I have just finished your book.[3] And besides trying to convey to you something of the impression it has left on me, I am setting about the difficult task of putting our two approaches into a perspective under which they can be compared and evaluated.

"Let me begin with a true story which I had long forgotten. During the early '20s, when I was a civil servant in the Weimar Government, I often said jokingly: 'I am looking forward to the day when I can sit down and write a book: Ten Years among Civil Servants: Their Mores and Customs'. I never even tried, but you have, on a much broader canvas, given us the insight into a world which, though more and more the center of our social experience, is an almost unknown planet—unknown even to those who inhabit it. One participates in a close-up view and in slow motion in live processes, of which most of us have only vague and utterly abstract notions.

"But it is not storytelling which you present. Though no one could have written this book unless he could speak from real experience, the observations have been conceptualized just to the extent necessary to offer *typical* descriptions based on a classifying instrumentarium. Only Chester Barnard has to my knowledge attained this degree of 'ordered concreteness'—like you, a man of affairs before he became a thinker. I do not want to embarrass you, but this seems to me a first attempt to do for a prime sector of the social cosmos what DeBrahe and Kepler did by way of observation and generalization for the planetary system. And what a propitious subject matter these guys chose for themselves, namely one where observation could concentrate on 'public behavior', and a sort of behavior that was easily quantified. What subtlety of interpretation of intangibles has been required to present a coherent, and yet not too coherent, picture of your field!

"I am not in the least surprised that, in emerging from this work of intellectual empathy, my book must be a real stumbling block for you. Its message seems, and in fact does, come from an entirely different dimension of reasoning. I have been aware of this difference for a long time—I had it easier than you because you gave me over the years many more formulated indications of your thinking than I have done. And I told you before that I regard your very existence as an observing and speculating mind as a constant challenge and warning. Still, I think that what I am aiming at, though not necessarily what I have so far hit upon, has its own and equal right. More than ever I am convinced of what I wrote in my last note: our approaches are complementary, and neither can achieve its goal without the other.

"Even so, I too do not find it easy to define precisely the difference between our two approaches. It is one of the level of abstraction, and thus of the generality of the ensuing propositions. But it also concerns the subject matter itself: you dealing ultimately with the microscopic issues, even when you speak of agents of the most comprehensive kind of policy framing; myself being ultimately concerned with macro-structure, even when I try to relate it to micro-forces. Finally, using terms which I don't like much but which have a conventional meaning: your interest is primarily positive-descriptive, whereas mine is normative-construing. All this is not quite true—there are admixtures of the other element in either book. But I think it describes the major emphases correctly.

"Now you spoke the golden truth when you wrote in your letter of April 16: 'You want a lot of people talking and thinking like me to prepare the ground for you'. Indeed, even if my 'program' were fully adopted by your or my Government, it could not be carried out without full awareness of the issues you are dealing with. But conversely I would say: Not before a framework of 'orderliness of the whole' is created along my lines will your insight into the 'art of judgment' be offered its true field of application, namely a field in which 'balancing' and 'optimizing' become socially and not only privately, generally and not only incidentally, effective."

On May 10 1967 Geoffrey writes to tell Adolph that he will be able to spend two evenings with him on his forthcoming visit to New York, and to comment on a position paper which Adolph had sent him. (Adolph makes a number of marginal notes on the letter.)

"This makes much clearer to me both what your position is and what is the position of those you are trying to persuade, and this in turn explains why I find your book difficult. Rightly addressing economists, you assume in your readers not merely knowledge but—far more important—attitudes towards the science itself, which are far from mine, which I didn't even realize until you spelled them out here. So the way you formulate your conclusions seems to me, even now I understand them better, a bit strained and unnatural, although it is probably the best way to express them to professional economists.

"It has always baffled me that economics, alone of sciences, seems to claim to be both a pure and an applied science; in other words, both a science and a technology. Sciences purport to formulate laws, invariant or statistical, which enable one to understand and even predict outcomes. Technologies use these laws to formulate procedures by which to achieve outcomes. We can call both the result of an experiment and the achievement of a goal an 'outcome'; and we can regard both as the achievement or the falsification of a prediction. But we should not, I think, allow this to mask the difference between a science and a technology.

"So I get worried when you describe an economic objective as a *'datum'* when in fact it is a *desideratum*, to be achieved, if possible, never fully but to an extent varying both with what the technology can achieve and with what the policy-maker may decide to aim at, when he knows the cost, in other *desiderata. (Adolph: it is a 'desideratum' in reality).*

"I get the feeling that you are trying to preserve the appearance of economics as a pure science, rather than accepting the implications of regarding it as a technology. I ask myself in what respect political economics differs from any other kind of political science? And in what respect 'instrumental analysis' differs from what in other political fields is called 'operational research' or 'system-analysis-and-design' or even (grossest shorthand of all), 'program budgeting'. *(Adolph: It is operational research applied to the market.)*

"In every other field of human endeavor, including that huge section of our economic activities which are not regulated through the market, we are today accustomed—far too accustomed perhaps—to choose our goals and our paths to them by a circular process of planning and policy-making, in which the planners, drawing on every relevant science, devise 'best' paths from the present state to the desired state (or as near thereto as may be attained) and analyse the costs and benefits which would attend the following of the path. Among the 'pure' sciences on which they draw there is perhaps room for a science which describes the market as a generator of signals. But what meaning these signals will have, how they will be interpreted, seems to me to be part of a much wider and still unformulated science of human communication. *(Adolph: True!)*

"And this brings me to the only other comment I would risk trying to make now. There are two kinds of open system, radically distinct. One kind is open to the exchange of matter and energy only; the other is open to the exchange of matter and energy and *information*. It is a reproach to science and a most significant one that it has not yet felt the need for a special word for the second type (which) itself is of many degrees. Human and social systems are mediated by shared and self-generated systems of 'appreciation' which need special consideration.

"The difference between a meteorological and a social system seems to me to be both more radical than you describe, and capable of more precise definition. *(Adolph: Please explain!)* I won't add more to this now; but I will send you under separate cover a copy of a paper which is coming out in *The Political Quarterly* in July or October and which has some bearing on all this."[4]

Disabilities

In 1968 the letters become a great deal more frequent and more intimate, with both Geoffrey and Adolph opening their inner, extremely personal, thoughts and feelings to each other. Both wives are in ill health, and it is a year in which Ellen's illness becomes considerably worse, making it difficult for Geoffrey to maintain his professional commitments. His letter to Adolph of August 17 1968 is particularly introspective:

"Over the last 8-9 years I have been occasionally haunted by two images. In one I am being driven fast in a closed horsedrawn cab. The doors are shut and the windows curtained. I don't know where I am going. I want to get out and I can't. I can see only through a small window between me and the driver's box, and this is almost obscured by the driver's back view. I can't reach him, he doesn't look round, I know he hates my guts and bodes me ill. The uncanny thing is that, seen from behind, he looks very like me.

"The other one dates from the year we met in Brig. I am in a train going up the valley from Lausanne to Brig. I am sitting in a first-class carriage, very comfortable, but with my back to the engine. As the line bends, new stretches of the sunlit valley come into view; and with each new view I say to myself—'So that's where I was'. But this is hell, because I at once remember that, when I was actually there, it didn't look like that at all, I never saw it at all, only immediate, irrelevant bits. Then I know that whatever I think I'm seeing now is equally unreal, I shall only see 'now' later, when it's too late to do anything but wonder why I couldn't see it then. And I think: better be in the coming tunnel now than travel sitting this way round.

"The first of these daymares marked a time around 1961-64 and has never quite returned; but the second is a fairly frequent visitor and at the moment I am living with it rather closely, because a turn in the valley has shown me something beautiful, demanding and so obvious that I just couldn't not have seen it at the time. And yet, so far as I can remember, I didn't. I can't even be quite sure. Yet it's only last year.

"July seemed all set for a carefree month, of which I was to spend the middle ten days at the Wenner-Gren's castle in Austria with a very attractive, small group of people, discussing a theme that was right on the beam of my book—and I had reached that stage in writing when you just must stop and talk and have some input. Ellen had made what looked like fine arrangements for the time. Then her illness crept up on her quickly but quietly, and in the end I first postponed and then cancelled the trip when I was packed—but apart from the disappointment, the frustration had the hateful quality of feeling unnecessary, that but for some failure of mine it wouldn't have happened. This upset us both rather deeply.

"Then at the end of the month, I heard that a very old and close friend in America had died; and though the news wasn't unexpected, it disturbed me so wildly that I knew something was amiss beside just grief—the same feeling of something irrevocable, obvious but at the time unseen that was done or left undone. And after a fortnight's reconstruction of the past I have just seen it—a letter which so obviously (now) invited me to write as to one who knew that her only remaining job was to die a prolonged and painful death, and whom I knew quite well enough to write to on that basis, though probably no-one else did. So I am back in my train and almost in my cab.

"The only worlds in which I seem fit to live are the vegetable world and the conceptual world. The garden outside looks at this moment as people describe things seen when under mescalin. In a winter wood every dead leaf looks different from all the others. And in this world of ideas that I have been exploring and/or creating this last fifteen years, the pursuit, reaching after appreciation of form, is as enthralling as it is in a winter wood. And into this second world other people enter as fellow hunters, fellow explorers, fellow artists. As such I can communicate with them and enjoy them like anything. But what they think of as the real world they live in is the world I bumble through in the train, if not the coach. Does this eerie confession make any sense?

"In September you will be getting from Basic Books your copy of *Value Systems and Social Process*. The new book, once called *The Conditions of Hope* but now tentatively called *Being Human Now*, goes on apace. It has fallen into three parts—the trap, the trapped, and the way out. I've finished most of the trapped and half the trap. Let's hope I can find the way out. This is to be published by John Lane, going into Penguin soon after. I hope to finish it by mid-November.[5]

"Forgive me for beginning this letter by spilling all my disturbances over you. They had to get out first and you have already helped by being their still unconscious recipient."

Adolph clearly writes back immediately, and although we do not have his letter we can imagine the warm affection it conveys to Geoffrey, who replies August 24:

"What you say helps and is, of course, true, so far as it goes, which is most of the way. The bit you don't explicitly cover is the second of my images. I don't think this is very obscure. It isn't true of everyone that they don't know where the hell they are until they have passed it. Some people are most sensitive to the actual present moment and what is going on around them and its present meaning for them.

"The trouble with me, I think, is partly the self absorption common to writers and creative folk, but crossed with a fear of some types of situations which is liable to block them off until they are safely passed. I vaguely know what these situations are and why I fear them. I don't remember what it was in the Brig year that made the image of the valley so sinister and significant, but the trigger doesn't matter now. It wasn't the first time that I have been shaken by the knowledge that there is an uncertain, selected area in the "now" that I won't let myself see until it is 'then'. But never so bad as this last time.

"About *Being Human Now*—this has come pouring out these last weeks and is almost finished. I would very much welcome your comments, at least on one chapter. The book, as you will see, is written for the general public but I don't want to put the professional off unnecessarily by the way I express my heresies. Since I am so much ahead of the date I promised the book to the publishers, I may be able to try a bit more on you if you could bear it.

"It is strange to think that Czechoslovakia[6] has happened during the four days it took your letter to reach me. I say in the foreword of my book that, writing in April 1968, I cannot guess what new disorder, at what level, will have broken out before it is finished. Before I send it to the publishers, I will list them. This last thing is very hard to bear. How terrifying human history is."

Freedom in a Rocking Boat

Together with this letter Geoffrey sends Adolph the chapter headings for the new book (which was to be published under the title *Freedom in a Rocking Boat*) and an extract from the Foreword:

I was born in Victorian England. I have travelled in a Europe where frontiers still asked no passports and the golden sovereign was an international currency. Freedom and order, security and stability, progress and unity seemed to my young eyes to be operative standards, enjoyable realities, even natural assumptions. The illusion was total but I am glad to have known it. It has kept me fruitfully surprised by every new assertion of reality, as it emerged.

The world I live in now differs from my childhood's world as night from day. This difference blends most subtly gain with loss, as all who appreciate the night will know. As wartime blackout let the stars be seen again above the darkened streets, so the eclipse of our small certainties has revealed processes on an ampler scale of space and time. They are the processes of regulation on which order depends—not this order or that but any order which humans may aspire to impose on life, at any level from the planetary to the personal, in any aspect from the economic to the ethical. It is with these regulatory processes that this book is concerned ...

The only reason why I write the book or why anyone should read it is that, however partial or personal, it reviews a predicament which, as I believe, involves all humans alive today as no common fate has ever done before. To be human *now*, in the last third of the twentieth century, is to share a common threat—not primarily the threat of nuclear war—and a common responsibility so great as to transcend the imperatives of our warring political ideologies and our obsolescent economic mythologies, and to need with corresponding urgency a common understanding of them. To this understanding I would make such contribution as I can ...

These words remained in the final text of the Introduction to *Freedom in a Rocking Boat*, in both its hardback and paperback editions, as did his acknowledgment to Adolph:

One debt at least I can identify and am glad to acknowledge. It is due, with many other less explicit, to Professor Adolph Lowe, whose enduring faith in freedom as a positive, ordering process crystallized and ultimately qualified the still somewhat different view expressed in the last chapter of this book.

In November Adolph writes "under the immediate impression of your book which—as I had suspected—I find a genuine achievement. It is much more of a whole than is *The Sociology of Management* and much more explicit about the fundamentals than *The Art of Judgment*. Only now in retrospect do I understand some parts of the latter, because I can now visualize the frame of reference within which your ideas must be evaluated. At the same time, the new book is as unpretentious as befits the extreme difficulties of the subject matter—an open *Gestalt* in the best sense to be elaborated, perhaps modified, in your further thinking and that of your open-minded readers.

"In many ways the last chapter is the climax—a truly pioneering effort to which I shall return when I take up that topic again, which has always been close to my heart. You will find some casual remarks in the document that I sent off a few days ago—the concluding chapter of the Symposium Report. You will see that we bark up the same tree, but your bark is much more articulate. I find your tripartite schema and the 'circularity of the process of appreciation' a great help for my own thinking, even if I am not yet fully convinced that the physical theory of communication will be as helpful for our concerns as you think—its analogical use is certainly most suggestive. I take it that we basically agree.

"About the manner in which 'hypotheses' are generated, you will find some comments in my draft. (You will have to remember that there I argue against a convinced logical positivist. At the same time I think it important to realize that ratiocination does play an important even if subsidiary role there). We also seem to agree that our available schemata of thought do not help us in even properly posing, not to say solving, the most burning issue of our age: the conflict of values.

"I am a little surprised that you regard the politicians as the major architects of the value system. Don't they receive their values second-hand? Is it not the great 'thinkers', religious and other, from whom the changes in ultimate values issue? Even a Hitler had to fall back on the pseudo-prophecies of a Gobineau and others of this kind. Incidentally, speaking of race, I was amused that you call difference in colour a 'conspicuous perceptual difference'—it is 'conspicuous' only for those who are already conditioned that way, which is demonstrated negatively every day here when white and colored children play together. True, some gentlemen prefer blondes, but it should make us think that no one has based a theory of discrimation on different hair colors of 'whites'.

"But the significance of the book for my own work lies in another direction, namely in your emphasis on ecology in the widest sense, and on the limits this sets to 'progress'. As several times before, your work is a most important corrective for my own thinking, and after having digested your warnings I shall have to modify a good deal of what I have been provisionally committing to paper. I profoundly wish that I were able to render you a similar service by tipping the balance, not of the facts but of your 'values', a little more in an optimistic direction.

"What I have in mind centers on the notion of 'emancipation', which you interpret in a possible, and indeed dangerous manner, but which can be understood in such a way that it meets your major concern. One can, as I do, basically approve of the breaking of old fetters—of nature, of man dominating man, of tyrannical gods—without forgetting that the mere negation of old bonds is not enough. Part, and the truly difficult and unsolved part of the task of emancipation, is the conscious establishment of rules of self-restraint and of the accomplishment of wider identification. From the 'tactical' point of view you may be right in stressing the dangers, but only after we have remembered, and reminded others, that the world from which we come is one of material misery for the overwhelming part of mankind, of profound injustice and of paralyzing superstition.

"It is not for the first time that we arrive at a point where we temperamentally view the world differently. I well remember your reservation against my—very bad—first draft on 'Equality' in Brig. A clear conflict of values exists between us on this fundamental level, which can hardly be resolved by one of us accepting the position of the other. But there is probably also an ecological balance of ideas, in the search for which—let me speak crudely—the country squire and the displaced Jew have something to learn from each other. I am deeply convinced that both of us have got hold of one aspect of the totality of our situation, and that, in pursuing the 'sociology' of our respective knowledge, far from refuting any position, we may overcome 'in some degree' as Bacon would say, our limitations.

"Let me for the moment stop here. I still have something to say to other parts of the book, among them of course your discussion of norms. I conclude today with my deep thanks for an exciting experience and a quite unusual stimulation."

Geoffrey's next letter is sent before he receives this from Adolph. On November 29 he writes:

"How pleased I shall be if the book starts you off on your next creative cycle; or, more exactly, gets you over your present egg-bound phase. I haven't seen any significant reviews or had any comeback, except from two friends. But to my great surprise Penguin have already bought the paperback rights, which is a good sign. I let them read it in draft, when I was discussing the new book with them, but I did not expect it to have this result.

"Next, what is the relation in your mind between originals, rebels, and independent individualists? I would never have thought of Darwin as a rebel. And if you just mean that he had original thoughts, what about Newton? Locke? Hume? Blake? Bentham? And the scientists, such as Clerk-Maxwell? It may be an insular delusion, but I thought quite a lot of original-minded blokes had appeared over here from time to time. But you evidently mean people whose originality took the form of rebellion against current views—not scientific views?—in the name of individualism. Right? No, it can't be right, or you wouldn't have included Darwin. You must expound.

"I have been asked by Christopher Wright, who runs the Institute for the Study of Science in Human Affairs at Columbia, to write an occasional paper in a series they do. I am glad of this, because the length (10-15,000 words) will be just right to say something about science that I want to say. It may also be relevant to what you are gestating. I think you know that I have long had the feeling that creative thinking is the same process right across the board, from science through politics and ethics to aesthetics, and I think I am now ready to say this with some clarity. On that again I shall welcome your thoughts."

Emancipation

The letters cross. Geoffrey's of December 4 assumes that this has happened, and may happen again, but he is anxious to answer Adolph's letter of November 26, "first because it has given me so much pleasure, and then because there is so much to answer ...

"As you know, it is always lovely when someone likes and finds a use for something one had written, and I am especially pleased that you should have done so. It encourages me a lot. I'm especially glad you find the last chapter useful. I wrote it 2-3 years ago to clear my mind and did not publish it, though it has since appeared in *Human Relations*. I think I can do a bit better now, and think I have done in the new book, but I'm very glad if this was useful.

"On the conflict of values, I think it is only the scientists who have made this conceptually difficult. The more I see of science and read of scientists, the more I feel that science has cramped the human spirit conceptually worse than all the dryads and demons put together. I've a chapter called 'The Scientific Distortion' in BHN[7] but I mustn't expand on that now.

"Yes, the politicians are odd architects of value; but after all, it is they who prepare and push through the national budget. You may regard them as mere interest brokers but they are really more than that, advocates of policy, responsible for executing what they get through. True, it is the social reformers who do most of the seeing and the pushing, more outside than inside. It's a less than half truth. But I'm not sure that the great thinkers are more than half the story either. England had no counterparts to Bentham whose names are so clearly linked with the evaluation of utiliarian values; but it happened and men did it.

"I know about the white and colored children, but they move me not at all. To a child, another child must look far more like itself than any of these enormous, hairy adults. But never mind that one ... You remind me, rightly, that misery, injustice and superstition, each in its own way, are bad or at least worse than their abatement, as such. I agree, and I feel as well as think it, though not enough. But I hate none of them nearly so much as I *loathe* the idea of emancipation. The following is from BHN:

> If we review the patterns of human life from the earliest we know to the present time, we find that men's relations with their surround, whether physical or human, have been growing more demanding on them in precisely the same measure in which men have increased their demands on their surround. The industrial age was no exception: the coal measures shaped the mining communities at least as much as those communities shaped the coalfields. The post-industrial age will be even more demanding ... The industrial era managed for a time to conceal this fact, even to pretend that the trend had been reversed. For a contractual society, in which so many commitments had become voluntary and so many goods had become buyable, appeared to be one in which the individual, *given money*, could maximize his demands and minimize his obligations almost without limit.

> In its last phase, our age is trying to universalize this dream by making the double freedom of the rich open to all. But this makes no sense even in the twilight of the industrial era, and it will make still less in the post-industrial age. Mutual demands mount not only between men and their physical milieu but also between each and all the others; and these social demands become harder to meet as they grow less structured by custom, less governed by authority and more widely extended beyond the social groups which used both to contain them and to sustain them. The demand of the other can be ignored for a time ... but the more sluggish the response, the more violent the ultimate adjustment and the greater the chance that the system will have passed some point of no return. This is the lesson, surely the oldest in human history, which technology has obscured, both by its practical innovations and by its conceptual distortions, which have penetrated our whole culture.

"Emancipation seems to me to be good only if it means that the commitments we can choose or have to accept are a bit more meaningful than they would otherwise be. It doesn't even mean freedom to choose our commitments; nearly all of them are built into our situation or just happen. Anyway—I had better stop, or I shall start surprising myself, as well as you". The following morning, he adds a postscript:

"I am wrong about the black and white children, to this extent. The fact that they don't notice the difference up to 5-6 shows that skin color, though conspicuous, has not by then become eloquent. But nor have many other symbols. A child's channels of communication are more limited than an adult's, and no doubt the inter-child channels develop in quite a different pattern from the adult-child patterns. But all this tells us nothing about whether the messages which the opening channels pass is right or not.

"This is terribly interesting, and I've not right now the time or the clarity to pursue it. But I believe that I am right in criticizing the unspoken assumption that lies behind the argument based on the fact that color difference becomes eloquent later. There really are tensions between black and white adults that there are not between black and white children. The fact that the difference becomes eloquent later is no evidence at all that the message which it comes to pass later is wrong. I agree that in fact it is very largely wrong. But the object of the exercise today should be to make it right, not to silence it. Shouldn't it?"

"I have waited for your second letter before answering the first", writes Adolph December 7, 1968. "And I will try today no more than to give you my immediate reaction to what is to me the central point of the second one. We have indeed reached a, if not the, fundamental issue in our discourse, a point so central that the maintenance of the 'universe' of our discourse may well depend on it— I am not saying: reaching agreement, but reaching agreement on the reasons for our disagreement.

"I have tempted you with my last letter into a confession which may have surprised yourself, as you indicate—it has not surprised me. The particular perspectivism which determines, and limits, my vista has made me sensitive to your perspectivism, of which, until now, you seem to have been less aware. Neither one of us can jump over his own shadow—only a vision arising from deeper regions than arguments can penetrate can widen, or possibly even alter, our relative perspectives. What is essential is to realize that the 'conflict of values' which separates us is neither due to different readings of the historical record, nor to what 'scientists' have done to the human spirit.

"When Amos, my great ancestor, stood up against the custom and authority ruling the Kingdom of Israel, the two perspectives and the values emanating from them clashed, as they did at the time of Hamurabi or the Russian Revolution. I could make my task easy by asking you why you think that only the old customs and authorities, not to say commitments, can make a society viable. I know that the ancient anarchistic utopia, according to which all will go well once all existing structures are razed to the ground, is rampant again. And your warnings are only too true when you speak to these opponents. But not only are they a small even if loud minority, but your real opponents, among them myself, are those for whom *emancipation* from Nature's stinginess, from human exploitation and from false gods who were invoked to support the privileges of the 'rich' (your word), is and remains the fondest dream of man.

"But this is not yet the true conflict of values. One may, like myself, cherish this dream and may yet be doubtful about the extent to which it can be realized. (Your book has amassed powerful arguments for the support of such doubts, which is one of its great merits.) What really matters is whether the all too possible disappointments are anticipated with tears or with glee. And when you say that the idea of emancipation, understood as I just circumscribed it, fills you with loathing, you take your side of the 'barricade' not from a sense of realism but—I want you to supply the proper term yourself. And I ask you to do so, not because I really do not grasp this ultimate determinant of what I called earlier your perspective. I can, of course, speculate, and I had done so when I called you a country squire.

"Certainly our respective life histories, our country of origin, our involvement in the 'ongoing' process of society—corporation lawyer, governmental war work, Coal Board, versus a persistent 'maverick' as a civil servant, academic teacher, and for 35 years an 'alien' in two countries—all the more enters into the shaping of our perspectives and the underlying valuations. In my case I must stress again the Jewishness—not only in view of the actual troubles which this has created during most of my life, but even more because of a 'prophetic' tradition which has only been confirmed by those experiences.

"Now the issue is not that these perspectives are wrong or bad, or even that they could be evaded. But whereas I am well aware of mine, I wonder to what extent you are aware of yours? This is a problem for the clarification of which I strongly recommend 'free association'. The very fact of your outburst—'loathing'—after all, the Utopians from Plato to Morus and Marx were not just criminals—shows that Reason has not yet fully penetrated this layer. We cannot know now what you will 'dig up' in the end, but it would be shadow-boxing were we to try to discuss the substantive issues before this issue is clarified."

December 15, immediately upon receiving this letter, Geoffrey attacks his typewriter:

"Your letter of the 7th has just come and I must dash off an answer to it, though I have not yet done all the free association you commend. What I loathe is the atomism of the British liberal era, moulded and expressed by the market economy and its underlying ideology and reinforced by an analytic and reductionist scientific tradition: everything implicit in Rousseau's statement that men are born free and everywhere they are in chains (O hell, was it Rousseau or

Marx?). Anyway, it posits both a valid protest and a false conceptualization. You are carrying on the protest; I am warring against the conceptualization. Both in their contexts are, I believe, right. It is just a question of which, in a particular context, is the more important thing to say.

"The thing I am saying is that, in Joe Oldham's phrase, life is commitment, that we are scarcely free even to choose our commitments, and that any concept of emancipation which ignores these basic facts is a delusion. The reason why I feel so strongly about it is partly, I think, because I have been myself a prisoner in this specious freedom, have not accepted my commitments, have not fought on the barricades, only talked about them and written books about them.

"Equally, of course, I have never been oppressed or hard up or dominated by authority. If I had, I might be insisting on the other side of the coin. But my side is equally valid and there are at least as many folk who need to have their noses rubbed in it. Indeed, I think there are more, I think my message is the more topical today, though it wasn't when I was born. But this may be wrong. Mine is what my experience has fitted me to see and say.

"So I agree with you entirely that what I am seeing and saying is the fruit of my own life experience; but I don't think that is any reason why I should doubt it. This country and yours too is stiff with people who have been emancipated from what you call (I rebel!) the stinginess of nature *and* the dominance of man *and* the tyranny of superstition and who are lost, miserable, alienated and in revolt, and I'm trying to tell them why. And the bit I quote from BHN is to me the guts of the matter. This three-fold emancipation leads us into a world far more structured by commitments than any men have had to live in before—so much so that it may well pass the ability of men to meet its demands. If they fail, I shall not be 'gleeful'. But I shall not mourn the passing of the illusion that led them into such an impasse.

"So much for that for now. I find no difficulty in seeing your half of the picture and yet insisting on mine, just because mine is the half I am fitted to see. What about you?

Deficit financing

"One other thing which I was going to ask you some time, so I'll add it now. It may be absurd to expect an answer in a sentence, but my doubt is this. First, a straight question. Did Keynes advocate deficit financing to reverse a spiralling depression? I know he persuaded his generation that public investment was the best way to inject purchasing power into a depressed economy; but this, presumably, would not have had its trend-reversing effect if the money had had to be pulled out of the private sector as quickly as it was pumped into the public one.

"To put my doubts more broadly: I think I understand that the health of an economy depends amongst other things on (a) the relation between the flow of buyable things and the flow of money to buy them with, which determines whether the general situation is inflationary or deflationary; and (b) the relation between consumption and investment, which determines on a longer time scale the power of the economy to survive and grow. But I can't see why the relation between total spending in the public sector and total spending in the private sector should be very important anyway.

"If the key to the recovery of the '30s was deficit financing, and if our state today is the reverse of the '30s, presumably the key to recovery today is the opposite of deficit financing, i.e. the reduction of relative purchasing power; and presumably this would be equally effective for its purpose however the squeeze is distributed between the two sectors. If so, it is false to argue that, because we need to cut purchasing power, we *necessarily* ought to cut government expenditure. Given the amount of the cut it is a separate question of policy how to distribute it between the two sectors.

"Is this right? If so, it is very important if, as I argue, public investment is becoming far too important to be played around with as a balancing instrument. If that invites too long an answer, you must just say so. But most of all I want to know whether the first page of this letter supplies a sufficient basis for our dialogue to proceed on."

Again, we do not have Adolph's reply, but Geoffrey's habit of recapitulating an argument allows us (in his letter of December 22 1968) to have a good idea of what Adolph said:

"Your 'rejoinder' arrived yesterday and I spent a most interested evening reading it. I should be wiser to wait and read it again before replying; but I woke up this morning with many thoughts in what felt like order and I had better get them out before they are submerged by the set they have for the moment replaced. First, let me see whether I have really got the argument right. As I understand it, you are saying:

1. Economic behavior is no longer sufficiently regular to support hypothetico-deductive study of a classical, scientific kind.
2. This is terrible both for economists who thought they were practicing a science and for businessmen whose behavior can only be rational if they can detect regularities in the economic world in which they live.
3. Since Keynes we have learned to apply controls (called primary controls) to the economic system, but these do not suffice to make it sufficiently regular, because they are based on the assumption that they will evoke regular and predictable response and this they no longer do.
4. We must therefore use, in addition, controls (called secondary controls) aimed more directly at making behavioral responses regular.
5. This would be easy, but also unnecessary, in a world in which everyone agreed both on the macro-goals to be pursued and on the economic behavior-responses needed to achieve them; but this is not the world we live in.

6. At the other extreme, it can be simulated by the kind of controls used in Britain in wartime (rationing, direction of labor and so on). But these take effect by restricting the field of economic choice, rather than by making it predictable. So they do not really qualify as secondary controls, even if they were possible and acceptable.

7. Let us then seek a repertory of secondary controls which (i) leave choices open, whilst they (ii) influence behavior sufficiently to make the choices sufficiently predictable; and which are (iii) practicable to use, (iv) not intolerable to experience, and (v) not self-defeating in protracted use.

8. Let us further accept the fact that economics, being a goal-less science at the service of any political program, must accept the political setting of its objectives—must be content to be Political Economics.

9. Let us further accept the fact (which follows from 8) that, being reduced to a technology, economics like any other technology must work regressively back from its objective to determine what path will reach the desired end, rather than working forward from the given present state to predict where it will arrive.

10. Let us call this plotting of paths *Instrumental Analysis*, and accept that it must involve the use of secondary controls.

Question A: Have I (despite the provocative wording of (9)) got the argument right? (In a marginal note on the letter, Adolph has written *'Yes'* .)

Question B: Am I right in excluding controls of the type mentioned in 6 from the definition of secondary controls? *('No'* says Adolph's marginal note.)

Question C: Do I rightly understand the character of a secondary control from the following examples :

(1)   In 1931 HMG launched a major campaign to persuade people that patriotic duty required them to buy British if they possibly could. A secondary control?

(2)   Today there is an official agency to help firms choose office sites out of London, and a major publicity campaign to persuade them of the advantages of moving out. A secondary control?

(3)   A friend of mine, a big industrialist, says the government should support all its incentive schemes for encouraging investment, development in depressed areas and so on by major advertising campaigns, rather than assuming that economic men will read the signal and act accordingly. A plea for secondary controls?

Question D: Do you assume that there exists, for the finding, an adequate repertory of secondary controls? If you don't, I would have expected to realize this from your book and paper, from a tone of 'this may not be possible but it's the only hope'. If, as it seems, you do, why don't you give your readers reason to share your hope? I, for instance, though ready to be convinced, can't imagine what you are relying on.

"Now for a few comments: It staggers me that any scientist should fail to distinguish between an historical and a non-historical system; but since they do, you clearly do well to disabuse them.

"Surely every *science* is goal-less, in that its only goal is to understand its subject matter. And equally (or more so) every technology is goal-less, because its business is to find ways of doing what others choose as good to do. Do answer this specifically, for I am utterly at sea here on what is evidently crucial. Are you saying any more or less than that economics is a technology? And if so, isn't instrumental analysis the normal procedure of technologies?

"Does some confusion lurk in the unique position of economics in claiming to be *both* a science *and* a technology? An engineer knows the sciences he needs for his particular doings. He may even become a professor of engineering. But he won't become a professor of physics. Similarly a doctor may become a professor of medicine but not (unless he changes his *métier*) of physiology. Nor is medicine as such a 'science'. Lawyers, on the other hand, may become professors of jurisprudence, and nearly all professors of jurisprudence have at some time 'practised' law. But the position of economists corresponds to neither and seems to me to be snarled up between the two. Is this because, alone of the social sciences, they tried to pretend that they were observers of a natural, non-historic field?

"But I have already said enough to reveal more than enough confusion. I do hope it is understandable confusion. It frustrates me greatly not to have got hold more fully of this obviously important and radical argument ... You already have one letter from me—about emancipation—which bears on this only in that I see no reason in experience or logic to hope that further emancipation will leave our resources less scarce, relatively to what we want to do with them. But we have been round that one before.

"Now I will return to my Columbia paper about the intimate relationship and wide relevance of those apparently separate powers of the human mind to (a) recognize and (b) create form, pattern or order—'three words which I regard as synonymous but often use together, since each has collected a somewhat different connotation.' I think we may find it easier to understand each other when we get on to that field."

Adolph's reply was written on New Year's Eve, 1968 : "This letter is an important send-off into '69, and I answer immediately. With one minor exception your 10 points are an excellent summary of my views, so good that I plan to use them myself in further discussions. The exception is point 6, referring to rigid command controls. They do fall in the general category of secondary controls, and it is my 'liberal value system' which makes me relegate them to the background. I may be wrong in this, as the experience with our surtax of last summer shows. It has been quite ineffectual so far, because of a tendency to dissaving on the part of both business and consumers. Therefore it should have been combined with a policy of compulsory saving—certainly a 'command' measure. But all this is not of basic importance.

"Now, to deal with what you call your 'confusion', let me start out from the question whether economics is a science or a technology. Your troubles arise from the fact that, paradoxically, you do not argue historically enough. If my interpretation of the events in early capitalism is correct, there was a historical epoch when economics could behave as if it were a science. In contrast with the historical school and other critics, I maintain that the alleged 'laws of economic behavior' were applicable to that era. Of course not because there ever *were* 'innate propensities' as the classical economists asserted, but because the natural-social pressures of that age induced a homogeneous behavior pattern which could pass as a sort of law of motion analogous to the physical laws of motion. Certainly there was always a difference in 'degree'—apart from the difference in 'causation'—therefore even then economics was only an 'as if' or pseudo-science. But conventional deductive analysis was applicable to a large extent, and though the welfare effects were dubious there was a minimum of 'order' in the sense of macro-predictability. Therefore, under the aspect of 'functioning', the problem of 'goals' did not arise.

"I will not repeat the reasons—that is, the historical changes—which have vitiated this law of motion, and have now indeed transformed the economic problem into a technological one, in which stipulation of macro-goals takes the place of the earlier 'knowlege' of a valid law of motion. So it is the very historical nature of the actual problem that placed economics at one time near the science end of the knowledge spectrum, and at another time near the technology end. And it is even more complicated, because neither is micro-behavior simply chaotic, nor need the irregularities be accepted as final—control can approximate actual to suitable behavior and, to the extent to which such controls work, processes can be approximated which again permit generalizations, thus approximating—logically—the former state of a pseudo-science.

"It is not you who are confused, but the state of affairs is double-edged: by doing an effective technology job we economists can recapture that minimum of predictability which is indispensable for maintaining decentralized decision-making. So it is not just a 'whim of scientism' that makes me strive for this, but my original value decision against collectivization.

"You are right that instrumental analysis is the 'normal procedure' of technologies. But in agreement with Polanyi it seems to me that no one has as yet worked out the detailed steps of such a 'logic of goal-seeking', and rightly or wrongly I regard my methodological exposition of this procedure as an attempt to elaborate the logic of the procedure.

"Now you chide me for not having been more explicit with regard to the 'repertory of secondary controls'. It is true, I have not given a systematic survey, though I have given a number of examples. I clearly state that this is a field which needs further exploration, and that the actual practices of a number of 'planning countries' offer important suggestions. Let me just remind you of an excentric but very important type of such controls which I have mentioned repeatedly: education of business leaders during their college years. If, in contrast to the thirties, the New Economics as well as collective bargaining are backed up by the majority of influential business leaders today, this is the consequence of what they were taught at Harvard Business School. But this is a wide field.

"I am most eager to hear more about your Columbia paper. This is certainly a topic which we both regard as fundamental. The last section of my rejoinder actually deals with the same issue, without offering a solution as yet."

Geoffrey's reply was dated January 8 1969: "I have two letters to thank you for, and your paper, 'The Third Force'. First, on your letter of December 21, I had one go at answering this properly and got bogged down; so for now I'm not going to try to answer the questions you put. 'Yes-but' answers take so much longer than plain 'No's'. I think the idea that significant life begins after economic needs are satisfied is wrong, anyway for the purposes of today's argument. But I could not do justice to all this without writing another book. I am much better for your three emancipations, and I have hung the last section of my Columbia paper on them. But I think the best thing I can do now is to send you BHN when I can get a copy—if you really want to see a book-length MS— and the much shorter Columbia one. We are barking up the same tree and seeing different bits of the same animal, and it helps me a lot to compare what we see. But there are differences in the 'setting of our appreciative systems' which at the moment I cannot identify and express clearly enough to be useful.

"Now on your letter of the 31st, I am glad I have got it so nearly right. But I am puzzled about my point 6. There is a difference between controlling imports by licence and controlling them by persuading people that for the time being they ought to buy British. The first merely restricts the field of economic choice. The second makes it more predictable, as well as more apt, whilst still leaving to the individual his own, now better informed choice. So I thought you would think it important.

"You don't explicitly answer my questions C or D. They seem to me to be relevant to your 'Third Force' paper. If a population were sufficiently well informed and motivated to avoid incurring liabilities in foreign exchange to an extent neither less nor more than the economic situation demanded, wouldn't that be the sort of spontaneously conforming society you have in mind? It isn't impossible. In the early '30s, in a train to Paris, a Frenchman said to me: 'You are the most extraordinary people. When other people have a currency crisis, they send their money abroad; but you folk bring it back'. Today we aren't even asked to.

"I am most grateful to you for confirming my understanding of Keynes and anti-Keynes."

As the Sixties drew to a close illness dogged the two men and their wives. Ellen's death in 1972 was to create a vast chasm in Geoffrey's life. Bea was to become housebound with Parkinson's and other ailments. The growing weight of old age was to strike both Adolph and Geoffrey during the next decade but interfered very little with their correspondence.

Notes

1 . Later reproduced as Chapter 3 in *Human Systems are Different*, Harper & Row 1983.
2 . G. Vickers, "Projections, Predictions, Models and Policies", *The Planner*, Vol. 60 No. 4, April 1974.
3 . *The Art of Judgment*. See Bibliography.
4 . G. Vickers, "Planning and Policy Making", *The Political Quarterly*, Vol. 38 No. 3, July-September 1967. Republished in G. Vickers, *Value Systems and Social Process*, Tavistock Press, London and Basic Books, New York, 1968. In paperback by Penguin Books, London 1970, New York 1971.
5 . Published as *Freedom in a Rocking Boat* (sub-title: *Changing Values in an Unstable Society*), Allan Lane, the Penguin Press—an original Pelican, 1970. See Bibliography.
6 . The 1968 invasion by the Soviet army.
7 . 'Being Human Now.'

4

The Early Seventies

During the next decade the correspondence between the two men becomes increasingly philosophical and wide-ranging, and ever more intimate. Geoffrey begins the decade with his letter of January 28, 1970:

"I've just been reading a rather moving little book called *Man's Search for Meaning*, by Viktor Frankl, an Austrian Jew who survived Auschwitz, Dachau and two other camps and now professes neurology and psychiatry at Vienna, where he has founded a school of existential psychiatry which he calls logotherapy. You may know all about him. In case you don't, the essence of what he is saying seems to be roughly this:

"The essential human pursuit is neither the pursuit of pleasure nor of power but of meaning. Meaning is not the answer to a question addressed by men to life about life in general, but the answer given by each individual to a question asked by life of him about each specific situation. The question is, what does this situation require of you?

"The answer may be in terms of doing, of experiencing or of suffering, including dying. Whatever the situation and whatever the mode of answer, there is always one and only one right answer, which is always accessible to anyone's search and which infallibly supplies not meaning in general but the specific meaning of that situation for him, which is the only sensible kind of answer to the search for meaning.

"Thus, unlike other existentialists, e.g. Sartre, Frankl distinguishes between no meaning and wrong meaning. Meaning for him is not just the actual answer, whatever it may be. Men, for him, are not to that extent their own creators. This is partly because he is evidently either a believing Jew or a believing Christian. He stoutly maintains that *requiredness*, hence 'responsibleness', hence meaning, are within the reach of everyone, of any faith or none. His examples are not, for me, nearly strong enough to carry the heavy burden of this proof; too often they come down to no more than defining something for which to live, which for a prisoner might be no more than revenge. But however unconvincing his examples on this point, the fact that six years of concentration camps left him with this faith commands attention and respect—especially from one who has never been more than comfortably hungry. I could give him much more puzzling examples of the question: 'What is the right answer—or any significant answer—to a situation like this?' but I would be very interested in his answer.

"Anyway, logotherapy is a fine supplement and antidote to psychotherapy. He instances a US diplomat who came to him with a terrible neurosis—an inexplicable rejection of the policies which his government expected him to implement. Frankl suggested that if a man's profession required him to implement policies of which he disapproved, the situation required him to change his profession. The diplomat was relieved—and amazed. Five years of analysis had convinced him that his scruples could be nothing but the projection onto a symbolic father-figure of his infantile resistance to the authority of his dad.

"Do you know Wolfgang Friedmann, a professor of international law at Columbia? I have known him for many years and spent some hours with him in London yesterday as he passed through after giving the Tagore lectures in Calcutta. He is a very sociological lawyer, largely engaged on research into such things as the working of multinational corporations. He is now looking for models of the mixed economy which he wants to study on a comparative basis. I think you may find that his work isn't far from your own line on ecological economics and may throw some light on it. He asked me for guidance on the literature. I told him sadly that your report, after much more thorough search than mine, had not yet revealed much that was any better than Vickers.

"They aim to publish *Rocking Boat* in August. My other book—tentatively called *Making Sense*—has gone uncannily fast. I've begun to make a typescript from a fairly large MS, from which I shall soon see both how much there is and how much is undigested and still in effect to do. Have you yet found your economic ecologist?"

Correspondence is made considerably more difficult by a long postal strike in the UK at the end of that year. On February 20 1971, Geoffrey is sending his letters to Adolph by special courier.

"I can't remember whether I sent you a fortnight ago a copy of my Philadelphia paper; I fancy I did. Anyway it is a long time since we exchanged letters.

"I wish I could send you a packet of cheerfulness. Spring has come, the weather invites one for the first time to stand still out of doors, all the usual magic is on the way. I have finished a paper for a journal here called 'Changing Ethics of Distribution' and am at last more or less free of deadlines.

"But the corresponding spiritual lift has not yet come. This may be just fatigue; or old age; or the usual reaction after the end of one of Ellen's illnesses. But consciously it focuses on the sad state of my country and the world, but especially my country, which seems to be in a dark, confused state. I wrote a paper (before the last) about the containment of conflict, tracing the ways in which a society mutes the conflicts that it generates; then resolves those that remain; then contains those it hasn't yet resolved; and then? We are getting to the point where we have to answer the ultimate query. Or are we? I don't know. I'm ill-equipped to think in conflictual terms.

"Our postal strike especially distresses me. These are intelligent, civil-service-minded men, employed by an undertaking whose 'capacity to pay' imposes a limitation far more real and assessible than any other public or private corporation I can think of. It is a revelation of the criteria that now tenant people's minds about absolute and relative levels of pay. Who under 60 ever heard of real incomes going down?

"How are you getting on with costing what it would take just to stand still on the ecological butter-slide? It's a terribly important figure.

Lecturing at Berkeley

"I am told that Basic Books will after all do a hardcover edition of *Freedom in a Rocking Boat*, and that the paperback will come out on both sides of the water at the end of this year, but no details yet. Meantime, a voice from Berkeley penetrated our strike to ask if I would give a lecture there end-April. Erich Jantsch seems to have funds to organize a series of guest lecturers. I am trying to put a program together, within the usual limits of time and support at this end, and also within an unusual sense of limited energy. At present I don't even see the usual chance of a weekend in New York. If indeed I have to fly over you without stopping, you will know that time and/or energy must be very short indeed." As he is sealing the letter he finds a paper written a week or so earlier "to cure a sudden nausea at the fate which kept me using words for such sterilized purposes as analyzing changes in the ethics of distribution." The experience it describes happened a few years earlier.

The track led abruptly upwards from the road, at first a chalk butter-slide under black yews, then shoe-slippery grass tussocks, to be trodden sideways and climbed zigzag at its steepest. It rose in three successive waves to a beech wood on the summit. Even from the crest of the first, the valley, with its winding river, railway and road, seemed already far below and far away. From the crest of the second they appeared foreshortened in remote detail, like the background in some Book of Hours. No sound reached that high place from the ant-like traffic or from anywhere but the wind in the grass.

When I turned to climb the third wave, I saw at my feet a small leaf, perhaps an inch long; pointed, withered to bright chestnut but still smooth. It was supported above the soil on the grey points of short grasses which did not bend beneath its weightlessness. It was curved in all three planes. Fibrous veins displayed its structure. It was quite still.

And as I watched, its stillness spread; first to me. I wanted not to move by a hair's breadth, lest the bond between it and me should break. The stillness spread to the grass around us. It encompassed the hill. The beech wood became attendant on it. The whole valley slowly filled with it. This leaf and I, its participant, had drawn the miles-wide landscape into an attentive, breathless synthesis, focused here on this inch-long form, poised on its supporting grass points. And for some timeless space there was no movement, no sound and no distinction or identifying of parts in all that had been there united. For there was no 'I' that gazed. No tiniest fraction of me stood aside to watch me watching. I and what I watched were one; and through that tiny gateway, I became one with what was boundless.

Then this lostness slowly passed. I became aware of my feet in their heavy shoes, upholding my weight on their arched muscles; of the grey winter grass around me; of the vigilant wood above and the shapely valley below; above all, of the leaf, but now as a separate form, fugitive and transient, beautiful and still charged with a strange excitement, fading now as from some happening which was over and would not come again.

So I climbed to the summit and walked through the wood, enjoying the forms of bough and trunk, the colour and shape of old bramble leaves, the heap of evocative delights that is a winter wood. But I knew now, as I had never known before and should never again forget, that this familiar joy was only joy in a sensed potential, in forms seen through the estranging glass of myself; that these delightful leaves were closed doors which I was enjoying only from outside; that if they opened, I should have a different experience—at a cost that I had not yet learned to pay.

This different experience, I have read, people can learn to receive, though at the cost of thinning their protective walls of self in ways both wearisome and frightening, especially to Europeans. I do not know why once, without preparation and without seeking, I should have strayed into the antechamber of the place where, could I have spoken, I might have said: 'I am That'."

Politico-economic ecology

In a letter written January 9, 1972, Geoffrey tells Adolph about a number of arguments into which he has been drawn with regard to politico-economic ecology.

"In the last ten days or so I have been involved in the same argument with three different people. First, an enthusiastic young Englishman, Edward Goldsmith, who edits a magazine called *The Ecologist* and recently edited a book of essays called *Can Britain Survive?* He sent me a long MS beginning with an excellent ecological analysis and ending with a puerile politico-economic conclusion. Then another young Englishman from the Tavistock, spelling out the same dream future when universal affluence sets everyone free from the demands of organization. And in the middle of all this a letter from Bertram Gross, to whom a friend had sent a comment by me on a paper of his about the danger of 'friendly Fascism'. The comment was: How can any society get by which mistrusts its institutions so much as Americans do?

"All this is relevant to your request to me to say what I think about the transition more clearly than I have in the *Rocking Boat*. The most convenient step towards that at the moment will be to send you a copy of the letter I wrote to the young man from the Tavistock. This is being copied so I'll hold this until next Friday.

"I have also been drawn into the argument now current here about the organization of government-sponsored research. I'm sorry about this, because it makes me angry and I can no longer afford or support that passion. There are times when I am overwhelmed, as by a distillation from my last seventeen years, by a hatred of natural scientists as being authors of the most poisonous mythology that has befouled the mind of man since Baal. Don't expect me to justify that generalization in every detail. But I feel better for having made it. I wonder whether you ever feel the same?

"I feel as if I were coming to the end of a creative bout and hope soon to tidy it up and have a rest. Meantime the world is hard to live in or to think about."

He sends Adolph a copy of his letter to Firth Higgin, of the Tavistock Institute of Human Relations, dated January 1 1972 :

As always when I read an essay on this theme, I am frustrated by the fact that I share many of your views and values but utterly reject your basic assumption. As I see it:

1.   We have not defeated scarcity. Millions of our fellow-countrymen are in real want now.

2.   We have not even discovered how to defeat scarcity. We thought we had until 20-30 years ago, but the myth is already exploded. For at least three reasons:

(i)   The self-exciting production system cannot of itself direct production where it is needed (in the world it is making) or distribute incomes in a way that world regards as acceptable. It has been kept going by calling in the state increasingly as director of effort and as redistributor of income. The resultant mix of rights based on political membership with rights based on employment cannot in my view be carried much further without radically changing the system. We do not know what, if any, system would do it any better.

(ii)   Anyway, the self-exciting system is not maintainable for ecological reasons. Growth rates must come down, perhaps growth must cease. Of what is produced the share going to collective use (notably environmental control) and investment must increase much faster than even present growth rates. So the amount available for personal consumption must shrink, heightening the problems of distribution.

(iii)   For Britain, dependent for necessities, notably food, on a world economy which will be even more affected than the domestic economy by the failure of the mainspring of perpetual growth, the foregoing difficulties will be multiplied. The risk of famine in England in your lifetime is far more real than it ever was in mine, except at the peaks of the two submarine offensives.

3.   It follows that the responsibility of the state as director of effort and as distributor of income must greatly increase. No smaller unit will be large enough to

cover the area over which ethical claims to equitable distribution are paramount. No larger unit could generate the consensus needed to make such a redistribution.

4.   What this will mean for us in political terms is hard to guess. It has been the only common theme in every revolution of our century from Ataturk to Castro, from Mussolini to Tito, from Lenin to Mao Tse-Tung. The nearest foreshadowing in our experience is Britain mobilized in the last war. Necessities were rationed, luxuries unobtainable, railways advertised 'Is your journey really necessary?' The disparities, physical and psychological, of private capitalism were much abated. There was also direction of labour, some control of prices and wages, heightened control of land use and private wealth. And so on. Which of its features would be less, which more, developed in a society mobilized to deal with national scarcity is an interesting question.

5.   Most odd and important, however, is the fact that this wartime Britain realized many of the states which you rightly desire. There was more fellow-feeling, more mutual help at the personal level. The dominance of state organization coincided with a more social and more personal community, more ready to prize and enjoy the things you rightly think it should.

6.   But it was not a society in which people went to work when and if they felt like it and did what, if anything, they pleased. Still less, if I am right, will be the best sort of England in which you can hope to live the rest of your life. On the contrary it will be a society in which public responsibility is accepted and expected by everyone, to an extent only faintly foreshadowed by the last war (in which, you may remember, farmers implemented agricultural policy, housewives implemented rationing and so on to an extent the post-war generation can scarcely imagine). This may not prove possible. If not, so much the worse. But if it is realized, it will be a world in which many of your psychological aspirations can be fully realized. It is, I think, the only kind of world in which, in the next thirty years in England, they could be realized.

This has been written at least as much for my own benefit as for yours. Thank you for the stimulus. I wrote on the same lines a few days back to Edward Goldsmith of *The Ecologist*, commenting on a paper which began with a splendid analysis of the ecological trap and what it would take to get Britain into a stable ecological state, and followed it with political recommendations for decentralizing into self-supporting localities, without a word about how they would support either themselves or each other.

A horror of large-scale responsibility seems to blind the counter-culture both to its necessity and to its potential humanity. This seems to me unimaginative and defeatist, in psychological and ethical as well as economic terms. Am I imprisoned in an old "palace of ideas" or dreaming of a new one?

With a subsequent letter to Adolph, January 13 1972, Geoffrey sends a copy of *The Ecologist* containing "a major sound-off about cutting Britain down to a stable state", together with a copy of a letter to its editor. "I declined to be one of the sponsors, but think now this may have been too cautious." He continues:

"I'm not aware of attaching any particular weight to persuasion. I list it as one of the agencies of change; and I include in it persuasion by the situation, by other people and by ourselves, not really separable processes but worth distinguishing in order to give a more adequate meaning to 'learning'. The other two agencies I see as impotence-and-coercion, and 'conflict'. Persuasion plus impotence-coercion is the limit of peaceful change. Beyond that you start fighting, with irreversible and unpredictable changes in both the objective and the subjective situation."

Geoffrey's letter of 13 January to Edward Goldsmith, editor of *The Ecologist*, concerning his 'Blueprint for Survival' is enclosed and carries further the argument in his letter to Firth Higgin.

> The ecological analysis is most cogent and comprehensive; you have done a most useful job in bringing all this together. I fully agree with your analysis of the self-exciting and therefore self-limiting if not self-destructive character of the governmental-entrepreneurial system and the economics which goes with it and supports its assumptions. I have some reservations on the social analysis. But my main criticism is that you seem to me unduly to mute, if not to misread, some of the political implications.

> Obviously the policy includes everything most hateful, at least in the short run, to government, business and trade unions—shrinking tax base, falling revenues, higher costs, shrinking markets, more work, lower wages, eroded differentials, lower GDP. The only current 'goal' in the program is reduced unemployment, through the encouragement of labour-intensive industry. This is important and will become more so if, as I expect, the present expansive policy comes to be recognized as incompatible with other than rising unemployment. But even your promise of lower unemployment looks like being realized more slowly than the corresponding costs.

> So it won't be easy to get it accepted by both political parties, industry and the unions. But given that you do, I ask myself, among other questions:

> (i) how could we implement it without starting a major recession (and having abjured in advance most of our present controls, such as they are)?

> (ii) how, whilst implementing it, could we remain sufficiently competitive in international markets? (It would obviously be absurd to wait until everyone else has agreed, especially since many other countries can afford to wait much longer); and

> (iii) would fiscal measures be enough to boost labour-intensive industry quickly enough, and if not, what are the alternatives and supplements?

> There are answers of a sort to all these questions, though some of them would go best with Fidel Castro as prime minister and Dr. Schacht at the Treasury—I choose two names for which I have high respect—and I won't begin to elaborate. But two points seem to me to be clear; these changes postulate an ideological revolution and a strong central government.

> To bring this country from its present state to a stable state will, I think, require centralized control at least as strong and far more extended than in the last war. I see no chance that greater physical dispersal would mean greater devolution of political power. There would indeed be much for local government to do, even more than now. But the weight of decision and control at the centre would surely be much

increased. (How else, for example, could your prosperous local communities support the starving ones or arrange to share limited and therefore probably licensed imports?)

Such a society may be highly democratic, highly participatory and socially well-knit. It will only work—and only happen—if everyone is frightened by events and prospects into an enormously enhanced level of responsibility, which will be expressed *both* in accepting centralized control *and* in implementing it at grassroots level. And for the same reason there may well be, as there was in the war, more humanity, mutual help at the personal level, social intercourse, community spirit and mutual trust, including trust of government and its officials. But I think the paper plays down the blood, sweat and tears to an extent which may make it (or its authors) sound a bit unrealistic.

On coercion and conflict

Geoffrey replies January 28 1972 to a January 20 letter from Adolph with regard to his formula 'maximum tolerable disorder':

"Your formula seems to me to miss one crucial element in the ordering process. It doesn't follow that we can command even tolerable disorder; and on the other hand, more than one level of order might be attainable though at different costs. I have been writing a paper about this for some time and I won't develop the thought further now except to say that in cybernetic jargon it all turns on when the feedback becomes positive, but I would commend to you, if you have not seen it, Karl W. Deutsch's *The Nerves of Government*, first published in 1963 and re-published with a new preface in 1966 in paperback by the Free Press.

"I find this book enormously helpful and important, both because of the writer's own insights and because of the summary that it gives of other people's work. The first part is a summary of the various models of society and politics which have been used up to the time when modern ideas of communication and control began to affect them. The second part describes the new models and their effect on the old models; and the third part uses the new models to draw some conclusions. This is the first book I have read which even tries to apply modern ideas of communication and control to the full scale of personal and societal problems which ordinary people have to face, and I have found it extremely useful.

"When you write that we all want to avoid conflict, you mean that we want to avoid the threshold beyond which the prosecution of conflict disrupts both the political and economic system on which we depend, and the personal and social expectations on which these in turn depend. A high degree of conflict can be, and is, continually being resolved and contained within this threshold; which shows that the word 'conflict' is used in two very different senses. This is the subject of the paper I am writing.

"I do attach a lot of importance to what I call mutual persuasion, partly because its importance and its nature have been so largely ignored by writers on the subject but chiefly because it is both the product and the mediator of communication at those higher levels on which any kind of tolerable society under present conditions depends, and it is indeed one of our safeguards against crossing the threshold beyond which conflict escalates. But I am equally interested in it as a major means by which conflict in the first sense is resolved and contained.

"Similarly I would not bracket coercion and conflict as you do in your letter, because coercion often serves to contain conflict rather than to escalate it. Here again what matters is the threshold. Sociologists are prone to argue the merits of a conflictual model of society as against an equilibrium model as if they were alternatives. In fact we all know that the system depends on both, and I think that systems theory helps us to understand in any particular situation what mixes, if any, will be stable." He refers again to 'Blueprint for Survival' and *The Ecologist* whose editor "has got a large number of scientists to attest their agreement to his thesis that within the next 100 years, or much less, the world will have to return to a 'stable state' in which it uses no more energy than it gets from natural regenerative sources, i.e. the sun, the wind and the tide, and no more material than it can make good by recovery and re-use (if it is mineral) or replacement (if it is vegetable).

"There are some qualifications to this thesis. Energy by nuclear fission, if it became possible, would greatly increase supplies of energy, although even this would be limited by the difficulty of getting rid of waste heat. Similarly, the recycling of inorganic material could be supplemented to a diminishing extent by the use of the remaining natural resources extended by synthetic processes but these, according to the paper, should be thought of as qualifications on a picture which is basically 'stable state', whereas at present even the most ecologically-minded economists and politicians think in terms of an economy of flow modified by increasing constraints to mitigate specific threats of pollution and wastage.

"The publication of this paper was accompanied by a press conference at which some of the scientific sponsors were present. It received a great deal of favorable comment in the newspapers, but has been universally ignored or derided by economists and political scientists. This is partly because it contains some naive social and political suggestions. Nonetheless, I am shocked and disappointed that it has attracted so little interest in these quarters. The only English economist to sign as a sponsor was Mishan, whose work you doubtless know. The only political scientist was William Robson. It seems to me very important that some competent economists should devote themselves to the problems which will arise insofar as a world economy of flow has to be converted into a world economy of stock circulation.

"Suppose, for example, that we started from the assumption that every use of material should be charged with the full cost of bringing that material back to the state in which it can be used again or replaced by its equivalent, and that anything which cannot be so replaced should not be used. This sets us two problems. The problem of identifying the constraints which prohibit some uses altogether, and the problem of measuring cost in those cases where regeneration or replacement is possible at some cost. This seems to me to be a fruitful line of enquiry which would, incidentally, produce some indication of that missing figure which you and I have discussed before now, namely amount of GNP which ought to be allocated to the maintenance of the physical and social environment.

"Since any move in this direction is going to result in a reduction in productivity as we now measure it, another field of enquiry will be into the dependence of the present financial system on continued economic growth and into the way in which world economy, at least in the developed countries, might move backwards, developing the labor-intensive industries employing less rather than more capital per head of person employed and yet devoting a greater proportion of total resources, at least in the first instance, to collective use rather than to consumption. This enquiry would be connected with the present intractable problem of unemployment, and might suggest an effective approach to it. This would be important, especially if the previous enquiry had shown that our present attempts to deal with unemployment by still further speeding growth are doomed to failure.

"In this last connection it seems to me that our present efforts in this country—and I think in yours too—to produce sufficiently full employment by stimulating the activity of an industry which has every incentive to reduce jobs will seem, a few years hence, even more absurd than our pre-Keynesian efforts of the 1930s. A corresponding political enquiry might pursue the implications of my paper 'Changing Ethics of Distribution' in its conclusion that the real net personal incomes available for consumption by persons in developed western countries over the next decades is bound to fall steadily, and in some cases dramatically, towards a much more equal level and that this will now affect more people in the high paid weekly wage earner class than in the high paid salary class, though it will also have great repercussions on the use, enjoyment, profitability and even ownership of private wealth.

"This in turn has important political implications. Our Labour Party in its present form seems to me no longer capable of socialist policies because of its dependence on trade unions, of which the more important have attained for their members privileged positions depending on the existing system. It is significant that although individual MPs of all parties responded eagerly to the ecologist's blueprint, and are developing an inter-party group, the only political party which expressed interest as a party was the Communist Party which averred, perhaps rightly, that it was the only party capable of carrying out such a program.

"I do not know whether I can generate over here sufficient interest among economists or political scientists to pursue any of these questions, but I shall try to do so. Meantime I write you this long letter to clear my own mind and to share with you the present product, such as it is. Do not let it divert you from your labors in hand. But at some point I am sure that all this will become relevant to your problem of identifying 'maximum tolerable disorder'.

"It is too late in this letter to tell you why I increasingly dislike natural scientists for reasons quite distinct from those which make me dislike technologists. It is not their fault, I agree, that they mislead social scientists into imitating them. But it is their fault when they themselves set up as social scientists, assuming that any serious problem can be reduced to their terms. And it is even more their fault when they allow the simplicities of their professional life to affect their political and human judgment, even in their capacities as ordinary men. If you know more than a few not affected in some degree in one or both of these ways you are luckier than I."

Moving towards a stable state

In March, Geoffrey replies to a letter from Adolph in which the latter had spoken of the sadly defeatist reaction of a friend with regard to the impotence of policy in moving towards a stable state.

"I enclose copy of a letter which I have just written about this, and I am writing a paper about it. It seems to me that there is a lot to be done and that every clarification in our thinking will be reflected to that extent in an improvement in our current policy. Of course, this will not be enough, but what does that matter?

"As to the ethics of the EEC, it depends which side of the account you think is the more important. We shall help Calabria, well and good, but what are we doing to the Caribbean? We shall help French agriculture, well and good, but what are we doing to New Zealand in terms of current ethical obligation? I have no doubt that we are breaking more ties than we are responding to.

"My own underlying feeling is that the EEC is mainly the rationalized selfishness of five rich strong countries seeking to be richer and stronger at the expense of their neighbors and particularly of the Third World. I think it is anti-American, anti-Russian and anti- all developing countries except those which the big powers bring along; and as to these, my impression is that our ex-colonies will not fare so well as those of France.

"The EEC builds into its constitution all those liberal principles which I think are least appropriate to the world into which we are moving. It is typical of EEC that it commits us to allow free emigration by Frenchmen, Germans and Italians at a time when we are denying it to our own citizens. It measures its present success as well as its future hopes by the yardstick of GNP, the inadequacies of which you know as well as I. And what it has achieved even in this direction has,

I gather, benefited the high technology, low labor industries and prejudiced the others. We shall have to go in now, but viewing it thus you will not expect me to glow with altruism."

The enclosure was a copy of a letter to the editor of *Futures:*

It is widely repeated, though not yet widely believed, that currently accelerating rates of economic growth will be arrested or stopped and then reversed within decades by four related but partly independent factors:

(1)   the exhaustion of fossil fuels
(2)   the exhaustion of metals and minerals
(3)   pollution
(4)   increasing populations.

The recent 'Blueprint for Survival' by *The Ecologist* seemed to me to put the ecological argument commandingly, whatever be thought of its political and social quotient; and we are promised a more authoritative and alarming pronouncement shortly from the Club of Rome. Yet even those who take this seriously mostly confine their responses either to passing on the message or to dealing with some particular and relatively tractable issue, like Britain's water supply or marine pollution.

Clearly the main answer to (certain) problems ... is to shift on to the natural production process everything possible from the human conversion process, both by reducing the amount of human processing and by substituting regenerative natural materials wherever possible for metals and minerals.

This is a huge and open-ended invitation to technology. On the face of it, the possibilities have hardly been scratched. The Amazon basin is the size of Europe and collects one-sixth of the fresh water of the planet. Yet the mammoth explosion of natural production there supports at present, very poorly, only 100,000 aboriginal Indians. The solar energy that falls on the Sahara supports even less human life. Sea farming has barely begun, though sea mining may already have gone too far. Hasty conclusions should not be drawn. The world's ecology may need the Amazonian wilderness; and in any case, when cleared, it has proved almost valueless for agriculture. Long-term artificial irrigation has its limits, I understand, through problems of increasing salinity. The oceans may be poisoned before they can be farmed.

The only conclusion I want to draw is that these changes pose new technological problems, born of a new concept of the relation between natural production and artificial conversion. In time its attention will be focused on these by rising costs and constraints deriving from scarcity. These will be anticipated by acts of policy by countries owning and countries using the exhausting supplies of unregenerative materials, the metals and minerals. These acts need to be still further anticipated by technology and its associated R & D, so as to ease these changes and to be ready for them when they come.

The changes grouped under 'exhaustion of fossil fuels' raise three sets of problems, all largely independent of those raised above. The first is the future of atomic energy. Atomic fission promises a long-term supply of energy but at a cost in radioactive pollution which is difficult to count or to face when counted. Atomic fusion, producing no pollutants except waste heat, is not yet invented, and when invented may be limited in its application by the requirements of very high technology. The whole question is also shadowed by the fact that our present atomic energy program is historically a by-product of the military demand for plutonium. Assumptions have to be made about the future of atomic energy and they need to be more carefully examined and more widely agreed than they are now.

The second group of problems concerns the possibility of generating energy directly from the sun. Photo-electric cells are already in practical use in spacecraft, but so far as I know, there is no prospect of generating energy by such means on the scale needed to do physical work, as distinct from sending signals. I do not even know whether this is within the bounds of theoretical possibility. We may link with this the unsolved problem of storing energy on a large scale by any means other than those time-consuming ones which have produced the fossil fuels.[1]

He writes to Adolph again July 31. "I remember our talk at Brig better than I remember what we talked about—though some of that is clear. You are probably more conscious than I of your ultimate objective. Mine, I think, is to see and express more clearly my conviction that there is a vector in human affairs, developing the more human from the less human, and that this is basically transcultural and more than individual, even though its only expression can be in cultural and individual terms ... The vision comes and goes. When I wrote last it was clearer than it is now. I expect it will go on returning."

In August, on holiday in the Ticino, he writes in happier mood. "I do not really like this vertical landscape so much as our gentle, long-tilled chalk. But the abundance of hardwood is lovely, the sweet chestnuts, birch, ash, acacia, cherry that cover almost vertical faces, and the islands of alpine husbandry (getting smaller now; there are wholly deserted villages by the railway from Domodossola to Locarno). And this country seems to be largely free from a feature I dislike in the Haute Savoie, where the delicious farmland is often framed in impenetrable and sombre conifers and above that crags as bare and tormented as anything in the background of an early Italian painter. Also it is free from the smell of blood which for me taints Haute Savoie from resistance days. (This may sound or be neurotic, but I have a particular horror of the kind of moral polarization which must have reached an all-time high in Vichy France. We may beat it yet in Ulster.)

"The only plus, such as it is, to set against the huge and multiple minuses of your absence is that, if you were here, my wish to catch up on many years of conversation would conflict distressfully with my wish to stop thinking and talking about anything human at all. The lizard on the terrace and the sparrows on the grass outside our window inhabit a dimension which I badly need to re-enter. Before I left I was very stale. And travelling begins to tire me.

"We left three old English friends dying, the country in the second week of a national dock strike, and Ulster in what seems an impossible alternative to civil war. My new book has not yet found a publisher. The tentative English publisher seeking a US publisher drew blank with Random House and is trying the Beacon Press. This is, after all, a book of previously published material (most of it) so I can't fly very high with it. And I realize more and more that it is only a diagnostic book after all. And like you I feel the need to offer something more than diagnosis before I finish. But here I hope to write nothing; perhaps to draw and paint a little; and certainly to read. I have begun with much pleasure to read the latest version of a book by my old friend Wolfgang Friedmann about *Law and Social Change;* his approach to the social scene is very topical as well as central. When does the legitimacy of authority break down? And how, when it is threatened, does it maintain itself without sapping its own foundations?

"Such questions are irrelevant to lizards and sparrows, and I shall try to be like them for at least a fortnight."

It is obvious that Ellen's death, in October 1972, must have been reflected in correspondence between Geoffrey and Adolph at that time, but none of Geoffrey's deep sorrow at this momentous event is reflected in what remains to us of his correspondence with Adolph. The next letter that we have, dated March 1, 1973, is wholly concerned with what he sees as a multiple crisis.

Closing the gamut

"As to our respective attitudes to the general mess, we seem to be saying exactly the same things to each other. So I shall stop trying for the moment to discover why the result does not sound like agreement. We both agree that we are in for a multiple crisis in the regulation of human affairs, political, economic and social; that each of us has a duty to do what he can to increase the chances that the course of affairs will be less disastrous than they might be; and that all we can do about it as agents in our present position is to write books and give lectures.

"I have no idea why I regard the gamut as closed, or even what you include in the gamut. I have no doubt that there will be (a) some social learning from experience, (b) pressure to adopt a more common view of the things that matter, (c) increase in coercion of those who don't, and therefore (d) more conflict and (e) worse regulation, perhaps leading to (f) self-exciting breakdown of international and/or national organization. But what this mix of these horrid prospects will be, in this or any other country, I have no idea at all.

"Now about the book: I am sorry that the title *The Price of Membership* does not seem to you sufficiently clear, and that you have the same criticism about *Freedom in a Rocking Boat*. Perhaps those who don't find these titles clear would not find the books readable either. But if you have a better idea I should love to hear it. Do you prefer the old title *Conflict and Membership?* Or *The Cost of Having Rights?* Or *The Duties of the Done-By?* Or *The Costs of Belonging?* If neither *The Price of Membership* nor *The Costs of Belonging* will do as a title,

I wonder whether the book will do as a book, because neither title seems to me more abstract than the contents of the book.

"Now for your book: I am awed by the thought of you finishing and then revising a book of 130,000 words. It must be nice to leave such a memorial even if the publishers' mills are going to grind even more slowly than usual. Even the thought of proof-reading such a work makes the mind boggle.

"What you say about Monod's *Chance and Necessity* confirms what I expected of it from the reviews and clears my conscience about not having read it. We can't blame physicists and biologists for talking nonsense about human affairs quite as much as they might blame us for talking nonsense about physics and biology if we had not studied these subjects at all, because even a physicist or biologist can't help living in the world of men and societies. Nonetheless, the extent to which they become imprisoned in their own metaphors is frightening. They tend to know less rather than more about human affairs than they would if they hadn't studied their own specializations.

"I have just been reviewing a book in which the author makes an interesting distinction between touch and sight as generators of contrasting metaphors— one relevant to man the observer and the other to man the agent or manipulator. He fails to notice that what he says makes no sense when applied to man the communicator—i.e. that people see and even touch each other.

"I offer no comment on what is going on here. The question whether the conditions for social learning will disappear or have already disappeared can only be answered by historians of the future. Meantime we must assume they have not; even if they have they may reappear some day.

Statesmen and writers

"Next about men of action and men of thought—or better about the difference between statesmen and writers. You and I cannot order out the troops or even promote legislation. We can only contribute to social warning. We need not therefore worry about the chances that it will make much difference or little difference or none. It is our field of action. It is as much our ship as anyone else's. But since we don't have to decide whether to jettison cargo or to take any other decision which is affected by weighing the chances of the ship reaching port, we can just go on doing our duty.

"This would be so even if the analogy of sink or swim was valid. But it is not. The antithesis between autocracy and democracy seems to me as unreal as the antithesis between success and failure. Of course we shan't 'succeed'. But if we do our duty it is possible that the mess will be fractionally less than if we don't. Neither we nor anyone else will ever know. Nor need we.

"Similarly with autocracy and all that. Our polity here today has elements of autocracy (more outside than inside government), elements of populism, elements of anarchy, elements of revolution, within a tradition of representative democracy; also elements of syndicalism which have been here for years but which may for the first time be in sight of controlling our trade union movement. The outcome might be guild socialism or a corporative state or dominance by property on new terms or who knows what. Any of these would only be labels for new mixes, political and social.

"All I know, or need to know, is that the more widespread and adequate is our common understanding of the situation, the greater is likely to be the unforced consensus on what it requires of each of us and the less the coercion, mutual frustration, innocent suffering and so on; also the more possible will it be for power to be attained and wielded by men of tolerant and non-revolutionary character.

"So I as a writer, analyst and exponent of criteria have my marching orders. Whereas if I were, for example, Whitelaw in Ulster, I should often find that the choice between tough and soft policies, each with its own costs and benefits, really depended on my estimate of how quickly who could be expected to learn what. That and that only is the kind of action-decision which it seems to me that you and I are spared.

"And inner-directed or outer-directed—once again, why think in antitheses? I am deeply conditioned by my culture but have chosen a path nearly always different from what that culture expected of me. Revolutionaries are conditioned by what they are trying to destroy. They may be nonetheless inner-directed, at least in this or that, if not the other. My personal 'journey into the interior' makes me a little more conscious than before of compulsive areas and blind spots which impair the quality of my inner-direction. I shan't sort it out at 78 but I might manage to make it less of a nuisance to others and even less of a burden to myself. I shall never know the answer, but I'm sure if I did it wouldn't be in terms of either-or.

"I don't want to belittle the general value of Riesman's polarities, so long as the poles are regarded as the ends of an axis. Even then, if used for an individual, I think you would need an awful lot of parallel axes to plot him on. You remember my story about the end of the world—'Let lights be brought' so that the statesmen *and* the revolutionaries can better see what they are doing. We are trying to shed light—however great our personal darkness."

Communication

We have no further correspondence until one from Adolph dated December 12 1974 subsequent to Geoffrey's visit to New York, during which they discussed an experiment undertaken in Atlanta with an ape called Lena.

"I don't know what Nanda[2] told you about this—she has most of her information from me. Now when you call the story 'not particularly interesting',

I don't know what your yardstick is. Compared with the issues you and I discussed the other day, the discovery that higher apes not only have a language to communicate among themselves but that a non-verbal 'language' can be devised which makes it possible for us to communicate with them is no more interesting than the rocket reports of what goes on on Jupiter.

"But if we are willing to digress from our immediate concerns I find the Lena story as important as the report on Jupiter. It demonstrates—what I have always suspected, to the chagrin of most of my philosophical colleagues who see in this a threat to the 'dignity of Man'—that the means of communication form a large spectrum in which what we call 'language' is one point. Still more important, it strengthens the hypothesis that the 'transition' of ape to man is a gradual one and not a 'leap'. True, all of us who ever lived with a dog must be inclined toward that hypothesis. Still, Lena seems capable of 'articulating' and this goes beyond what we have so far experienced."

He sends a brief note to Geoffrey February 8 1975 to explain his long silence, due to a 'flu epidemic.

"We also had a strike at the School[3], by now settled, but term starts a week later—for me a real boon. I am still waiting for Cambridge to send me the copy-edited text of my book—like God's their mills grind finely but very slowly.

"I don't know whether your or my country is in a worse mess. Our Government has now told us that we shall stay in the slump for at least another two years—nice effect on business expectations! *Fiat* free enterprise, *pereat mundus!* What does the rebellion in the Conservative Party mean—moving toward my friend Enoch Powell? Here George Wallace has the largest share in the polls predicting our next President. On the other hand the Near East looks a shade more favorable, but not before May shall we know what will happen."

The Berkeley lectures

Geoffrey's reply February 19 says that he has been much obsessed during the last month or two with writing the four talks he is to give at Berkeley (University of California) in April/May.

"I forget whether I told you about this. As talks, they will be of an informal seminar type, but they are to be developed into a short book which will be published, if it agrees, by the University of California Press through the mediation of the Gaither Lecture Fund and the Center for Management Science. The current titles are:
1. Making Sense
2. Alienation
3. Education for Sense-making
4. The Process of Design.
I look forward very much to hearing your reactions.

"This afternoon I am to be visited by a young political scientist from Oxford (Z. Pelczynski)—not so young, he is vice-regent of Pembroke College—who has a student in a jam over a thesis. Pelczynski is an authority on Hegel and I hope to continue my slow education in the original concept of the dialectic process.

"Since you wrote you will have heard that our Conservative Party has redefined itself on what it expects to be more traditional lines, although Margaret Thatcher is, I hope and believe, a far cry from Enoch Powell. Throughout the Western world the political spectrum is polarizing and the middle ground appears to be giving way. In this country I am not at all convinced that this is a permanent trend. Our vulnerability to external constraints and particularly to the need to buy food abroad will, I hope, ultimately be a unifying influence as well as an accelerator of learning. This however is only a hope and as we have often discussed before, is much more likely to reflect differences of past experience or even difference of temperament, rather than well-founded guesses at what is going on.

"I am afraid I shall not be able to visit New York in April/May. I have however been asked to spend some of the Fall term again at MIT, and I hope we shall have another chance to meet then. I enclose an article from the London *Times* by Peter Jay about 'Indexation', knowing that you are an interested authority on this. I wonder whether you agree with what Peter Jay has to say."

On inflation

Adolph replies March 9 that he agrees with the content of the *Times* article on inflation but finds it excessively 'scholarly' and unnecessarily 'profound'.

"What is at stake is the elementary fact that inflation is a tax, which must be borne by someone. If all receipts are indexed, no-one is left to do so, and the effect can only be a rapidly spiralling price level. One can well say that this procedure will kill inflation because it kills the currency. My proposal was much more modest. I wanted to prevent speculative borrowing by forcing the borrower to pay back the 'real' value of his loan. But this has in the meantime become superfluous, because with the progress of recession the problem is rather how to make people borrow. I fear that the proposed tax cuts will not do the job of stimulating employment because much of the 'gain' will be saved rather than spent. The answer is public works, which create income for the unemployed who are sure to spend it. But this goes against Republican ideology. So we shall have to slide into double digit unemployment rates before something effective will be done. If on top the situation in the Near East should turn to the worse, nothing will help.

"Whether the 'middle ground' will give way permanently will depend on the intensity and duration of our present troubles. I can only admire the patience of our housewives ... Did your Pembroke man reveal the depth of the dialectical problem?"

Geoffrey's March 15 letter reveals his admiration for Adolph's explanation. "You put the issue beautifully simply. If indexing is regarded as a form of tax exemption, one can follow any particular proposal in terms of the effect which it will have on the exempted class, including any indirect results which flow therefrom and also in terms of the added burden left for other people to carry. This makes clear (1) the absurdity of indexing everything, (2) the theoretic inadequacy of dealing with a taxation problem in this way, i.e. by using one's discretion to exempt but not to tax, and (3) the degree of impotence which operates to make even this kind of discretion so much better than nothing at all.

The Common Market

"You will have read about our approaching referendum. Everybody will be relieved when it is over, and most people I hope will by now be praying and working for an affirmative result. Whatever one may think of the Common Market, its merits or otherwise have now become almost insignificant compared with the prospect of being stuck with a national referendum expressing a preference for a policy which none of the three political parties wants to implement, and which indeed they have all declared against. Nothing would do more to move our parliamentary democracy, such as it is, in the direction of the delegate democracy which is common and appropriate in trade union politics, and therefore is the only kind of democracy familiar to this huge slice of the working population.

"When this is out of the way, we shall see what our political parties look like. Assuming that the verdict is favorable, the relative profiles and strengths of the Labour and Conservative parties will, I think, have changed more than would have seemed possible a year or two ago. But the change will by no means be completed—only one 'still' in a sequence of increasingly rapid change. Let us hope that a lot of tacit learning is going on under the surface."

Adolph writes equally enthusiastically, March 18.

"I always knew that you have a knack for the essentials of economics. Can you believe that I cannot get that simple truth across to luminaries like Milton Friedman or Abba Lerner? The superstructure which has been built over the elementary truth—all matters of common sense—has by now obscured the essentials to a degree that the 'summit' of economics which Ford[4] assembled last fall could only be compared with the Tower of Babel. And it is by no means only the underlying 'value' prejudices—they do play a big role—but the incapacity to add two and two. Another example is the struggle about a tax cut as a stimulus for raising demand thus employment. Of course it will not work, at least not to the degree expected and necessary. The reason is that most people will save the windfall and not spend it under present conditions of uncertainty. The proper way would be a large program of public works. But there political ideology enters—that would be 'socialism'.

"About staying in the Common Market—honestly, from earlier remarks of yours I had concluded that you favored the other side. Though I was always aware of the burden this implies for Britain, I still thought that, over the long run, even the economic advantages predominate. To this you have now added a very significant political argument. So let us pray ..."

"I am still inclined to wish that there was not a market," replies Geoffrey April 4, "and that we were not in it, but as there is a market, and we are in it, I am quite sure that we should stay in it since we could not restore the original position by withdrawing. I am also influenced (though no-one else seems to be) by the fact that our membership is embodied in a treaty which we have not reserved the right to break or vary. But as I said in my last letter, even these weighty considerations are now dwarfed by the fearful constitutional problems which would arise if a referendum negated a policy to which all our three parliamentary parties are committed.

"Even without this complication our present situation is bad enough, and if you read our news you will see that it is getting worse, politically at least as much as economically, through the growing use of means, illegal even by our present elastic laws, to enforce political rather than industrial objectives. This no doubt will reach a crisis some day and the sooner the better, but neither of the present political parties looks adequate to deal with it at present. As you know, I always retain a residual hope, if not belief, that people learn what they need to learn in the end, even though this be so late that they and others pay a very heavy price for the delay.

"I take off on Monday and feel extremely ambivalent about these lectures and the whole project."

"We have just heard the result of the plebiscite," replies Adolph June 6, "and I want to tell you how happy I am that the good sense of the common man in Britain has again triumphed. I also know how crucial this decision is—less with regard to the narrower content of the vote but for the maintenance of parliamentary government and political stability. Looked at narrowly, the blessings of the Common Market will remain doubtful in the short run. But I trust that Britain's influence will make itself felt the longer her participation lasts. And though my Germans have been behaving very well in recent years, a compensating force is the best guarantee that they will continue to do so.

"For the rest I am frankly worried about your silence. You must by now be back home for almost a month. Needless to say that I want to know how you feel about this visit, but even more, whether you are well and fit in body and mind."

He has now started on a popular version of his book *On Economic Knowledge*: "Harper has let the original book go out of print, since it sold only 700 copies last year. (They did the same with Myrdal's *The American Dilemma!*) So my book can be bought in German, Japanese and Portuguese, but no longer in English. My new venture will be written on a quite different level and should make use of what

I have learnt over the last 10 years. But it is all still tentative and nothing may come of it."

"I am sorry that I have not written before," replies Geoffrey June 17. "There is nothing sinister in my silence. My stay at Berkeley was the happiest of my American visits, and also by all accounts the most successful. I enormously enjoyed living in the middle of the beautiful campus. I also enjoyed being drawn into current work to a much greater extent than usual. As you know, the diaries of both students and faculty tend to get very full and extra-curricular activities, like visiting lecturers, are normally peripheral. The four lectures which were my main preoccupation were peripheral in this sense, although they were well attended and kindly received, but I was also asked to take seminars in at least six different ongoing courses already in peoples' schedules, so I made contact with far more students and far more faculty than I did at MIT. I also found it a much more congenial intellectual atmosphere. So it was altogether a happy time.

"I spent a busy week on the homeward journey, including three days at Ottawa, where I found the climate among the federal civil servants I met much less happy than I have learned to expect from Canada. Since I came home I have done various lectures and seminars in courses given by the Architectural Association here, and I have found some baffling contrasts between these and Berkeley. But I will not expand on that now.

"I do hope that, by the time you receive this, the manuscript (of the *Growth* book) will have come back (from Cambridge) and that all will be in order for publication. A lot of people, including me, will be awaiting this. I am intrigued, too, to hear that you are starting on a popular version of *On Economic Knowledge*. The problem of keeping books in print gets worse and worse, though I should have thought an annual turnover of 700 would have been sufficient. I hope the popular edition matures.

"Yes, we are still in the Common Market. We have debarred ourselves from controls which I think we shall, nonetheless, have to use within the next few months; and we have given a lot of people a scapegoat which they will blame for measures which we should have had to take in any case, and should have taken long ago. On the other hand we have avoided a major constitutional crisis, checked the growing power of both political extremes, and got ourselves into a better position to negotiate special treatment which we shall probably need. So I think we are up, on balance, or at least less down that we should otherwise be. The situation hardly merits any higher praise. I continue to wait, with such patience as I can muster, for the triggering of that tacit learning which I believe to be going on. The crucial debate within the trade union movement and within the Labour Party is taking its course and will, I think, have its fruition. But they are uneasy days.

"I have been asked to attend a conference in New York November 27-30 next. This will make it possible to arrange a shorter visit to MIT than would otherwise be appropriate. I propose at present to spend a weekend (October 25-26 or November 1-2) in New York, where I shall hope to see you and other friends. Between then and the conference I plan to visit Ann Arbor and MIT and possibly Washington.

"I am just beginning the major bit of writing which is to emerge from the Berkeley assignment. This involves a commitment to make a book out of the four lectures. I have abundant material and I am beginning to see the shape of it. I have let it lie fallow so far, but I want to get the bulk of it done before I make another visit."

In July 1975 both Adolph and Geoffrey had falls which put each of them out of action for a while. But a broken wrist does not prevent Adolph from typing a letter on July 17:

"no, i don't go in for a new fashion in spelling! if it were not so sad it would be just funny: while you fell and bruised some ribs i fell and broke my left wrist. the arm is in a cast and typing is confined to the right hand, which is a little bothersome, but it is quite interesting to learn what one can do with one hand and what not. still—i am so moved by your letter (to a canadian friend) that i must tell you at least this, and also assure you—what you know anyhow—that i am in full agreement with you. as a matter of fact, this is the language of dr. rieux in camus' *plague*, and i see how right i was when i chose it for your 80th birthday. when i am more mobile again i shall have to say more. it is indeed a painful question whether the spirit in which our generation played its institutional roles is still prevalent, and to that extent the issue may well be a generation problem."

More on inflation

Geoffrey's bruised ribs did not keep him out of action for long. On July 22 he sends Adolph copies of two letters, one dated July 15 to William Robson, who founded and had just retired from being editor of *The Political Quarterly*, and the other dated July 17 to the London *Times*. They are quoted here because both are of direct relevance to the ongoing discussion between Geoffrey and Adolph.

My dear Robson,

Your birthday party was the most moving, as well as pleasant, occasion that I have attended for many a day. I am very pleased and grateful to have been included among the guests. I hated missing the last few moments of your speech. Tiresomely, I had left myelf with a last train to catch instead of arranging to spend the night in town. Apart from the fact that it was you we all most wanted to hear, I wondered whether you would have anything to say about what is my most darkening thought these days.

I was with you when you described the much better England of today (more sensitive, more equitable as well as more affluent) compared with the England into which we were both born. Did you, I wonder, add anything to explain why the members of this better England are so much less proud of being English than our generation was?

The great reformers (whose names, when you recited them, were like some potent spell) and equally the crossing-sweepers, no less than the landed gentry and the entrepreneurs, believed that it was an unique privilege to be born English; and if they were indignant reformers, it was through a burning sense that the present was unworthy of both the heritage and the destiny. Today's generation would think it both shocking and ridiculous to feel, still more to express, any such sentiment. Patriotism is a dirty word, even history a peripheral study. To whom do today's young look back as we look back on the Tawneys and all the rest of the great names you cited? The pantheon is empty—except, for a few, for such figures as Che Guevara and Mao Tse-Tung. And even these are exclamation marks, rather than landmarks. The sense of continuity, of belonging, of simultaneously making and being made by a specific community has evaporated from Western consciousness, or at least from British consciousness.

And not overnight. It was there in the First War. It was there in the General Strike. It was there in the Second World War. It was there in the first after-war years when the Beveridge packet went into law with such abundant general support—and when in the eyes of the world our society stood more highly than it has probably ever done in history. What has happened?

Were they all wrong, the reformers we revere, in thinking that a politically 'reformed' society would be more stable, as well as more human than a traditional one? Or were they simply ignorant of some underlying psycho-social condition which they or history were eroding even while they built their great edifice upon it? Surely the second. But if the second, what is this ignored essential and how compatible is it with today's social insecurity?

I don't suppose you answered this question in the last few minutes of your speech. And insofar as I have a tentative answer, I won't let it get into this letter. But I woke up this morning with these thoughts in my head, and as a background to them a sense of tragic irony that you should be making your confession of faith and recalling your spiritual progenitors in, of all places, the Reform Club, surrounded by pictures of three generations of 'reformers' who for all their differences had shared so much of the elusive connotations of 'reform'; that we should be celebrating a life and a journal devoted to that very idea and that nonetheless the idea itself should be fading and sickening around us, perhaps sinking under our feet, not because it had completed its span of usefulness, still less because it was false in itself, but—?

Your reference to *The Art of Judgment* warmed me as I haven't been warmed since I read your review of it ten years ago.

To: The Editor of the London *Times*, July 17 1975:

In pursuit of sanity let us distinguish between checking inflation, redistributing the burden of inflation, and altering differentials apart from inflation.

Checking inflation will take some years at best; the degree of our success will determine day by day its total current burden. This will fall as an unvoted, inescapable, pro-rata tax on all incomes and property expressed in money, except insofar as we choose to shield some, wholly or partly, at the expense of others. Every such act of shielding will alter differentials, perhaps in ways quite different from what would otherwise be the outcome of forces which would be making for rapid change even without inflation.

The Government's package aims both to diminish the burden and to redistribute it, though at the cost of hugely reducing the scope for changing differentials for other reasons. MPs have now been included in the shielded class for three disparate reasons, all in my view bad. First and chiefly, to make up for rising cost of living. But to shield a class from the rising cost of living is precisely to pass their share of the burden, either to someone else by denying his identical claim or to everyone by more inflation.

Secondly because they have had no rise for three years. True; but it is too late to alter that now, for them or for others. If most people's earnings are to be reviewed every year, all must be. If most take account of time worked, all must. Differentials are difficult enough without our making jobs and earnings even harder to compare than they need be.

Thirdly because they deserve more by comparison with some others, including legislators abroad. So do others, including many with skills far more exportable than British legislators. Moreover, as David Wood observed (July 14), their allowances give them elasticity almost without parallel, which I accept as right, though he does not.

There *is* a right answer (your leader of July 17)—an answer at least as right as we expect from coal miners and public corporation chairmen. If we do not get it from you or the Government or the MPs concerned, we shall not get it from the chairmen or the faceworkers.

You know the alternative. You have been telling us for years. If conservative and liberal members as a body were to decline to accept more than their £6 a week they would not directly affect the going rate of inflation to any significant extent; but they would begin the rehabilitation of Parliament as a thinking body and as a moral force, hugely increase their chance of returning to power and challenge the government far more effectively than they can do by their votes."

In September Adolph's cast is off, Cambridge has finally shown signs of life and he has inserted all the changes and corrections, but he doesn't expect the book to be published before spring. He will not teach this term. Geoffrey writes September 11:

"I am glad that you have the cast off; it must have added to your burdens. My bruises cleared up, my Swiss journey was fruitful. The weather since I returned has been enchanting, my occupations have been sufficiently varied. But—what?

"There is the corrosive loneliness of Ellen's absence, which other presences and absences leave quite untouched, though a few of them comfort. Then there is the book, which proliferates and grows ever more formless. It is now called *The Pursuit of Order* and warns the reader in the foreword that the title is chosen to avoid implying that such creatures can be caught, let alone kept. But if the book exemplifies its own message so completely as not to get written, it will be a self-defeating exercise.

"And of course there's the general mess—how odd and human that that comes last. Things are being done now in Ulster which are as bad as anything in Timor or Angola; and any time now we shall again have to try to govern the place. Our own politico-economic crisis is bad enough to live with but, in time short or long, with varying degrees of misery, I can see one of various outcomes emerging, none very pleasant but at least not a sadistic orgy. But Ulster—!

Ecce Homo

"You have probably never heard of a book called *Ecce Homo*, written by an English historian in about 1870 about the recorded life and teaching of Christ and their extraordinary results. It scandalised the Victorian world but couldn't be ignored because Gladstone of all people said it was fine. I have just re-read it, for good though obscure reasons. What it tells one about the life and times of Seeley (the author) is even stranger than its actual subject. Reading it, I realized how utterly remote is the culture in which I was bred from today, as remote as Seeley from the Jerusalem of Christ's age. Seeley didn't know much anthropology but he knew all the classics could tell him about the ethics of the ancient world from Homer to Cicero and he compared the ethics of the Victorian world and found them better; and this he traced to the moral initiative of one man, which he found remarkable. He makes a good case. What can happen in three generations!"

"Most interesting what you write about Seeley" Adolph replies on the 17th. "Is he the man whom I know as the author of *The Expansion of England*, a book which taught me many things?[5] I am convinced that it is true that the New Testament only changed some emphases of the Old—but this is not little. I will see whether I can get hold of the book. I will not write about the 'big' world today—there are only too many Ulsters in the world."

"Life continues to treat me kindly", writes Geoffrey, October 3: "I had a curious experience last week. I went to the annual general meeting of our Operations Research Society to give its closing address and surprisingly to receive its silver medal. They were all very kind to me and I was glad to think that such a mixed bunch of technologists had found anything sufficiently useful in what I had to say to honor me in this way. The initiative came, I think, chiefly from their chairman, a nice man called Tomlinson, who incidentally is engaged on one of the most interesting large-scale bits of O.R. that I have ever heard of. He is one of an interdisciplinary team, half of whom come from Iron Curtain countries, which is to examine and compare the Tennessee Valley Authority and a similar Authority in Siberia. The visit to TVA is concluded. It was chaired by an East German for whom Tomlinson has high regard. The visit to Siberia is due for next year, and Tomlinson will probably be chairman. This is O.R. in a big way. Indeed, I am interested to see how wide a meaning O.R. has for some of its practitioners. I called my talk 'Where does O.R. stop?'

Consulting in Washington and at MIT

"My American journey I expect to begin October 31. The first week I expect to spend consulting in Washington, and perhaps Philadelphia, about health policy in connection with what seems to me a very interesting development, namely your National Health Planning and Resources Development Act of 1974. The next two weeks will be spent at and around MIT. The fourth week will be spent partly at Ann Arbor and partly in New York, where I shall be fully engaged until Sunday November 30 with the Fourth Meeting of the International Conference on the Unity of Science. This, I am told, has become politically controversial. The members who accepted are dropping out in shoals. It looks as though our only opportunity for a meeting would be on Monday December 1."

Adolph, October 9, says that December 1 will be fine, and congratulates Geoffrey on his silver medal.

"I had not heard about the fights within the Unity of Science movement—does political controversy mean recognition that values are involved? In this country we have so far been spared the struggle between 'realists' and 'ideologues'— simply because the latter are at the fringes and are not taken seriously by anyone. But, as you know, the same fight threatens to destroy social democracy in Germany. Is there a middle position? I have been asked to join the newly-founded Committee on Economic Planning, which tries something in this direction, and I am in close contact with Galbraith in this matter, who is mellowing without losing his bite. At the moment, the possible bankruptcy of New York is in the foreground—if this happens we may have a repetition of 1931 when the final breakdown was initiated by the failure of two central European banks. We shall know more when you are here."

On October 13 1975 (his 81st birthday) Geoffrey replies from Cambridge during his period as visiting professor at the Massachussetts Institute of Technology.

"Last Saturday I spent largely in reading *The Plague* and comparing my lot with the journalist, trapped in a plague-ridden city to which he did not even belong. That, however, was after a week in which it appeared that my main concern here was a non-starter and that I was the only one who seemed to feel any commitment to it. A week later the prospect looks bright, and I may have contributed something to the change.

"My weariness is induced by a combination of intellectual shock and culture shock which are hard to dissociate. I spend my time trying to understand the language of good minds, better in many ways than my own but so differently formed that language often cannot bridge the gap. I am also inadequately used, which makes the isolation greater. Moreover this speeds a process which has been going on since Ellen died, of realizing the self-made boundaries of my world, without as yet having been able to get much beyond them. I have two students—or rather they have chosen to take occasional talks with me—and this is refreshing and easy. They too are transients in the Ivory Tower. I feel much more at home with them than with any of my hosts.

"I am told nonetheless that my presence is making enough of a difference for my hosts to be glad I'm here. I have never been good at knowing what difference, if any, I was making and this enormous doubt, growing now for two years, produces on my 81st birthday what I think must be my first identity crisis. Well, perhaps it is good for us to be displaced persons—you should know far better than I. But this is a curious kind of displacement—perhaps only the opening of closed gates.

"*The Plague* is a wonderful book. I have just finished it. It leaves me in one way dissatisfied—but every statement is bound to beg the questions about which complementary statements might be made. It is too big and I am too tired to comment. As to the affairs of our two countries, I know nothing at all. I suppose some news of Europe, even of England, must reach Boston but I have formed no habits of connecting with it. In any case I pursue what I came for with obsessive persistence, and the time each day that I can effectively read or write is too little for the demand. Both my tacit back-room and my explicit parlor are almost too full to work in.

"My major preoccupation is to understand a book, *Theory in Practice*, just published by two men closely associated with this project, Chris Argyris and Don Schon. I don't commend it and I won't try to describe the issues it raises in my mind. But they challenge most of the assumptions on which I have written for 20 years and lived for 80, and in this challenge there are important messages which I need to get. Time is needed.

"Tomorrow I go to Rockport, a small community near here, with a bunch of planners who have there, it seems, performed a remarkable feat—of organizing, advocating, coalition-building, and other entrepreneurial skills that I did not associate so nakedly with planning. We go to celebrate their success."

"Just a word of welcome and of sincere thanks for your moving letter," Adolph replies November 6. "I perfectly understood what you meant to express. And I am the last person to take a friend's dark mood amiss—I am suffering from that disease much too frequently. As a matter of fact, I am just now going through such a period, for known and unknown reasons ... work is not going well.

"I have finished the first part of a new book discussing the various paradigms of economic theory, with a long critical chapter on Marx—the new academic 'folk hero'. But I am stuck with the transition to the next part. All the more I admire you that you, in the short time of a number of months, should have written practically a whole book, and I am very eager to see the draft. In case your visit coincides with the arrival of the galleys—it is too much to hope!—I trust that you can leave it with me.

"About New York—we shall talk. Do you remember from the war, when the home front was in great excitement whereas the people at the true front were quite calm? It is a little like this, and I am actually more worried about the national and even international repercussions of a bankruptcy than about the discomfort it will, no doubt, bring in the long run. When I read what Wilson has decided to do to meet the emergency, the ineptness and frivolity of our Government looks even worse. I do hope your stay here achieves its purpose and brings you— especially at MIT—more satisfaction than last year."

Money and credit

Geoffrey's letter of December 5 looks forward to reading Adolph's chapter on Marx, and returns to the subject of inflation.

"In the manuscript I left you there is a small passage about 'inter-subjective reality'. This owes a good deal, at least by way of confirmation, to Berger and Luckmann's *The Social Construction of Reality*. The example is money and credit. Money and credit are certainly facts of the world out there. Although this is not the world which astronomers and physicists study, it has a reality of its own. The relationship between the generation of money and credit on the one hand, and the generation of goods and services on the other, determines the rate of inflation as surely as the law of gravitation—or rather, it determines the minimum speed of inflation. If we generate money and credit faster than we generate goods and services the value of the money will go down however much we believe in it. If, on the other hand, we stop believing in it, its value will evaporate like dew irrespective of what may be happening in the real world of goods and services.

"It thus seems to me to illustrate the kind of reality which lies between what Galileo insisted on and what the solipsist maintains. Nor is it an unusual example. It seems to me that all our realities participate in some degree in the character and limitations bestowed on them by the fact that they are collective creations of human minds.

"But I do not want to engage you in a philosophical discussion on paper, still less to invite your attention to me on the book while you are wrestling with the last part of that edited proof."

Adolph, whose December 2 letter crossed Geoffrey's, has questions about the manuscript.

"I have read the first nine chapters, and I am deeply impressed by the profundity of ideas, the sweep of presentation and the range of your 'knowledge'. At the same time I confess that it has so far been difficult reading—mainly because so many strands of thought are followed without my seeing as yet how all this will converge on the subsequent chapters. Therefore no more today in terms of 'appreciation'.

"I also wonder—and this is an intrusion into 'substance'—whether you really mean to convey the impression that the 'order we are fit for' coincides with that represented by the small East African tribe described on p.11, and that the 'contractual role' is the villain. After all, this was not invented by the Moderns—at the latest by the time of the Punic Wars Roman society had a fully developed contractual order, at least within the city itself. Incidentally, your emphasis on 'contract' coincides with Toennies' ideas as expounded in his *Gemeinschaft und Gesellschaft* [6], which you probably know—if not, it might be worth your while to look into it—there is an English translation."

"I am sorry that you found Part 1 of the book difficult reading," Geoffrey replies on the 11th, "and particularly that it was not clear to you how this would converge on subsequent parts. There must be something wrong with the foreword.

"I realize that this is not an ordinary kind of book, and in the foreword I try to spell out the relationship between the three parts. In the first part, 'The Human Endowment', I try to spell out all those mental capacities with which we cannot help crediting ourselves even though some of these have got buried under current scientific ideologies. In the second part, 'The Western Heritage', I describe aspects of Western development which seem to me to explain why Western men today are unable to introduce any acceptable kind of order, either into the course of their affairs or into their understanding of what is going on. The first part is supposed to illuminate the second by showing the kind of order we are naturally 'fit for'.

"I think I shall find you are right in accusing me of having pinned too much blame on the contractual role for our current state of confusion. The world into which I was born was a world structured by contractual roles, but it nonetheless seems to me to have been, in its self-confidence, far more like a traditional society than like the societies of today."

Letters crossed again after Geoffrey's return to England. Adolph's is dated December 10.

"The world has not become a better place since you left—with all the complications in the UN, the continuing strife in Lebanon, the sudden coolness of the Russians, and British plans of protectionism. With us the situation is, if anything, more confused. Kissinger's fate is in the balance, and though much can be objected in his past actions I don't see who can take over just now. Richardson, who is the favorite, may in the long run work out well, but he simply lacks the experience for the immediate problems. So we are going into another year full of gloomy foreboding.

"My days have been spent with a thorough checking of what the copy editor has done to my text ... so I had to interrupt the reading of your manuscript. This may not be so bad in view of my questions in the recent note. I also wish that you could send me the final chapters—I have a feeling that they are necessary for a real overview.

"Now a word regarding the 'reality' of money and credit. I fully agree that we deal with an 'inter-subjective' reality and have been fighting for this since I wrote my little book on *Economics and Sociology* in 1935. Perhaps you have a copy left, which would make understanding much easier. There I discussed precisely your problem. But my conclusion, and I stick to it, is very different from yours. The 'objective' relationship—quantity of money (credit) created and of goods produced—does not by itself determine the rate of inflation. It does so only if the increment of money (credit) is *spent*. Whether it is spent or hoarded depends on 'expectations', a phenomenon for which there is no simile in the physical world. In other words, there is no 'law of inflation' which could be set side by side with the 'law of gravitation'. If, instead of saying 'by *generating* money faster' etc., you had said 'by *spending* money faster' etc., you would be right.

"The technical term that must be added to the quantity of money is the 'velocity of circulation'—a highly volatile phenomenon, influenced by innumerable 'extra-systemic' factors, factors for which there is no parallel in the physical world. In the social world the 'pull' can even be negative, that is, in spite of the fact that today more money is 'in the hands' of the public than yesterday, the amount actually spent may be less than yesterday because the public wants to build up its cash holding (especially at the end of an inflation) or because lower prices are expected tomorrow. Frankly, I don't see why you insist on that parallel with the law of gravitation—my position squares much better with your general attitude to human and social phenomena."

Geoffrey's December 18 letter thanks Adolph for correcting his economics.

"I get the point and I will revise the passage. There still seems to me to be a significant contrast between the relation between goods and services produced and money spent, on the one hand, and between a currency which does and does not command confidence on the other. On the other hand I realize that the amount of money spent, like the amount of money in credit generated, is a variable dependent on all kinds of human factors. I must think what to do about it in view of your reaction.

"I have not got, and have never had, your 1935 book on *Economics and Sociology*. I will try to get hold of a copy. I cannot think why I should have missed it when your *The Price of Liberty* is such a landmark in my mind. It is probably because it was published before we met.

"As for my book, I am proceeding at present very slowly. Christmas makes increasing demands and there are patches of lethargy. I hope nonetheless that the back room and front parlor will in time cooperate sufficiently to get it done. We are at the moment digesting the Chrysler settlement shock, which has alienated both Left and Right from the government. It may be that this is not wholly deserved, since we have not been told what was the threat to which the government capitulated. An economic colony is vulnerable if the coloniser threatens to withdraw with the most, rather than the least, possible damage."

Adolph writes December 21 1975, and again on the 27th. His *Economics and Sociology* was destroyed by a German bomb and had not been reprinted, but a copy should be available in the Library of the London School of Economics. As he reads on he continues to be puzzled by the 'architecture' of Geoffrey's manuscript.

"In your letter you have withdrawn your denunciation of the 'contractual' role, and I am very glad. Certainly this is as old as classical antiquity, and I don't think that one can make the contractual order of the Roman Republic responsible for the final decline. But this raises a larger problem—the only substantive one which I want to raise before I have seen the final chapters. Though I am inclined to agree with you in your position that we are not 'fit' for the world in which we live at present, we must be extremely careful in positively limiting the worlds for which we can become fit. As chapter 9 reads, you seem to reject the entire development beyond primitive society. You cannot really mean this. But the main point is that I firmly believe that we cannot know—either by 'existential reflection' or historical study—what Man is capable of mastering. There *are* limits, but how to know where they are? This need in no way weaken your positive propositions. What is required under all circumstances is a *temporary* slowing down of man-made change—were it only to afford Man the necessary adjustment time for building a 'more sensible' world. Perhaps we disagree on this important point—I hope not."

Notes

1 . G. Vickers, 'The Management of Conflict', *Futures*, June 1972, and 'Towards a More Stable State', *Futures*, December 1972. Both articles were republished in G. Vickers, *Making Institutions Work*, London Associated Business Programmes Ltd., The Halstead Press, New York.

2 . Dr. Ruth Nanda Anshen, founder and editor of the *Convergence* series published by Praeger Publishers (Greenwood Press Inc.), New York, including A. Lowe: *Has Freedom a Future?*, 1988.

3 . The New School for Social Research, West 12th Street, New York City.

4 . US President Gerald Ford.

5 . Seeley, Sir John Robert (1834-95). *Ecce Homo* (1865), *The Expansion of England* (1883).

6 . *The Community and the Society.*

5

The Late Seventies

The New Year begins with another letter from Adolph, dated January 17, 1976.

"The *New York Times* had an article which was somewhat optimistic about Britain overcoming her worst economic troubles. Is that also your impression? On that occasion the *Times* spoke of 'Lord' Kaldor—I did not know that he had followed in the footsteps of his countryman Balogh. And with Dahrendorf the Director of the London School of Economics, Britain can no longer be accused of xenophobia. Incidentally, I read the latter's pamphlet on 'The New Liberty'. This raised my blood pressure by 20 points, especially since the Bicentenary Issue of the *Public Interest*, which represents the American 'neo-conservatives', spreads the same nonsense. I am debating with myself whether I should not prepare a new edition of *The Price of Liberty*, extended by a second part which applies the idea to the present. That the extreme individualism of German idealist philosophy—made respectable in Britain through Mill's *On Liberty*—should be offered as the newest wisdom is beyond comment. You might have left Dahrendorf to the Germans!"

"As for Britain's economic troubles", replies Geoffrey, January 24, "I have no idea what is going to happen, and as you know I do not draw these distinctions between success and failure. Manifestly a lot of learning has taken place in the last ten years. I do not think we should have a Jack Jones now if Wilson and George Brown and Barbara Castle had not tried, however unsuccessfully, to bring in a statutory incomes policy and statutory control of trade unions ten years ago. Nor should we have had the recent proposal in one trade union to reduce wages in order to conserve jobs. On the other hand, I think it unlikely that a socialist government can hold its present line with one and a half million unemployed without doing more than it is doing. FDR in similar circumstances invented, amongst other things, the TVA. Wilson's scope is narrower. We shall see. There is a sinister lack of new thinking on either Left or Right—but so there was in 1932. Perhaps providence will send us a new Keynes. Who knows?

"I have not read Dahrendorf's book, but if it moves you to produce a new version of *The Price of Liberty* it will not have been published in vain.[1]

"As to my own book, it is in an almost complete log jam. The attempt to meet your criticism, which I hoped was valid, has disposed of the original architecture, but not yet replaced it with a new one. The minimum changes envisaged at present are a new foreword, two initial chapters, and some rewrite of the rest of the first part. I do not expect to be sending you any more of it or showing any of it to anyone else. If it is to survive at all I must concentrate on getting it into some form and getting it away."

In his February 25 letter he indicates that he seems to be making progress.

"My wrestle with the book seems to have reached some sort of a conclusion. It seems probable that the enclosed list of chapter headings will in fact be the final one. I do not know whether this will seem to you a more acceptable architecture for a reader. I still have to go through the book in its new form and remedy the duplications and omissions which are bound to have got in from such a drastic exercise. I have, however, committed myself to send it away to be copied at the end of March, so for good or ill it should by then have taken its final form. What has been thrown out will be almost enough to make another book.

"I have been perplexed throughout, and still am, by the fact that the book is both a study of science and technology as a contribution to culture, and an analysis of a specific historic situation, especially the British one. I hope the two themes will be found to ride sufficiently together. After cancelling (the American visit) I received another invitation, with a transatlantic fare attached, for the weekend April 30/May 1. I plan at present to go over for this and to spend a few days before and after at MIT. If I do I will ring you from there, though I am afraid I shall not be able this time to come into New York."

The attachment gave the four parts of the book, now called *Towards a More Human Order*, as: 'Western Culture in Disorder', 'Disorder in Personal Culture', 'Designing Cultural Order', and 'The Resources of the Person'. Adolph (March 6 1976) finds the new outline a real improvement and wishes Geoffrey "all the best for the final spurt". On March 13 Geoffrey writes again about *The Price of Liberty*.

The Price of Liberty

"I had a nice time yesterday at a lunch-time seminar with some students at Oxford. In the course of this I mentioned *The Price of Liberty*, and this led me to read it again last night when I got home. What a wonderful little book it is! How much I wish you could spend a few years here and now and write a sequel. The desire for 'spontaneous conformity' is still there and has some real political significance, but it is nothing like what it was in the 1930s. History has not yet answered the questions you ask us—the doubts which you express.

"My book is still an unstable and unsatisfactory collection of papers. Its table of contents and even its title are different from those which I last sent you. I have no idea what it will really be like when it is finished, even though I am committed to finish it within three weeks and expect to do so. I have never had an experience like this.

"Part of the reason is that I am dealing with culture at three levels, if not four—with changing English culture, with changing Western culture, with disintegrating personal culture and with the concept of culture generally. Moreover my understanding of the fourth of these is not strong enough to support the other three. Nor, so far as I can discover, is that of anyone else. It seems to be a curiously neglected study. My young host at Oxford yesterday teaches in an interdisciplinary course called 'Human Sciences' which contains no history and no more study of culture than is supplied by a small contribution from ethnology. The social anthropologists at Oxford, I gather, keep rigorously clear of cultural problems except insofar as these creep in inescapably in studies of kinship and suchlike transcultural subjects.

"This is why *The Price of Liberty* is so refreshing. It is not only such a good book in itself, it is such a good sort of a book and an example of a sort of book which is extraordinarily rare. Do you know of any other? Surely I must be missing out on some cultural historians?"

Adolph thanks him (April 3) for his "good words" about *The Price of Liberty*.

"But you must not compare it with the big canvas of Tocqueville—one of its merits is its brevity, but for this very reason it is little more than an *aperçu*, as I said in the preface to the 3rd edition. Reissuing it with an extensive *Postscript* relating to contemporary America is one of my possible projects.

"While I write this your new Prime Minister is still unknown. What a strange step on the part of Wilson. In the meantime the European Community is falling apart and we here are doing our best to mess up matters within and without—though, contrary to my dire predictions, the economy is recovering albeit with a large technological unemployment.

"I expect my proofreading to be finished within two weeks and then I can sit back, pondering what to do next. The book will not be out before July, which means that I shall have had it on my mind for six and a half years!"

Geoffrey is finishing off notes and references to his book. "Unless it provokes some frightful reaction when I read it through next week, I hope we can regard my last book as completed—or at least my last of that kind." May 14 he writes to Adolph about his visit to the United States.

"I finally posted two copies of the book to the University of California Press on Thursday April 22, and left for Boston the following day, taking a third copy with me. MIT made me three more xerox copies, one of which I took to Washington. My host at Washington xeroxed it again and promised to send a copy to you, so I hope you have received it by now. Do not allow the reading of it to be a burden to you. But if and when you can get through it I shall be interested to know what you think of it. No one at present, so far as I know, has read it. In any case, no comments have yet come back to me.

"I found this visit a laborious one and missed more than usual through fatigue, but it went quite well. I made a number of new friends at MIT. I enjoyed my brief visit to Milwaukee and was impressed by the climate of the university, at which nearly all the students are part-time adults. If the people I talked with were a representative sample of mid-Western American businessmen, the prospects for America and the world are much better than I thought they were.

"The same applies to George Washington University, also a place with a student body which is largely either part-time or seconded from business or more usually government careers. I was amazed at the breadth of the education which my young host there, Bayard Catron, is providing for these mature seekers of a doctorate in public administration. He also managed to engineer a conversation with about 15 people of many disciplines, mostly faculty, which went on for four hours and was barely interrupted by lunch—a most remarkable achievement. I learned a lot from these people.

"Has the work on your great book really finished? If so, are you enjoying the respite, or do you feel lost without it?"

Adolph's reaction to receiving the manuscript is one of enthusiasm.

"What a book! If I questioned the 'architecture' of the first draft, I can now only say that it is a cathedral. Not only does it hold one's attention, it creates real excitement. And this is due not to dramatic over-statements, but to what medieval Germans called *maze*, for which 'moderation' is a bad translation. It is so well balanced and fair in its weighing of the future of technology, of the balance of centralization and decentralization, and the interplay of rationality with the tacit factor.

"I wish I had the leisure to go into details. I would have to say more about 'induction', which is quite close to the heuristic method which underlies my 'instrumental analysis'. You have also solved the difficult issue of 'dialectics'— there cannot be any misunderstandings any more. And what you say about the positive significance of 'constraints' is most important.

Problem setting and solving

"I would like to discuss with you the problems of 'problem-setting' and 'problem-solving'. The, for me, decisive sentence is: "It is easy to 'keep an open mind' so long as we do not have to act." I admit all the infinite complications in trying to arrive at a 'concept of reasonable appreciation'. But even in normal times the actor must cut through in a crude way, not to mention the simplification due to some 'overwhelming imperative'. And I feel that the latter is precisely our situation—in a real sense 'the enemy is at the gate'. Nietzsche spoke of the 'terrible simplifiers' who will rule the 20th century. When all is going smoothly we are concerned with 'regulating and controlling systems'. But in emergency situations specific 'goals' take over. Of course, they too are embedded in systemic relations. But—even Beveridge seems to me a case in question—the 'Bolshevik' attitude comes to the fore, as you seem to imply yourself. But all this is mere stammering. Let us hope that the day is not too far when we can converse about this and many more of your ideas.

"One last word about Camus: your description of Dr. Rieux's position is very fair. But—in contrast to Sartre—this is not the entire Camus. You must read for your 'enjoyment', if that is the word, his lyrical essays, where he speaks of Algiers, his home, and where you find a sentence like this: 'Yes, there is beauty and there are the humiliated. Whatever may be the difficulties of the undertaking I should like never to be unfaithful either to one or the others'."

"Your letter of May 26 has just arrived and has given me tremendous pleasure and satisfaction", writes Geoffrey June 5. "I awaited your response with special eagerness, not only because I have special regard for your opinion but also because it was you who led me to redesign the book. I am delighted to hear that you now find in it a degree of architecture which is adequate and acceptable. How glad I shall be if other people, including the potential publishers, react with anything like your enthusiasm. You praise the book on just those grounds which I most value.

"I am particularly glad that you are satisfied with what I say about the dialectic process. You know far more about Hegel and Marx than I do, and I have realized from previous criticisms of yours that you have not been satisfied with the way in which I have used the word. I am delighted that this statement seems acceptable to you.

"Yes, of course there is a real clash between policy-making and effective action. At most times in the history of men and societies there may be no scope for any real policy-making—the constraints are too severe to admit any real choice. But it remains an important act of faith, though doubtless (like all acts of faith) an unprovable one, to believe that, at least now and then, space can be cleared for a degree of choice which is important enough to matter and not too wide to be exercised.

"How strange of Camus to identify the 'humiliated' as his antithesis to 'beauty'. I think I know what he means, but there are so many worse things than humiliation. I will read his essays. I owe a lot to you for sending me *The Plague* when you did—it made a great impression."

Adolph writes July 9 from his vacation home at Hilltop. His wife's state of health had threatened a holiday of which he felt badly in need.

"From the above address you see that fate was merciful and permitted me to go away after all (but) there is a 'veil' between me and the beauty that surrounds me. My desire to do some work could not be less. I brought some, but have not touched it. As a rule, such days and weeks are the welcome opportunity for 'meeting myself'—a mental and emotional 'house-cleaning' which is very important to me. So far I have not succeeded. I have read Henry James' *Portrait of a Lady*, dating from another millennium but full of psychological insight (and) am now reading a history of Henry VIII—quite a useful lesson. I did not know that the age was that 'bad'—I do not refer to the wives, but to politics, national and international. Wolsey, Cranmer, Cromwell; the difference from the totalitarian regimes of our time is one of scale rather than of kind. Another warning against the centralizing trend. More and more I think that our criterion should be the 'maximum tolerable disorder'—alas, the limits of tolerance are steadily shrinking. This is one aspect which I missed in *The Price of Liberty*; what else is British muddling-through?"

Publishing practices, and a rejection

On the same day Geoffrey writes to tell Adolph that the University of California Press has not, alas, responded to the book with enthusiasm, finding that, while well organized and readable, 'by comparison with *The Art of Judgment*, it operates on a high level of abstraction and may not stay close enough to real situations to compel the reader's interest'. This is naturally a great disappointment to Geoffrey, who finds the decision not to publish difficult to understand and turns to his friend for enlightenment.

"Forgive me if I bombard you with letters for a while. I have decided to do no more about the book until I really understand what happened to it at Berkeley. And you are, amongst many other things, my closest and best interpreter of academia.

"Many books have been written in the last decade about the present and future of the West—Heilbroner, Toffler, Dubos, Michael and so on. Some of these have been best-sellers. My book claims to be in this genre. Is it unacceptable to the University of California Press or even to any University Press as such? (*i.e.* do University Presses confine themselves to the literature of 'discovery' or 'invention' rather than 'wisdom'?) If not, in what does it fall short? Callenbach has been to much trouble to pass on his readers' criticisms but I don't really understand them, and some are of a kind which no one has ever made of my writing before. Are they applying some academic standard not found elsewhere, or some general standard which would be equally applicable by a commercial press?

"Much has also been written in the effort to make systems theory a useful tool in understanding very large social systems. This interest I have also shared, and I have tried, especially in this book, both to make the idea useful to historians and to counteract its baneful influence as an oversimplifier in the hands of systems engineers. The Gaither Lecture Fund which sponsored the book has a special concern with systems theory (I think the money comes from IBM) so I had a special reason to emphasize this aspect of my thinking. But the concept of 'appreciation' as a 'system' is one which I have been stressing for 15 years and whenever I come across references to my writing it is nearly always as the author of this concept. So I did not have to skew the book to bring it in and develop it further.

"Well, now for the critics. One says I am saying nothing new, though I am saying it charmingly. The other says that whatever I am saying, I am not saying it rigorously enough to merit attention. I could list the unaccepted theories which I am asserting and could claim to have been as rigorous as space permits, e.g. about the relation of brain research to intuition. But this is not a case for argument. If this is what three people get when they read the book, many others will too.

"I could wish he had sent it to at least one historian. The criticism I was afraid of was historical criticism, because I know I'm not well enough read in history to do safely what I attempt here. But history is an even more unpopular subject than culture—among philosophers, even more than social scientists. I wonder whether a university press ever asks a student's opinion. I am inclined to seek a new publisher known to be interested in this approach; but first I shall await enlightenment from you."

Adolph's first response is contained in a postscript to his letter dated July 9.

"O, these publishers! *On Economic Knowledge* is now with the fifth one—all four others having declined a reprint with highly complimentary refusals. The 'level of abstraction' has become an obsession here—pragmatism interpreted as the outlook of the lazy mind is rampant. The difference between university presses and private houses is rapidly disappearing—books are becoming 'merchandise'." He expands in another letter July 13.

"I have by now learned to interpret the language used by publishers. In fact, Rosenthal was one of those who declined the reissuing of OEK though he knew 'how important the original version of the book was' and though he is sure 'that an updated edition would be very welcome'. But 'we are just so overloaded in this area that it would be unfair to the book (!) and unwise for ourselves economically to commit to publication at this time'. Now this does not mean that you should not try him first, especially since he knows you from *The Art of Judgment*.

"As to the comments of the two readers, I wish they could be broadcast all over the Western world. That a manuscript can be condemned because it reflects 'wisdom' rather than 'discovery' or 'research'—you might use this sentence as a motto for the book. Ultimately this situation is the justification for your writing the book. Who would today be willing to publish *The Price of Liberty* if these are now the criteria? We can only pray that there are some publishers in England who do not despise wisdom—in Germany there are such, another paradox.

"I need not tell you that, apart from my indignation, I am truly sorry about this result. My own book is, as you will see, 'technical', 'formal and abstract' as the 'specialist' likes it and certainly not 'in the public domain'. And yet I am sure that the present rulers of Cambridge New York would not accept it any more because it swims against the current, though in a way different from yours. It is this state of affairs which justifies the various enterprises of our friend Nanda[2] who ... has published some books of wisdom. Keep her in mind as an ultimate recourse. Onward, Christian soldier!"

Geoffrey's letter of July 19, 1976, sent before he received this, reports new developments at Berkeley.

"My sponsors there are much disturbed that the book was processed and turned down without any reference to them. They are now reading the book. Maybe they will persuade the editor to try it on a different sort of reader. In any case it is back in the Berkeley mill, and there is nothing for me to do until I hear more. Whatever happens I expect that I shall get more illuminating comments from my friends and sponsors there than from the unnamed readers.

"I am interested to hear that you are reading history. I feel a great need to catch up on a bit of history, and I have often thought that a study of our totalitarian period might be useful, particularly because in the light of history it seems to have been absolutely necessary." He writes again on the 22nd.

"Regarding my book, the thing which puzzles me in the comment of the more sympathetic reader is that it says nothing new. It has not been turned down on account of commercial pressures and so on, but on account of these adverse criticisms of its content. Now it is true that I write books only to clear my own mind, and it might well be true that such clarity that I reach is no more than other people have already reached. This, however, is not the impression which I get when I talk to people, particularly at MIT. So I shall wait with lively interest to hear what my hosts there think when they have read the book.

"Meantime I am having a delightful unintellectual time—broken however this weekend by a visit to the summer school of our Open University, to which I am just setting out. This is a most interesting institution, apparently free from all the handicaps to which normal universities are heir. They do a course on 'systems' which seems to me extremely well devised, and I am going up to give the closing talk on it on the last day of their summer school."

Meanwhile Adolph, having only just received Geoffrey's letter of the 9th, had written again July 20.

"This is not an individual case, nor special behavior on the part of that university publisher. I can only speak of the new American 'practice'. This is, as my own publisher—Cambridge—told me, largely influenced by the wish to save storage costs in view of the high prices charged by warehouses. Therefore, only books can be printed which 'move' rapidly. Now why publishers assume that books of 'wisdom' move more slowly than books of 'discovery' or 'research' raises a wider problem: the attitude of the contemporary reader.

"You mention Heilbroner, Toffler etc. Well, the successful ones—there are others—have all been 'popular' in terms of style and emotional appeal. Your book is certainly not popular in that sense. In fact, it demands from the reader a degree of concentration and even of previously acquired experience that is usually invested only in 'scientific' books. And this indeed narrows the market in an age of 'instantaneous satisfaction'.

"Don't get me wrong: what I say here is an attempt at explaining what is behind this attitude of publishers—I certainly do not defend it. What to do? Certainly not to fret—there is nothing 'wrong' with your book that you could change, except perhaps the title. I never liked it. Leave out 'Systems Thinking'. Perhaps: *Understanding Modern Culture* or something else which is simpler. And look for another publisher. I am by no means sure that the attitude described permeates English publishing to the extent to which it does American. If you give me the green light I will show the manuscript to Nanda.

"I am gradually accepting the fact that what people like you and me write about is not already in the public domain—if it were we would not write. This carries its penalty, well expressed in Boulding's letter to me a few weeks ago apologizing for his bad review of OEK 11 years ago: 'You were saying something very important which at the time I was not ready to hear'. This does not undo the harm he caused with that review—these experiences are the price we pay for our liberty!"

Updating On Economic Knowledge

On August 28 Adolph tells Geoffrey that he has been totally absorbed with finishing a piece for the *Festschrift* of his colleague Jonas, with which he had been struggling in vain for the better part of three months.

"It is done, not very good but satisfactory for the occasion. I have finally succeeded in finding a publisher who even feels honored to reissue OEK, though he has already three Nobel Laureates on his list. This will keep me busy to the end of the year, but I am happy that the book will again be available to the students.

"For the rest, our election circus is in full swing. Carter is certainly courageous, the way he told the American Legion that he wants to grant a wholesale pardon to all violators of the draft during Vietnam. But he will have to fight an uphill struggle, especially because his sister has just published a book on faith healing, based on their evangelical beliefs. Besides, he is called woolly and vague because he confesses that there are issues for which he has not yet found the final solution. It will be a real test of the country's moral fibre."

Geoffrey, September 9 1976, is delighted to hear that OEK is to be republished.

"Who is the lucky publisher? I am not sure whether I told you that *The Art of Judgment* has been reprinted in America but not in England?[3] I enclose copy of another letter about my book, this time from West Churchman, an influential figure at Berkeley. I have written to my host there explaining that whatever contrary opinions he marshals, I shall not expect the young publisher to change what is evidently his mind, as well as the mind of his first readers, and that the outcome which I should least welcome would be to have the book reluctantly published by a publisher who did not believe in it. I hope we shall reach finality soon.

"I am interested in what you write about Carter. We shall all be waiting, not only for the result of the election, but also to see what it does to the new President, if the President is indeed new. I have just read a book by Brzezinski called *Between Two Ages*, an old book published in 1970. I wonder what you think of it. I gather that he may be politically important if Carter comes to power."

"I know who Churchman is" writes Adolph, who finds this letter upon his return from Hilltop, "and his word should carry considerable weight. Concerning his queries, I am ashamed that I did not catch that mistake with 1776. More important, he is wrong with regard to Kant and *Mathematics*. But there are certainly some voices insisting that mathematics is an empirical science. He has a point in stating that the first few chapters are slow going—I found the same when I reread OEK which, otherwise, I found a very good book! The style is somewhat turgid in some places, but I cannot do anything about it because the old text will be photographed. What will occupy me during the coming months is the *Postscript*. The publisher—the International Arts and Science Press, a small but distinguished house—and I are not yet clear how long the *Postscript* should be. It should cover the factual events since 1964, especially the failure of the most sophisticated institutions to predict correctly. And it should clarify some of the theoretical issues, which I discussed partly in my Rejoinder in *Economic Means and Social Ends*, which by now is also out of print.

"On top of this I have been asked by another publisher to write a short book in the area of your own latest manuscript. Provisional title: *Prometheus Unbound?* The question mark is essential, because it would show the pluses and minuses of the process which I call 'emancipation'. Finally I have been asked to organize a panel on 'What is wrong with modern society?' for next year's session of the American Economic Association. I am not at all sure whether I will accept—not only does my agenda get a little too crowded, but I cannot see that much useful purpose can be achieved in such a session.

"Did I tell you that *The Path of Economic Growth* has appeared? The book is an artistic achievement, which is not, and should not be, the prime interest of the reviewers. Your copy will soon be on its way, but don't read more than chapter 1! I don't know the Brzezinski book; I will try to get hold of it. He is very clever but an utter cynic, and I pray that Carter will not make him Secretary of State. It was from our telephone that you settled the republication here of *The Art of Judgment*. I trust they will exploit the English market too."

Money, wealth and instrumental analysis

"You are indeed a wonder of creative energy", replies Geoffrey on the 29th. "My very good wishes to your new book and to your panel, if you decide to take it on. I find it hard to say no to invitations which I should like to accept, but which I know will crowd me unduly, and I will not add my persuasions to those who will be trying to make you say yes to this one. I think, nonetheless, that there is a field in which the right sort of economists could make a useful contribution— that is, to a better understanding of the relation between money and real wealth.

"People born into a money economy experience money as a more direct reality than any of the productive processes, even perhaps the one on which they themselves are engaged, and it has of course developed real systems independent of the realities which it mediates, or rather interdependent with them. I wonder how much education of this kind is given in primary and secondary schools in America or elsewhere in the Western world, and how much could be given without unearthing real controversies between people who claim to be economists? If there is not a common understanding among the experts, we cannot expect there to be a common understanding among the laity. And the things you have told me about your colleagues' views on inflation suggest that the amount of agreed content is very small indeed. If money were only a veil, as I think Keynes said, it would be relatively easy to explain. But although for some purposes it functions only as a veil, for other purposes it functions in many other ways.

"No doubt there are many things the matter with Western society in addition to its misunderstandings about money. But it is these to which we chiefly look to economists for enlightenment and it seems to me that we look in vain— although not perhaps more in vain than if we asked corresponding questions of epistemologists, historians, linguists and many others.

"No further word about my book. I am content that it should lie quiet at present, because when it moves I shall have to do quite a lot of work on it and I am not yet ready to do that. I will stir things up if need be when I am ready to deal with the response."

Adolph tells him (October 19) that his old friend Tommy—now Lord Balogh—had visited him.

"He was much more disciplined and sober than in the past. All the more I was impressed by his pessimism about Britain's economy. He thinks that both labor and management are hopelessly behind their competitors, and expects an early development to an autocratic regime which, in my terminology, will apply 'command controls'. Our election process deteriorates from week to week. Again, it can only be the choice of the—assumed—lesser evil, which is Carter. The pettiness of the issues discussed by the two candidates cannot be described.

"No, I have decided to turn down the offer to set up and speak on the panel. It is a waste of time, and I cannot say what I would like to say in ten minutes, which is the maximum allowed for a paper. I would rather try to say it in 80,000 words, which is the length allowed by my second new publisher. Incidentally, money is much too controversial a subject to be taken up in schools. It was Keynes who first attacked the idea of money as a veil, but much more is at stake. The award of a Nobel Prize to Friedman has restarted a heated controversy."

"I am not surprised that Balogh is depressed by what he sees here" says Geoffrey October 25. "We all are; and I could fill this envelope with recent cuttings from the *Times* analysing the political impasse. You may have seen that Harold Macmillan returned to public activity in a BBC interview in which he advocated a government of national unity, *i.e.* a coalition on the model of the one which ran the last war. In discussing what event could trigger such a change with emphasis comparable to a war, he mentioned bread rationing. I was very surprised that his interviewer did not take him up on this and invite him to expand his understanding of the situation in which the country's total food supply would be in such jeopardy as to need rationing. This would have given him the opportunity to rub in what I think was much the most important thing he had to say.

"This is the more important if, as you say, money is far too controversial a subject to be taught in schools. Is it not odd that we understand the working of this man-made device so much less than the most complicated workings of nature—but perhaps it is not so odd after all. I have been saying for a long time that that is what we ought to expect. And so have you.

"I have been very busy the last three weeks with guests. The next four weeks are busy with lectures and engagements of various kinds. Then I go to MIT for 2-3 weeks including, I hope, a brief visit to Yale, but I am afraid that I shall not have enough steam to get to New York. I will certainly ring you up from Cambridge. It will be nice to be that much nearer. Meantime, this is just to keep in touch."

On November 4 he reports receiving Adolph's book.

"I am delighted to have it and I have read the introduction with the greatest interest. It is beautifully clear; and though I have a comment, I will not try to express it now because it links with a correspondence which I am having with at least two other people about the relation of social scientists to each other, and equally—a distinct issue in my view—about the relation between the pure and the applied elements in each of them. I hope to have something to send you about this soon.

"Just one anticipatory remark. You would agree, would you not, that the President's Council of Economic Advisers is there to do instrumental analysis not positive analysis (except insofar as the second is needed for the first)? The President wants advice on what he can feasibly do and at what cost, not just prophecies of what is going to happen. By far the greater proportion of your economic students, as of the whole out-turn of economic departments, must I should think be engaged today as operations researchers, systems analysts, cost-benefit analysts, planners and all the other techniques which have grown up in the last 30-40 years for the assistance of the policy-maker. I have learned from you in the last ten years to accept, as a fact, the great difference in outlook which seems to exist between most academic economists and their former students now practicing the many professions to which economics is relevant. But I am still surprised at the gulf, and more aware than I was of the need to bridge it.

"I spent two days last week at a conference in London organized by the British Operational Research Society under the auspices of the Royal Society. Four practitioners of operational research and its many related disciplines discoursed on their methodology and their theories. Four satisfied users from among the largest undertakings in the world (Shell, Unilever, the British National Coal Board and a department of the British Government) described how valuable this advice had been to them, not only in finding the best way to carry out given objectives, but to compare possible objectives in the light of analyses made by these professions to show the feasibility, uncertainty, risk, cost and benefit, which attach to different hypothetical courses.

"This large body of professionals is trained in universities, in proliferating schools and institutions, and claims in effect to provide precisely that body of applied social science which policy-makers want but often fail to find when they go for advice to academic departments. These new 'applied social scientists' have very seldom had any training in social science. The exception is the economist, precisely because he has, until recently, been regarded as less softly social than other social sciences. I am not happy with this take-over bid, which is being made largely by mathematicians, computer scientists and communications engineers to provide policy-makers with advice on how to run the world and, therefore, by implication with their model, of how the world works. It is nonetheless a powerful and confident bid which is being made by a very large body of highly competent men, and which is encouraged by the fact that there is a vacuum to be filled.

"In one sense this only underlines the importance which you attach to instrumental analysis made by people who know about both the political and the social process, including the obscure and culture-bound field of personal motivation, but it seems to me to raise more questions than your introduction answers, and I hope to be a little more explicit later on. Meantime I will read the book. I would not have ventured to send you the little paper that came with my last letter if I had known that I was about to receive such a comprehensive answer."

Growth and zero-growth

A "Guy Fawkes Day!" letter from Adolph tries to persuade Geoffrey to come to New York.

"Look, if you have the time to spend 2-3 weeks in Cambridge, and 'afford the additional luxury of a visit to Yale', it should be possible for you to add a one and a half hour train ride from New Haven to New York. Now I have been sensing for quite some time that it is not so much preoccupation with other plans as an aversion to our blessed city that keeps you away. Alas, there are indeed enough reasons to dislike NYC, and I won't argue about this. But you should realize that, considering the situation in which I find myself, which makes travelling abroad impossible, this attitude if perpetuated will cut off our personal contact for good. Forgive me if I speak so bluntly, but it shows you how much I wish that it were otherwise, and that I have not given up hope that you might find it possible to put in at least one day in New York.

"Now there is an additional reason this time. It concerns your little draft of *Growth*. I am afraid I have strong objections against the way you pose the problem and the ensuing answers. If I had much time I might answer with a counter-memo. But even then I fear that the complexity of the problem would prevent us from an easy understanding. For this reason I do wish that we could devote a quiet hour to talking the matter over. Do give it a thought. As a preparation for such a talk, I will jot down a few comments to show the direction of my reservations:

1. You treat as a micro-economic problem—as a decision on the part of firms—what basically is a macro-problem, namely the question of how to maintain full utilitization of present and increasing resources.

2. Seen in the latter light, 'growth' or net investment has a basic function in any economy in which part of the current income is *saved*. Or to put it the other way round, we can dispense with net investment if all current income is consumed—either directly by the income recipients or indirectly by taxing away savings and using the resources thus freed for public consumption. I need not discuss the socio-political difficulties of such a solution, though economically it would be OK. To show you one example, the viewpoint of the firm is unsatisfactory because it creates the 'fallacy of competition'— you seem to believe that distributing all profits on the part of the corporation would solve the problem. Yes, if you make sure the recipients of the dividends consume them. If they save only part of it, a demand-employment gap arises unless you have compensating net investment—via the stock market which takes up new issues—or you tax away those savings.

3. What I have so far said concerns the *structure* of an economy in which both net savings and net investments = growth are down to zero. Another problem is how to transform an economy which does have net investment

into one with zero net investment—a problem discussed at length in the book. The transition is extremely difficult because it implies the shutting down of that part of the capital good sector which now produces the 'growth real capital', and the transfer of the resources hitherto employed there to the production of consumer goods. I estimate the size of that sector as between 10% and 15% of total output—differing in different countries with different growth rates. So you can imagine what turmoil such a transfer would cause. It can be done by a degree of 'planning' (central compulsion) that exceeds our keenest ideas.

"Now all I am saying here is a crude restatement of the basic proposition of Keynes' *General Theory*. (We, that is some of us, knew this before but he certainly raised it to the level of accepted doctrine.) Perhaps you should look into my Keynes chapter in OEK, which also touches on the relationship of Keynes' propositions to Growth, which he never discussed explicitly. Still—and this brings me back to the beginning—the importance of the problem might make it worth your while to conquer your aversion to NYC."

Geoffrey's note of the 15th replies to these comments but does not refer to Adolph's insistence that he come to New York. (Alas, they were never to see each other again.)

"I do not think I confused the micro-problem of zero growth in a firm with the macro-problem of zero growth in a national economy or a global economy. On the contrary, I thought my correspondent had done so, and intended the note as a caution.

"The fact remains that zero growth in an enterprise does pose a real problem for managers. I was much concerned with it when I was on the board of Parkinson Cowan. The chief executives were so unable to envisage success independent of physical growth that they went on pushing their size up until they exceeded their capacity and came to grief. But even if they had accepted the fact that it was unwise to enlarge a cooker factory in boom years to a size which was unlikely to be fully occupied in other years (our break-even point was nearly 80% of full capacity), they would have found it hard to give effect to this policy because distributors were unwilling to stock cookers which could not be delivered in whatever quantity the market required.

"In the old days, when direct labor costs were the major item, businesses could shrink as well as grow simply by dismissing men but, as you know better than I, both the dominance of indirect costs and the dominance of growth ideology has produced the wretched-like mechanism which I mention in the paper.

"Once again, I assure you that I am not saying that control at this level is either/ or a sufficient contribution to controlling the growth of the national economy, still less the global economy. I am not saying it has anything to do with it. It may even be that the policies to which the managers of individual businesses are driven today are basically inconsistent with the national policies which need to be applied. Hence the need for the political constraints you mention. But, in the context of my correspondent's letter, it seemed to me important to make him draw the distinction more clearly than he was doing.

"I will re-read the references you mention in your letter to see whether I have missed anything. I will also re-read the paper to see whether it is misleading. The man I wrote it for is coming to see me next week.

"I am sending you, under separate cover, a longer paper which you may dislike even more. It refers expressly to your work and I want you to tell me first whether you have any objection to being cited in this way. I would like to know, as a separate question, whether you agree in substance with the paper. It is oversimplified in at least two ways. It may not be quite valid to identify the applied sciences with the professional schools. It may not be quite true to say that no-one in an academic discipline is usefully trying to teach an interdisciplinary course. Nonetheless, the impression I got, both in America and here, is that the huge antithesis described in the paper is substantially right."

Here, alas, we have a gap until Adolph's letter of December 16 in reply to a letter from Geoffrey of the 8th, which appears to have explained the delay in terms of fatigue.

"Naturally I was disappointed about your silence, since there was so much to talk about. But I certainly understand the reason and can only hope that the New Year with less pressure will restore you to the energy-emitting self that I have known for so many years.

"You will soon receive the draft of my *Postscript* to the new edition of OEK. If you should find the time for even a brief comment I would be most grateful. So far I have had only one substantive response to *The Path*—from Hicks. He even writes that he 'enjoys' reading the book—clearly an indication of masochism. If we could have met I would have liked to speak to you about my present and very vague plans. This will have to wait now until I am clear enough to put something into a letter."

The first letter in 1977 is Geoffrey's of January 7, in which he comments on Adolph's *Postscript*.

"I hesitate to comment because I have already said most of the things I want to say and you have referred me to sections of your book which I have not yet re-read. But time is short—so here goes.

"I have three main comments. First, your economic macro-goal is balanced growth. I find no reference to distribution as an *economic* goal. Accepting this limitation, I observe that for at least ten years British governments have been practicing political economics by applying secondary as well as primary controls to the economy. And they have been abundantly helped by economists acting as instrumental analysts in devising means to this end, some hired by the government, some of the economic institutes offering their advice *gratis*. The result has been failure, partly because the economists differed widely in the advice which they offered and partly because sections of the electorate were strong enough to negate even those policies which governments dared to propose, and to inhibit even the expression of those which governments ought to have proposed.

"I cannot reconcile these realities with a world in which (a) everyone agreed on balanced growth as a dominant macro-goal, (b) economists sufficiently agreed on how to pursue it, and (c) all relevant sections of the electorate agreed to pay the costs, however heavy to them as a sub-system of the whole.

"Secondly and more seriously, our concern with balanced growth is relatively new. Since the '30s at least our economic concerns have been with distribution—distribution of work, i.e. full employment, and greater equality of income by redistribution in cash and services. Beveridge, writing in the London blitzes, assumed that there was and would always be enough for all. Distribution, he thought, was the only problem. And in the view of many, one effect of our efforts at securing these two kinds of distribution (of which the first at least has failed) has been to affect the motivation of both entrepreneurs and workers on which balanced growth depends.

"I don't know whether you call these distributive policies political economics or economic politics, but I do not believe that the politics of production can be separated from the policies of distribution. We are faced today with three rival solutions—(a) to increase the entrepreneur's confidence in his ability to trust his own judgment by assuring him greater rewards for guessing right, (b) to do the same by stabilizing his environment by planning agreements and such, and (c) by transferring his initiatives, especially his investment decisions, to the State. Your analysis shows that the first is unlikely to work. We have as yet no real experience of (b) and our experience of (c) is unhappy, partly because these decisions when politicized are always governed by the need to preserve employment, even by propping up ailing industries without reducing their employees' earnings. Your lack of attention to the distributive aspect of economic policy, especially employment, adds to my difficulty in translating what you say into the terms of my own experience.

"Thirdly, and greatest of all, I am stunned when I read that the pertinent laws of nature and engineering rules include 'those psychological laws that link a specific behavior to specific motivations'. You refer me to chapter 10 which I have not re-read, but as of now I firmly believe that there are no such laws. To affirm them is to affirm a disbelief in human culture.

"Humans are human because they are acculturated in a specific culture. Cultures are historical phenomena. The responses of Britain to 'going off gold' in 1931 would be unthinkable today and incredible to a generation of Britons too young to remember them. Swedes respond today in a way unthinkable to Britons today, though less remote from the Britain of which you wrote *The Price of Liberty*.

Are you saying that we can't have a science of economics until we have standardized world culture? If so, do you regard this as possible or desirable?

"All the social sciences seem to me to be blasted by this aspiration to escape from culture and so to make good their claim to be as scientific as the natural sciences. B.F. Skinner would agree—but do you really believe in Walden II, let alone desire it?

"I agree that it is a function of government to foster those elements of common culture which are needed to keep a society in existence and to secure as much of its shared goals as is compatible with sufficient learning and change. And this has an economic constituent. But this is a political and social problem infinitely wider than the pursuit of balanced growth. And even in economic terms, recent history has surely shown that balanced growth is not an objective which can be pursued without reference to the two great distributive objectives, full employment and reduced differentials in income, which have dominated the policies of Western countries for many decades and which are most unlikely to be compatible with balanced growth considered on its own.

"In your *Postscript* you mention three doubts which have grown in your mind over the last ten years. They reflect the protests expressed above, but not to my mind nearly enough. The question whether economics can be made into a science is no doubt important to economists, but the rest of us are interested in it only insofar as it may improve the understanding of governments and governed of the options which are open to each of them, each within the constraints of its own history and culture, in changing or maintaining the conditions of its corporate life. One of these is the role of paid work, the possibility of full employment and the cost of securing it if it can be secured. It is not the only one. But no-one can assume today that balanced growth, however achieved, will ensure or even be compatible either with full employment or with stable money.

"I woke up with this in my head so I send it for what it is worth. It may overlook much that is in OEK which I have read, and more in *The Path* which as yet I haven't. But it would not be so strong and spontaneous a reaction if there were not some great gulf either between what we are talking about or between our basic assumptions concerning it." He adds a PS to the effect that part of his letter is ill-expressed. "I would not deny that there are links between a given set of mixed motivations and the resulting behavior. Where culture comes in is in determining how situations are perceived and what motivations they evoke." A week later, he writes again.

"I felt bad at sending you my last letter without having first read some of your references to OEK, especially chapter 10 to which the *Postscript* refers. I have been doing so and trying to understand why I still find it so difficult.

"One reason, I think, is that the answers you offer do not seem to relate to the questions which our economic state moves me to ask, and sometimes depend on assumptions which you take for granted but which are different from the ones I take for granted. When, for example, you refer to changing motivations and therewith behavior, I think you must be thinking of the motivation of buyers and sellers, entrepreneurs and financiers. But my mind, equally spontaneously, thinks first of the motivation and behavior of workers and voters, the two bodies whose misguided expectations are so dominant in both the private and the public sector. Similarly, you talk of decentralization as a policy which authority is capable of willing. I think of it as a fact imposed by the semi-autonomy of a whole range of power groups each of whom, partly through its electoral power and partly through industrial action, can curtail the power of central authority whether that authority wills it or not.

"In a word, I live already in a syndicalist corporate state and I expect that the trends indicated by these two words will get much more acute before they are abated. This of course does not alter some economic 'facts', but it does profoundly alter one's picture of economic expectations insofar as these supply the motivations for economic behavior.

"But enough of this. Since I came back from America five weeks ago I have been unduly busy. I have sent off three papers to various publishers or editors, including one which has proved to be the most frustrating and frustrated thing I ever wrote; made two journeys, given one highly unsuccessful lecture, and had five sets of visitors, most of whom have been 'professional'. The last of these occupied yesterday. Now I have an unstructured diary for weeks ahead and I hope to live at a more human rate. Moreover, since I seem to be better at cooking than writing, I propose to do more of the first and less of the second. But this will not stop me writing letters, particularly to you."

Three days later (January 17, 1977) he writes again.

"I wonder whether you have read Daniel Bell's *The Cultural Contradictions of Capitalism*? I think you would find it interesting, especially the later chapters on 'the public household'. These bring out very well the sociological nature of the problem created by the need for national housekeeping in a household which has not developed the attitudes and concepts appropriate to members of such a household. Both the regulative function of the government in preserving the conditions of a market and its policy functions, and the dual task of deciding how much to spend on the public household and how to allocate this amount between rival demands, have in fact passed out of the control of the policy-making process because of the rise in people's ideas of what Bell calls their entitlements, and because both the increasing power of particular groups and their indifference to old constraints leaves the government with inadequate discretion both for policy-making and for regulation. If this is true of the United States, it is infinitely more true of Britain.

Inflation and Distribution

"The word 'inflation' does not occur in the index to OEK. And although there are many references to 'money', none of them so far as I can see discusses the kind of instability which now threatens Western economies owing to the changes which Bell examines here. If you have time and interest to look at these chapters, I shall be interested to know whether you think Bell does justice to Marx and to contemporary Marxists in his frequent references to both.

"I know you may think that all this is not central to your efforts to persuade your fellow economists to be instrumental rather than predictive. If, however, the situation is such that no instrumental analysis will point the way either to sufficiently stable regulation or to any desired policy, then the question of cultural change becomes crucial. And this, as Bell points out, is not just a question of changing political institutions. I am not wholly in love with Bell's decision to separate cultural processes both from political processes and from social processes (though I see the advantages which he hopes to gain thereby), but I feel that he has said in this book a number of things which I have tried to say in *Western Culture and Systems Thinking* [4] and which today must, I would have thought, form the background to any economic instrumental analysis."

Adolph writes at length January 16. Reading Geoffrey's letter of January 7 has created for him the greatest puzzle in quite a long time.

"Again and again I asked myself whether words have the same meaning for you and me, and what at bottom creates such enormous misunderstandings. But one thing has been brought home to me most forcefully—how unfair it is for me to ask you and some of my colleagues to comment on this *Postscript*. After all it is intended for people who have just finished reading the main part of the book and are still uncertain about certain propositions, wondering above all about the topical relevance of the book. Most certainly I cannot expect that even a person such as you, who read the book carefully more than a decade ago, can remember the details and thus link up the statements of the *Postscript* with the essentials of the book.

"In your case this leads to the consequence—most surprising to you—that not only do I agree with the three points you have advanced as criticism, but I have made those very points very explicitly, both in the book and in the *Postscript*. Let me take up the points:

1. You find no reference to distribution as an economic goal. What else than distribution do I discuss on pp.17-22, and not only as a national but also as an international problem? I explain there why I played this problem down in the main body of the book, and stipulated stability and balanced growth as primary goals—perhaps a short-sighted assumption even then. But I certainly stressed redistribution as a central condition of all instrumental policy, today and in the future. You may not agree with what I say on those

six pages, in which case your objections might be very helpful to me. But your just saying that you 'find no reference' makes no sense to me.

2. Now, there may be a terminological misunderstanding at work. You subsume 'full employment' under distribution. This is a very unusual classification, certainly not the conventional one among economists. Since it is concerned not with 'shifts', but with extension of the aggregate, it is generally, and rightly, treated as a 'production' problem. As such it plays the strategic role in the book—just look at the references in the Index (under Utilization of Resources)—and is a major feature of 'stability' and 'balanced growth', the two macro-goals on which my entire analysis hinges. Again, what I say may be deficient, but I am certainly dealing with the issue very extensively. Incidentally, nowhere do I claim that 'economists sufficiently agree how to pursue balanced growth'—why would I write two long books if this were so? And I certainly would not admit that your economists advocated, or your government applied, the right kind of controls at the right time.

3. Still, your main wrath is directed against my statement that, once I know a person's motivations—in my terminology his action directives and his expectations—I can predict his behavior. You interpret this as saying that there are laws which 'determine how situations are perceived and what motivations they evoke'. Now I say the very opposite on numerous pages of the book. My 'laws' relate the effect on behavior to certain *given* motivations. You impute to me the statement that there are 'laws' which relate motivations to certain ascertainable 'causes'. If you will reread those two pages you will see that I deny the existence of such 'laws of social causation', and ascribe to any tentative prediction of the effect of a given control on motivations at best a probability value, largely based on common sense. And you will find there a passage in which I relate this effect to the 'rules on the observance of which the functioning of any society depends'—my formulation of what you define as 'culture'.

"Now, knowing you as a careful and basically sympathetic reader, I cannot help speculating what it is that makes you totally misunderstand my very explicit formulations. It is not for the first time, but seems to arise whenever the 'scientific' aspect of economics raises its, for you, ugly head. I find a clue to this when you say that the question whether economics can be made into a science 'is no doubt important to economists, but ...' What you fail to see is that the 'but' in which you are interested is conditional on economics being developed into some sort of 'science', that is, to the point where prediction with a limited prediction interval can be made. Why? Please read pp. 7-8 of the *Postscript*, and if this is not enough, chapter 4 of the book itself. Believe me, I am not interested in economic theory as a game, as a good many of my colleagues indeed are. My whole enterprise in revising the scientific approach in economics is inspired by the wish to make the result 'useful'.

"I know that you instinctively rebel against this attempt. But remember that our prejudices no less than our true insights derive from such instincts. You will find me open to any argument you will put forth against what I do say. But so long as you argue against statements which I do not make, that 'great gulf' of which you speak cannot be bridged." He continues January 24.

"Perhaps I should wait with writing until you have responded to my letter of January 16. But the two notes which you sent me since go a long way toward bridging that 'great gulf' which seems to separate us. In your first letter you have commented on what I have actually written about—in OEK and, especially, in the *Postscript*—statements which I still believe you have totally misunderstood. But now you point to issues I have not dealt with or only in passing—issues which I regard as important as you do. So why have I not taken them up at great length in the *Postscript?* My answer is this:

"OEK was written in the early Sixties. At that time, though the world was full of grave problems (Cuba crisis!), the economies of the advanced countries with which I was concerned were, though under-performing, in no serious economic crisis that threatened the socio-political foundations. This is true also of Britain, which seemed to make a real comeback. So if inflation does not appear in the index of OEK, the reason is that it was no problem—certainly not cost-push inflation. And no-one thought that we might be on the way to what you aptly call a 'syndicalist corporate state.'

"But, you may reply, why not take up these issues in the *Postscript*, which is after all to be published now? My answers are these:

(a) I *have* taken them up in the last six pages, though what I say there is geared to the main body of the book, specifically to chapter 12 (*not* 10, as you write). In that chapter I stepped over the limits set by my main purpose of debunking conventional economics and offering a substitute in instrumental analysis. There I deal with some wider aspects of what I call 'Political Economics', which extends to the socio-political framework of economic processes. Recognition that this framework has changed during the last decade is expressed in those six pages of the *Postscript*.

(b) But why only six pages? For two reasons. One is that my publisher has set the limit of 25 typewritten pages for the *Postscript*, so as not to unbalance the book. Now the published critiques of the book all deal with the narrower problems of instrumental analysis, and I had no other choice than devoting the larger part of the *Postscript* to those problems. But even if I had more leeway, I could not do justice to what Political Economics, or rather Politics in the Aristotelian sense, will have to become if catastrophe is to be avoided. This is possible only in a different book, with a different starting point and a different frame of reference. I have been struggling with such a book from the day when the manuscript of OEK was delivered to the publisher. I even showed you a—badly misbegotten—first chapter in Brig. *The Path of Economic Growth* intervened for more than five years. But I am at it again—have even a contract—though I have great doubts whether I shall ever get through with it.

"Now you may ask: why reissue OEK if it seems to be out of date? Obviously I believe that it is not out of date. There we come to the central point—the cardinal difference between our two countries. It is possible that the 'syndicalist corporate state' will overtake America too—it has not done so as yet. Though badly distorted by monopolistic manipulations on both sides of the fence, the market and its components are still the dominant reality in our economy.

"Two years ago I had great doubts about this. This was the time when Bell wrote his book, which I saw when it was published, and which I admire in many respects. But his diagnosis reflects the incertitudes of those dangerous years. It may be an image of the future—it does not represent the present. Against my own expectations, what I call 'organized capitalism' functions again here. Our rate of inflation is moderate at less than 5% in 1976. Our unemployment is much too high, but it is no threat to social stability. One reason is that the number of families in which at least one member does not earn is small. Total employment has increased over the last five years by many millions. In a word, we do have problems but none in the realm of economics that what I call 'secondary controls' cannot greatly alleviate. And we seem to have now a government which knows how to go about it—with great caution and, thank God, without Kennedy's flamboyance.

"The main reason for all this is the unbelievable discipline of our unions. As opposed to those in Britain, they are not out for a 'revolution through re-distribution', but by and large for maintaining their real wages. With many other 'foreigners' I often complained about the unpolitical nature of the US union movement. It has turned out a blessing. In such an environment Political Economics in the limited sense of OEK is not only feasible, but a precondition for maintaining the *status quo* during this dangerous period of international transition. I am by no means sure that this relatively happy state of affairs will last, and I have made this abundantly clear in my *Postscript*. Resigning myself as 'optimum goal' to 'a maximum tolerable degree of disorder' should absolve me from the suspicion of 'optimism'. What I actually mean by that phrase I do not know at this stage. If I should succeed in my new enterprise, I might be able to be more concrete.

"Incidentally, I predict that, though we may all head for a corporate state— a situation fully compatible with my Political Economics—the syndicalism which rightly worries you will not last. It will, in the worst case, be suppressed, from the Left or, more likely, from the Right. A far from pleasant prospect, but one that threatens what we mean by 'culture'—not economic viability.

"Finally, you ask what I think of Bell's criticism of Marx. Not only do I basically agree with him, but I have made the same point—Marx's neglect of the State as potential organizer of the 'substructure'—in my Marx chapter in OEK."

Geoffrey's reply, February 5 1977, thanks Adolph for his two letters.

"On the second, it is well to be reminded how small a cloud inflation was in the early '30s. But that does not for one moment question in my mind the value of reprinting OEK. It is far too fundamental to be affected by such changes. I cannot respond properly to your first point without re-reading the paper and my letters and recovering the point of view from which I wrote them. This I cannot do now, so for the moment I can only say how sorry I am that I should have so misunderstood you. The same is largely true of the second point, except that your letter shows me that your concept of balanced growth would, you think, provide sufficiently full and constant employment as a function of increasing production. I cannot conceive how it would or why it should, but that must be because I haven't understood what you mean by balanced growth. I know you have defined the term but it doesn't follow in the least that I understand it.

"Nor do I understand how a government can provide these pressures and constraints which you show to be necessary without using as one of its criteria their effect on employment. Is not the amount of employment a function not only of the extension of the aggregate but also of the composition of the aggregate? A more labor-intensive production system employs more people for the same output—hopefully at lower average wages! Increased production in labor-intensive activities presumably provides more employment than the same value of increase in less labor-intensive industries. You can also help to equate production with work force by reducing hours, early retirement and so on. I supposed that the pressures and constraints you had in mind would be much concerned with all this. It dominates the scene here.

"On the third point I can say a little more and it may help to explain why I so often just don't understand what you are saying. You point out that I was barking up the wrong tree. I was. I had realized this after posting my letter. But directed to the right tree I am no better off. How can you forecast a behavior from a motivation? What, I wondered, do you mean by a motivation? I thought maybe the wish to attain balanced growth would be an example. But as I point out, economists don't agree on how, if at all, this could be done, so you can't forecast behavior from that. And you agree in your letter of the 16th.

"Well then, you come to my rescue again with a definition of motivation. But again I don't understand your definition—'action directives and expectations'. Well, I can think of some expectations which would be likely to cause specific behavior. If, for example, I expect the price of my raw materials to rise, I am likely to stock up if I have the money and the space and the expectation of using it quickly enough. But what can 'action directives' mean? 'Directives for action'? Surely not. If someone has got so far as getting a directive for action, from whatever source has authority to give such directions, you can't, can you, speak of 'forecasting' the action from the directive? You know what he's been told to do. It's as simple as that.

"I often find myself, in this sort of case, trying to give specific meaning to some general words of yours, and absolutely failing. And often they have to do with your use of the word 'forecast'. I thought a forecast was always a deduction, however precarious, made from some proposition which is at least one degree more general. Starting from there I can't imagine how an action could be said to be 'forecast' from a knowledge of the direction to do it.

"I've set this out at length because it may exemplify some of my difficulty in understanding the words you use. If it doesn't, never mind. But it does grieve me greatly that I so often absolutely fail to understand your writing, although we understand each other very well when we talk and there's no-one I've learned more from than you.

"Of course you are right in wondering whether words have the same meaning for you and me. They often don't. This is very common in my own experience. No-one even among my closest friends outside the academic and professional areas involved can read a word I write, and those who try find it pure anguish. And yet I've spent all my life, not least in the law, trying to write what anyone can understand. (No use giving a lay client an agreement he can't understand.) I've ceased to wonder why and marvel instead when anyone understands anything.

"I am in a precarious state here. I have made all the changes in my book that I am going to make, except for re-writing the last chapter. I hope to get that done in a week. But I am much up-and-down from day to day, and I don't propose to undertake another effort of this kind. Maybe when it's over and I've had a rest, things will look different. Meantime, I won't pursue the OEK issues, although if my mind were up to it I would love to know what you think of our government's conflicting plans for creating a framework within which economic performance might be at least a little more predictable than it is now."

"Far from clearing up all the difficulties in our mutual understanding (your letter) goes some way to it" writes Adolph February 10. "Again I must say what I wrote earlier: the potential readers of the *Postscript* having read the book, will know what I mean by 'balanced growth', by 'action directive', etc. All these terms have been carefully defined, as the index will confirm. My definitions may be open to criticism, but they are there, and my argument needs obviously to be judged under that aspect.

"To give briefly two examples: balancing of growth has been expounded on two full pages (291-3) and indeed it includes the notion of continuous full employment. You ask why this 'would or should be so'. Well, here I think we meet the crux of the matter. You understand this term in the 'positive' sense, that is, as something somehow happening in the real world. I understand it as an instrumental term, that is, as a macro-goal which I stipulate, and for which I try to derive the means suitable of attainment. So I say: I will have 'continuous and efficient absorption of present and newly accruing resources', and the remainder of chapter 11 is devoted to a detailed analysis of the quite complex steps by which this goal can be achieved.

"Something similar is the case when I say that knowledge of action directives and expectations permits me to predict behavior. There we are in the micro-sphere, that is, I speak of individual producers and consumers in the market. By 'action directive' I refer to the 'micro-goal', more specifically 'modal' micro-goal, which the marketer pursues. One, and in our society the still outstanding, is 'maximization of receipt' and 'minimization of expenditure', briefly called 'profit motive' when we speak of the producer. And indeed I dare to say, if I know that a firm follows that action directive and expects demand for its product to increase, it will expand output. Certainly if there is a snow catastrophe, as many US firms have recently experienced, which prevents transportation of raw materials, such expansion of output will be delayed.

"There are possibilities of other 'extra-systemic' impediments—as even the law of falling bodies can be counteracted when a gust of wind pushed a feather upward. But I trust that, for the majority of cases, you will not deny my proposition. In the same way, a consumer, driven by the micro-goal of minimizing expenditures, will defer purchases when he expects a fall in price. So 'action directives', as you can read on many pages of OEK, do not refer to government directives trying to guide marketers, but to the 'inner dictator' who determines an individual's modal goal. Certainly the profit motive is only one possible directive—I have referred to other directives, very briefly only, because we know little about the precise consequences of these alternatives. In the new book I have tried to show that any action directive other than what I call the extremum principle is incompatible with a society which mainly relies for its provision on the market, that is, it presupposes far-reaching central control.

"I fully agree with you that many of those difficulties disappear when we talk eye to eye, because misunderstandings can easily be corrected on the spot. It is for this reason that I regret so deeply that this opportunity has not been given to us for a long time. I strongly feel that your mind is at the moment averse to pursuing these issues further, and I don't expect any answer to this letter. But I am happy to know that the revision of your book is almost completed. Has California made up its mind? Or have you in the meantime found other possibilities? As a last resort you might try my new publisher—not of OEK but of that other mysterious book—the Seabury Press here in New York. They are new and enterprising, and would not discriminate against a book of 'wisdom'.''

"You have more to bear than I have," writes Geoffrey April 7, "with the single though serious exception that I think you seldom have to wrestle with material in a field in which you lack competence, let alone mastery. This, however, is my constant experience and economics is one of those fields. I am getting tired of this, though I do not expect that I shall ever learn to prevent my enthusiasm wandering into unfamiliar territories.

"Meantime, I have not yet heard about the book (nor even that it has been received); the backlog which accumulated while I was writing it, plus a number of current things, has kept me busier than I would wish but I am slowly getting things more under control and more into a workable relation with the amount of physical and mental energy I still have. I will write again when the batteries are more fully charged."

Adolph writes to Geoffrey May 15 that during the first two months since publication *The Path of Economic Growth* has sold about 800 copies—more than half in Britain and the Commonwealth. Considering the price of $10, he finds this amazing. The new OEK is in printing and should be out sometime in July. He writes again June 9:

"Since I wrote last I have come to realize that the 'strait-jacket' of a book may well be what stymies me. I will now try to draft some independent essays—four or five—about matters about which I think that I have something to say. There is a hidden hope that, in the end, what emerges may yet be suitable for a coherent piece that can appear as a book." He expresses his total agreement that "without what you call a transcultural vector, there is no answer to any of our major problems.

Judaism and Job

"This brings me to your praise of Judaism in your earlier letter. Again I can only agree. Obviously I would never sever my ties with my Jewish tradition so long as Judaism is under attack. But very likely I would not do so even if this negative condition would fall away—a most unlikely possibility.

"Of course, one must be clear about *which* Judaism one talks about. Before the age of the Prophets it was largely a tribal religion, as many others—with two exceptions: monotheism and the absolute validity of the Decalogue as moral rule. On the other hand, the post-prophetic development, and especially the post-exilic evolution, led to an increasing legalization, and thus calcification, of the creed—so much so that possibly no Western religion is more in need of a 'reformation' or new *'Stiftung'*. The various mystical 'revolutions' in opposition to the prevailing legalism—Kabbala, Chassidism and, in a way, Buber— were useful as critics, but did not achieve any lasting influence—Buber is much more popular among Christians and Humanists than among Jews.

"Now I regard the prophetic period—from Amos to the second Jesajah—as the core of what is 'transhistorical' in Judaism. There is no dogma except the postulate of there being only one God. And there is no theology—a totally Christian invention and a *contradictio in adjecto:* trying to bring down to a rational level what by the nature of the case is ineffable. At the same time Jesajah especially humanized the ancient tribal supremacy into that delicate unity of individual and group which, later in the scholastic debate on Universalia, was logically but not empirically resumed. (Most important, Abelard's solution: the community of Jesus' disciples is neither the 'sum of the 12 nor a 13th entity besides, but the 12 disciples *when they are united in the spirit of Christ'*. I know of no better simile to what a real 'group' is.) This and the cry for justice, national and social, is the essence of the prophetic teaching, which makes 'history' and not some abstract 'world' the battleground between good and evil. There are the roots of what you rightly stress; the sense of personal responsibility to some absolute.

"But the picture is not complete without bringing in *Job*, the strangest and in a way truly revolutionary book of the Old Testament. I most strongly recommend to you to re-read it. As you know, there is an ancient 'framework story', with which the tale begins and ends, which somehow serves to soften the blow of what is said in the center part, and which according to the experts is much older and not really relevant to the main message. This is the experience of a man who, without having committed any moral trespasses, is struck down with all conceivable misfortunes and ills. His friends try to persuade him that, somehow, he is being punished for sins even if he is not aware of them. But he maintains that he is innocent and maltreated by what he thinks is a just God. And in the end the Lord appears—not to confirm Job's sinfulness, but to challenge him as a little worm who must not protest against divine majesty, just or unjust.

"Now the Lord's *Donnerwetter* has been a stumbling block for interpreters for the last 2000 years. It is indeed not to be reconciled with a 'loving' master, and not even with a just one. When I grew older I began to realize that, terrible as the Lord's behavior is judged by our moral standards, it truly reflects the indifference of the cosmic forces—indifference to human fate. But, and this seems to me the message of the story, in the face of such overwhelming and indifferent power Job, though admitting his 'ignorance', speaks the famous words: 'He may slay me, I will not quaver. I will defend my conduct to his face'. Now this is not the text as you will find it in the James Bible or in the revised version. As has been discovered only recently, the text was tampered with by the early Rabbis, reading: 'Though he slay me, yet I will trust in him.' (Should you be interested in the details, get hold of the Anchor Bible, Job, translated by Marvin H. Pope, Doubleday, NY 1965, which has all the critical apparatus.)

"Now, precisely, this seems to me the situation of modern man. He realizes that the Universe does not 'care' for him, nor even against him as some of the Gnostics taught. To maintain one's integrity in the face of such indifference, that is, to try to be 'more moral' than the universe—this is his affliction. I have no answer as to how this can be rationalized. It would require a total reinterpretation of the cosmic forces, cancelling all that has been believed since Pascal. Or one would indeed have to assign to Man the task of 'superman' but against Nietzsche's vision, investing him with a divine mission of 'humanizing' what is within his range of action. But we agree that, without an answer to this greatest of our dilemmas, no absolute standard can be established. And without such a standard, all we say is built on sand. I leave it at that for today."

Adolph continues the discussion July 29 in reply to a letter from Geoffrey dated July 24.

"Let me first say something more on the issue of the transcultural vector. You ask at the end of your letter whether you miss something. My answer is: No, except some incidental insights. I fully share your faith in man's power to design a humane order, though the cosmos is—may be—indifferent to this. In fact, this is all that can be said without involving oneself in wildly speculative metaphysics and theology. There are people—apparently they are even in the majority—who cannot live without such speculations. You and I do not belong to them.

"Of course—and this I mean by incidental insights—there is a mystery: how did the spark of insight and moral responsibility awaken in a being that himself is part of that nature which, beyond the human mind, is indifferent? I know that, since Aristotle up to Tillich and Teilhard, the hypothesis lingers that what comes to fruition in man is 'potentially' present in the amoeba and in every rock, and also in the primordial 'soup' which was the beginning of everything. Maybe such a speculation gives satisfaction to some—it does not to me. Rather, I am willing to be silent before the mystery of the awakening human spark. And, as you rightly indicate, since nature did give rise to man, can we call her truly indifferent? Another unanswerable mystery.

"If and when we meet again I want to add something about your last comment that we are fighting a losing battle. Of course historically considered this is true. But does it make the individual struggle meaningless? I have an answer to this which it would take a little book to put down on paper. But more than ever you and I are together. The rebellious part in Job is not the older but the more recent. There are speculations that the author was influenced by Euripides!"

In an August 20 reply to a letter from Geoffrey dated August 12, Adolph says that he is about to take up again *The Price of Liberty* as a possible chapter in the book with which he has been struggling so hard. He comments on a paper Geoffrey has sent.

"You know how profoundly I agree with the main thesis of your 'model'—there is no hope unless what you call the 'autonomous individual' can be 'tamed' again. With you I see this as the fundamental condition—more important than any institutional reforms which, after all, can work only in the hands of responsible persons.

"Still, if I had written this paper I would have shifted the accent slightly. For reasons that I understand very well, you have given much if not primary emphasis to the Luthers, Antigones etc. who feel compelled to *oppose* the current standards in the name of a 'higher authenticity'. I agree that these are the great 'models' of the human species and that, without them, conformity to even a 'good' tradition will degenerate. But are the Luthers our main concern today, or even the absence of them? Is our major problem not how to make Mr. Smith and Mrs. Black again into responsible persons?

"For this it is necessary to regain what you mention just in passing: the subtle web of ethical convention. In other words it seems to me that we shall have to worry, in Fred Clarke's words, how to encourage the type to develop 'beyond the type' only once we have regained what he called the human type who accepts 'ethical convention'. Or in my words, only after spontaneous conformity with regard to the fundamentals of a good society has been achieved does the 'dynamic' problem of the right way of superseding conformity arise.

"I am sure that you will agree. But if you plan to publish the paper, I wonder whether you should not stress more strongly that web of ethical convention, and should say a little more about what it consists of. The only other point I feel some hesitation about concerns what you call 'a sense of responsibility to the culture itself'. Unless you mean by this the largely inarticulate and even unconscious acceptance of that 'subtle web', it seems to me that, as a conscious commitment, this goes beyond the capacity of the 'common man'. I am indeed inclined to think that some 'metaphysical belief' is indispensable, though don't ask me to be more precise. With you I expect a 'turn of mind' only 'from collective hardship and collective need'—what this will reveal in terms of 'belief' we cannot know today, though all may depend on it.

"A final word about the national-international issue. We agree that, today, all true loyalties are still national. But we should also agree that a great danger arises from this in view of the insolubility of practically all political and economic problems on a purely national basis. It will have to be part of that 'subtle web' to include transnational commitments.

"I feel as if I were back in the trenches—comrades falling left and right. In the last six weeks I have lost four friends, among them the latest, Ernst Bloch. Except in the case of Achim Weyl (the son of the philosopher and himself an eminent mathematician) who died at 62 from cancer of the throat, none of these cases is 'tragic'. The others lived to a good old age—Bloch was 92—and they had more or less completed their life's work. So it is sheer egoism when I complain because they have left me lonely. The fact that, as you say, every moment has its own importance—the timelessness of the present—seems to me the core of a 'non-transcendental' religion. More of this another time."

Loyalties

Geoffrey's growing fatigue, due to the gradual advance of his illness, make travelling more and more burdensome and he is forced to decline a number of invitations. In August 1977 he is hospitalized; he writes to Adolph August 31/ September 1 from the Radcliffe Infirmary in Oxford.

"I grieve with you at having lost so many contemporaries recently, mine I think fell away earlier. But I find it a huge consolation to have so many friends in the cohorts junior to me, some younger than 20. I expect to be home in about a week. Meantime what leisure in which to write to you! And so to the paper and *The Price of Liberty* and the concept of responsibility to 'culture'. Perhaps responsibility to history would be a better way to put it.

"I am not personally attracted by the Luthers of this or any other generation. In the world into which I was born 'God, King and Country' seemed an adequate and harmonious focus for Everyman's loyalty. God was of special importance as being the most personal and the most comprehensive. But that was a culture in the heyday of its self-confidence. There comes a time when its self-confidence needs to be challenged. And if the challenge is 'successful', what then? An immediate, desperate need to recreate the 'spontaneous conformity' which has been deliberately destroyed and which cannot be recreated spontaneously, since its spontaneity was the fruit of its self-confidence.

"Nonetheless, spontaneous new loyalties do arise in the ruins of old ones and grow quickly. Consider how quickly the right to strike, most ludicrous of rights, has risen with the right to free speech, free movement, freedom to work, indeed, has dominated them all. Is not this now a huge 'spontaneous conformity' within the large sub-culture which shares it? The spontaneous conformity is so only because it has learned how to impose itself beyond the possibility of questions. Is not this as true in an English trade union as in a Chinese commune?

"And so to the problem of the dialectic process. In the paper I sent you I express the belief (1) that history is bound to proceed by dialectic jumps, rather than by an incremental process; (2) that times of dialectic change are dangerous and may lead to one of three outcomes, namely (a) a new phase of self-confidence reflecting but never repeating the past, or (b) to a phase of prolonged oscillation, or (c) and worst to a vacuum of loyalties and the dissolution of society. I also (3) express the view that the last phase of Western, especially British, culture has left us a specially dangerous legacy—and hence a greater risk of fate (c) above—by undermining the concept of responsibility itself, replacing it by the absurd concept that the common good is best served by the self-seeking of the autonomous individual, a new concept irreconcilable with a social, still more an acculturable species.

"It is on all this that I especially want your judgment—on beliefs numbers (1), (2) and (3). I don't get this from your letter. I agree that we need our Ismenes as much as our Antigones, perhaps today more. But I am contrasting these two 'responsible' types with the irresponsible because of the 'autonomous' individual who has taken the place of both of them and with whom neither can communicate except with bombs.

"I have sent the paper to *Futures* for consideration, but I shall reconsider it myself as soon as I get home in the light of your letter and of any more comments this may evoke from you. It is crucial not only to this paper but to the central theme of my 'Berkeley book', which still awaits a re-editing of its beginning and end. It has been good to spend my first day 'up' writing this long, leisurely letter to you. Be assured that your company across the Atlantic grows ever more precious to me as the years pass."

Adolph writes September 12 to express shock that Geoffrey had had to be hospitalized.

"I should like to say much more about the personal aspects, but I am at the moment under heavy time pressure. So I would like to answer, at least briefly, the substantive questions which I passed by in my last letter:

1. I don't think that 'responsibility to history' is a better key word than responsibility to culture. It is all much too abstract and may appeal to people like ourselves, but as I said before it is Mr. Smith and Mrs. Black who must be raised from the doldrums. Yes, God, King and Country—this is concrete, as are the slogans with which the Marxists adorn their banners. I do not see anything comparable in our arsenal at this stage—one of our main weaknesses.

2. True, there are new spontaneous loyalties in several sub-cultures. But being 'sectional' they make matters worse rather than better. The more passionately they are held by their respective groups, the more will they polarize the nation.

3. Frankly, I have no answer to the question whether 'history is bound to proceed by dialectic jumps'. What little we really know of the past—seeing some of the events in which I participated, now written up in German history books, confirms my old suspicion that so-called recorded history is a form of novel writing—only partly confirms this. I cannot see any 'jumps' in British history since the end of the 17th century. But more important, I do not care. I always disliked 'philosophy of history', partly because of my early fascination by the Marxist brand. And what does it matter for our burning problems of today? I certainly agree with all the dangers you stress concerning the present, as I do with the three alternatives—(a) new state of confidence—(b) prolonged 'oscillation'—(c) dissolution. For how long a time alternative (b) can be 'stood' is impossible to say. I am afraid that we shall have to stand it for generations if the good alternative (a) is to be realized.

"As you also know, I could not agree more when you stress the undermining of 'responsibility' and the wrong notion of individual autonomy or 'liberty'. I spend what little free time I have on clarifying in my mind what 'liberty' can mean 'tomorrow'. My *Price of Liberty* touched only upon some of the issues involved. You will hear from me if and when I see more clearly.

"Speaking of your paper, what seems to me lacking is a concrete specification of what 'responsibility to culture or history' implies. I know how difficult it is, not least because the phenomenon is 'sub-rational'. You will never exhaust the meaning—the most one can give are probably some striking examples: the former British conviction that certain things 'are not done'; the extension of the time horizon of our actions to the unborn whose life chances our present actions affect. Just two aspects, and probably not the most important ones. But unless we succeed in entering this dimension of concreteness, Mr. Smith and Mrs. Black will never know what is at stake. They may well reject it even when they know, but then their 'guilt' differs radically from that in the state of ignorance.

"I am sorry, this is all written in much too cryptic a style, but I must not keep you waiting because you want to make the paper ready for print. Yes, I remember well our first walk. I can only say that over the years you have become for me the embodiment of what it means to be truly English. In my growing loneliness—I have little chance of meeting even the few people still alive for whom I care—every one of your letters is balm."

Geoffrey has left hospital and is back in Goring-on-Thames when he writes September 23.

"I think you are right in criticizing my paper for being more concerned with responsible Antigones than with responsible Ismenes. The question arises whether these two kinds of responsibility are the same and how they arise. The Greeks, as you probably know better than I, had a splendid word, *aidos*, defined as meaning :
1. A moral feeling or sense of shame; shame, modesty.
2. Sense of shame, feeling of honor, self respect.
3. Regard for others, respect, reverence.
4. Mercy, pardon.
5. That which causes shame or respect, and so both shame and scandal, and also dignity and majesty.

"They attached great importance to this feeling of what should or should not, might or might not, appropriately be done in particular circumstances. It is common, even in Homer where it is usually regarded as an incursion from a divine source. *Aidos* could come upon you in a particular situation, just as rage could, and was probably directly excited in you by some benevolent or hostile God.

"This sense of reverence, including the obligation to oneself to obey the constraints and imperatives that one has accepted, seems to me to be the essence of culture, whether the impulse be in manifest accordance with society's idea of 'good form' or whether it be the individual's responsible attempt to amend the society's idea of 'good form'. What I have called a cultural vacuum is the antithesis of both.

"Friends of mine who have a house in a remote Swiss mountain village tell me that this year the place is strangely silent. Hitherto the natural silence has always had a faint background of cowbells. This year there are no cowbells. The peasants have had to stop having their cows with cowbells—because the tourists steal the cow-bells. Do the tourists lack any sense of *aidos?* Or are they trying to introduce a new morality? Clearly the first. Even if they were conscious pioneers of a society in which the idea of private property had been wholly displaced, they would recognize that the cowbells were significant not as private property, but for the necessary function which they performed.

"If a tourist would like to have a cowbell but is restrained from stealing one by *aidos*, what is the nature of his self-accepted restraint? To whom, and for what is he responsible? You may be right in saying that responsibility to culture or to history is a concept too abstract for Mr. Smith or Mrs. Black. But although the concept of responsibility may be abstract, it always presents itself in concrete cases—like the cowbells.

"It is said that the division of labor helps to weaken the sense of responsibility. I am not wholly convinced by this. You do not have to grow your own vegetables, but your responsibility for getting your references right in the books you write is not thereby impaired. Part of the trouble, I think, is that responsibility is a sense of constraint or obligation felt by an agent-experient and invisible to an observer. It is therefore not describable in the language of an observer or comprehensible to those who have not themselves experienced it in action. This huge field in which the meaning of words, even to observers, is wholly supplied by and limited by the observer's personal experience, or empathized experience as an agent, is a stumbling block to everyone raised in a scientific culture, or at least to everyone so raised who does not appreciate the basic distinction between facts of human life and other facts.

"In a world where *aidos* is taken for granted no-one violates the reverence expected of him for accepted authority, except in the name of some authority which he reveres and accepts still more. Even this, of course, can produce lethal clashes; but even those who clash most fiercely have a shared universe of discourse in that they both know what *aidos* means and respect it as an ethical governor even though they may differ radically in their understanding of what its imperatives mean for each of them. This came out very clearly at the time of Suez when those who regarded it as an ethical issue had a common universe of discourse even though one thought of it as a British Budapest and the other as a non-Munich. Equally, neither of them had any common universe of discourse with those who regarded it as a legitimate exercise in political power, and differed only in their judgment on whether it was a misconceived plan or a good plan badly executed.

"Somewhere in this field, I think, lies the issue which is crucial both to you and to me. No human society—indeed, no society of social animals—can survive unless it has a powerful and shared sense of *aidos*, shared constraints and shared commitments in situations similarly perceived. To permit even the minimal degree of adaptation needed for survival this shared ethic must be capable of changing over time, but its changes must be kept within the limits imposed by the equally strong need for a common ethic. This limit may be exceeded either because changes in the environment require it to change faster than its coherence permits, or because internal changes have the same effect. But when this happens, the society I think is bound to perish.

"Years ago, Ellen asked to lunch a Belgian Catholic priest who was deputizing for the Catholic priest in our village. At lunch she asked him, rather daringly I thought, what he thought of a certain Cardinal. The Belgian answered warmly, "I think he is a very good man, a very good man"—he then added thoughtfully, "But I think one needs only one." I think he summed up the problem very neatly; but he threw no light on how one can ensure that one gets enough but not too much of this terrible yeast. I wonder whether this will move you to any further reply. I hope it will.

"Sorting files the other day, I came across a copy of a long letter which I wrote to a friend on August 23, 1945, describing the political alternatives which I thought had been opened for Britain by electing a Socialist government. I enclose a copy. You will see that the final conclusion is that this issue would depend on changes of culture within the governed rather than on changes of policy among the governors. This I still believe to be true, but although in August 1945 I confidently promised another letter on this subject soon, I realize that I have in fact been trying to write that second letter ever since, and that I am not much nearer now than I was then."

Adolph replies October 1, and agrees wholeheartedly with the main substance of Geoffrey's letter.

"Your *aidos* is indeed a key concept and, as you defined its meaning, it is a big step toward the 'concretization' of which I spoke earlier. What you say could not have come at a more opportune moment: I am struggling hard with a clarification of what 'liberty' is to mean 'tomorrow' in contrast with its perverted meaning over the last 200 years, at least in the minds of the philosophers. I find it extremely difficult to be 'concrete' myself—in the little pamphlet of 40 years ago I circumvented the problem by being anecdotal. Your little story of the cowbells is along the same lines, and tells more than any conceptual exposition of which I know.

"And yet I feel that the problem must be treated on the conceptual level too if what is new—in fact it is very old—is to be brought home. Incidentally, it is not the concept of responsibility which is 'abstract' but that of 'culture', unless it is specified the way you have been trying to do. But I doubt that the ordinary reader will interpret 'culture' in that sense. And though responsibility is indeed a key concept, we somehow have to be specific in stating for what we are or are not to be responsible here and now.

"Your story about the Belgian priest points up the other problem: how much 'salt' can we digest, necessary as it is to have some salt. I sometimes wonder whether individual liberty is or should be more than a 'corrective' in an otherwise conformist context. No doubt, over the last 200 years and especially during the last two generations, we have greatly oversalted our daily meal. What you say about shared constraints and shared commitments could not be truer. And yet—commitment to what?—constraint of what? I expect that we shall stammer around these issues for quite a while... Indeed, we both have been trying to write your second letter for some time."

A long silence on Geoffrey's part worries Adolph. He writes to say so on November 12—a letter which naturally crosses Geoffrey's of November 11.

"This for me is a barren period, though I struggle with my essay on 'Liberty in Our Time'. It is among other things a translation of *The Price of Liberty* into prose, if you see what I mean—very difficult because the light tone of the original essay permitted me to gloss over a number of important issues which I now cannot do. For the rest, one looks in vain for a bright spot in the wider world. It is interesting that Britain has so far been spared the kind of terrorism the rest of Europe is subject to. I do not count your Irish excesses among this sort of anarchy. Altogether your news sounds better, whereas we are progressively disappointed with our President. He promises too much without having the ability—remember Roosevelt?—to swing either Congress or the nation at large."

"Humans are social animals and have survived from the beginning only by patterns of self and mutual expectation, taught by each generation to the next" writes Geoffrey on the 11th. "The sense of responsibility to honor these expectations seems to me to be basically the internalized acceptance of these responsibilities as something one accepts of oneself. Since individual experience differentiates us out of the social network as well as socializing us in, it does not surprise me that there is room for difference and debate about the criteria of rightness and their relative value in conflicting situations.

"But the most conflicting minds may still agree in taking responsibility for granted as a principle. Not so today for many reasons familiar to us both, and hence the danger we both fear. I am sure you are right in thinking that at least in the West today liberty should be regarded as a qualification on conformity, valuable both individually and socially insofar as it does not threaten unacceptably the basis of coherence, but to be accorded no absolute priority except where the context is 'responsibly' judged to demand it.

"Your search for the concrete: of course none of this abstract stuff means a thing without a context, and it is useful only insofar as it enables us to subsume different behavior in different contexts under a coherent explanation. The answer to 'responsible for what, to whom?' depends on context and is also subject to human innovation within the same context. I am conscious of responsibility for not wasting or polluting resources to a greater extent than I was twenty years ago, partly because I am more aware of the issue, partly because a volume of public concern has built up round it.

"I am even more conscious of responsibility for not endangering social coherence, even by advocating changes which are in themselves useful and timely, except insofar as I think the situation will stand it. If you are writing about liberty in America in the next twenty years, you have your concept. But what will make it acceptable, I think, is its conformity with a model of human social behavior which equally explains why at an earlier date a concept of liberty which now embarrasses us was what we most wanted. This in turn involves getting across a dialectic concept of history antithetical to that which governed the 19th century. And that of course is difficult, but not so far as I can see difficult in principle. The only use of general ideas is surely to make concrete examples understandable.

"I know my use of 'culture' is unusually wide, but I think it is needed and that my function is to try and widen it. The concept of the human heritage seems to me both comprehensible and inspiring, and I see no reason why ordinary people should not find in it both commitment and constraints."

"I agree with every word you write about responsibility" writes Adolph, November 19. "Also that we need a model of social human behavior if we want to criticize a specific historical situation, especially if we want to do something about it. Just there lie my difficulties, and when I wrote last time that I am trying to translate *The Price of Liberty* into 'prose' I have the construction of such a model in mind. In this connection I have realized that there is much sloppiness in that pamphlet. I failed to distinguish clearly between 'political' and 'personal' liberty—between self-government and the cultivation of the personality in that solipsistic sense that prevailed in Germany. The formula should be: *The price of political liberty is the restraint of personal self-indulgence.* Or: *In order to minimize political control you need a fair measure of 'social control'*, that is, agencies that induce spontaneous conformity. So far, so good. But now this must be made concrete, and there the multiplicity of cross-currents has so far overwhelmed me."

Commitment and constraint

In his letter of January 14 1978 Adolph says that his daughter Hanna, with husband and children, had come for Christmas.

"We talked a lot about the new *'incertitudes allemandes'*. As a consequence of the terrorist activities a kind of McCarthy spirit seems to be rampant, fostered by the opposition party. Anyhow the leading writers and scholars are much concerned. Alas, 30 years of *Wirtschaftswunder* [5] cannot make up for 500 years of social atomization.

"This brings me to your anxious questions: how can commitment and constraint be legitimated? I have been struggling with the same problem for the past few months, without even the inkling of an answer that would satisfy me. Thus, my new *Price of Liberty* has come to a full stop. By reading a little about the spirit of the Victorian age and some of its representatives, I begin to wonder whether I did not idealize the state of conformity. Or I may have just experienced the few years when the inherited spirit was still strong, though the worst abuses that were associated with its origin had been overcome.

"I do see the need for 'commitment and constraint' as overriding in the present state of emergency. But I cannot see how this need can be satisfied 'spontaneously' when British firemen go on strike, US Congressmen are bribed by Koreans, and the Governor of the State of New York reduces taxes—when New York City is again on the verge of bankruptcy—to assure his re-election next fall. I am sick and tired of listening to complaints about the non-conforming younger generation, when the 'old' behave much worse. Many of those youngsters, wrong as their means are, act out of protest against conditions against which you and I also protest.

"Of course, one can paint an ideal image of the way society should operate, but what sense has this if one cannot see even the beginning of a change of mind in those who wield power? Nor among those who drive 70 miles an hour on our highways in spite of all the sermonizing about an energy crisis. I am more and more convinced that only catastrophes, actually experienced and not predicted ones, will awaken both Kreon and Ismene—hopefully not 'end' catastrophes. And even then the democratic process is unlikely to generate the appropriate measures that are bound to be painful.

"What I am writing here is no more than a pouring out of contradictory notions that confuse me completely, and paralyze any attempt at rational formulation. Can you show me a beacon to orient myself?"

"As regards the issue with which we are both struggling," replies Geoffrey, January 23 1978, "I have got some light by reading de Tocqueville. It is interesting to see how even this great man found it hard to reconcile the idea of equality and liberty with obedience to constituted authority, however the authority was established and controlled. He was of course right in seeing that a society of multiple interdependence would produce structures of authority, but he seems to have regarded these as something which could, and should, be resisted and even reduced to trivial importance. He had no idea of the extent to which what he would accept as a free society would depend on what you call tacit consensus.

"You are right, I think, in supposing that in the 1930s you saw in England the remains both of an acceptance of authority and of a consensus in the criteria of individual responsibility which had hung over from a previous age and previous assumptions, both political and religious. I do not, however, think that your book was any the worse for that—rather the contrary. It convinced you that it is possible for a society to generate such tacit consensus and that widespread responsibility is consistent with coherent action. And the personal experience that this is possible is both comforting in these days and also useful, because it prevents one from ruling it out as a solution.

"For example, the British fireman who disapproves of the strike but strikes nonetheless because his loyalty to his union is dominant among his responsibilities is not to my mind acting irresponsibly. He is, however, illustrating what happens when the structure of loyalties in different parts of a single society become too different to be contained.

"The future would obviously be a much more disciplined one. The only question is whether the discipline will be imposed from without or generated from within. Even this distinction is not so clear as it looks, because a great deal of what looks like spontaneous consensus is in fact generated by authority. The Soviet Union and China are conspicuous examples, but all societies do it and need to do it to some extent. Indeed, the defence of liberty depends not, I think, on curtailing public powers of persuasion in favor of orthodoxy, but rather on the extent to which they can allow and can afford to allow dissenting voices to be heard.

"I am not sure how far this will make any contribution to your cogitation over the dilemma. I am in particular difficulties with it too, because I have just got back to the book and am realizing how inadequately I have dealt with this so far, but I send it to you for what it is worth."

The tacit consensus

"I think you are not quite just to de Tocqueville" replies Adolph, February 5. "He is also one of my heroes. So I know that he ultimately relied on the religious sense to make democracy work. There you have the roots of a tacit consensus.

"Look, I am not blaming the individual fireman, who really is in a conflict. I accuse his leaders, who place him and the country into such a situation. And this in the face of a declared national policy of recovery with which anyone of average intelligence can only agree. Of course, those problems hardly existed when Britain was the economic leader of the world, and tacit consensus was the result of the possibility of evading all dangerous issues.

"In a word, I was always aware of the objective conditions of the British case—isolation, economic advance, colonial outlets—T.S. Gregory told me in 1933 that it was a pity that I came 30 years too late. Then all the bullies could be sent to India. Now they have to be kept at home! But I see their importance as much greater now relative to the socio-psychological make-up, which anyhow was the product of a long history. Neither of these conditions can be repeated anywhere in our age. And though it is important to know that there was once a set-up conducive to generating discipline from within, it becomes a little like the dream of the golden age.

"So I think that, on balance, all tendencies speak for the imposition of discipline from without. Even this would not be tragic, if we had not every reason to ask: *quis custodiet ipsos custodes?* Or, to put it in positive terms: the 'education'—intellectual and moral—of potential leaders has become the foremost political task; how, where, by whom? I grant you that leaving room for dissent is an important issue. But even this is secondary compared with the 'enlightenment' of the ever more powerful executive. In this country the crimes of the Nixon regime have for a time caused a reaffirmation of the power of the legislative, which under our Constitution is the most pertinent issue.

"And if we want to avoid true tyranny the 'followers' need an equivalent education, especially one that brings home to them the overriding significance of long-term problems, for which again the oil business is a good test case. No 'man on the highway' will believe that there is an oil problem, and obviously, in the short run, there is none. How, other than through catastrophe itself, can this feat of education be performed?

"Well, there you have a list of my troubles. And there are, again and again, the voices of sirens which tell us that it is really not so bad and that, in the confused manner in which a 'free society' works, matters will be solved somehow. What happens at the moment in Italy, and is likely soon to happen in France, may throw some light on the new constitutional set-up that is painfully evolving. Alas, the 'old' democracies have so far made little contribution. This is enough for the day. But it is a consolation that you too try to bite this bullet. Luck to both of us!"

Systems thinking

Adolph writes again, February 12, to comment on a suggested 'presidential address' Geoffrey has sent him. He had "gratefully studied" it, but finds himself at a loss how to respond.

"I like its content very much, and agree with every major thesis. But I must ask: what does it help to use the systems terminology? As you say on p. 2: human systems are in principle unstable and 'of infinite complexity'. Now as I understand the intention of systems analysts it was their dream to be able to reduce both the instability and complexity to, at least intellectually, manageable proportions—possibly by way of quantification.

"And this is indeed the picture entertained by systems technologists. My resistance arose from the outset because of that dream of a not even pleasant utopia. But if their endeavor cannot be carried over to the human sphere what more than a catchword do we have in using the term? Of course, there is a world of difference between a 'relationalist' view of the world and mechanical linearity. And we do agree that it is the former that may one day help us to penetrate further into the mysteries of Man and Society. But again, what is gained when we use a term that was coined with a much more ambitious pretense, and one to which we must object?

"Now I must confess that, for the last 6-8 years, I have not followed the literature on systems. Perhaps much has changed in the intent and achievement of the 'systemers'. As I read your paper I feel that you could have made every point as convincingly without using the term even once. And by using it, you arouse expectations of 'exactitude' that you just do not want to arouse. Now take me to task and enlighten me."

Geoffrey answers both letters on the 24th.

"It is a pity that we cannot agree about the usefulness of this word 'systems'. It puzzles me too, because classical economics is by far the most elaborated and formalized systems theory in the social world. Of course I wholly agree with you that systems *technologists* over the last twenty years have made many brash incursions into the field of social systems and have done us a lot of harm, and I say so at the end of my paper. Indeed the whole of my efforts in this field over the past twenty years have been to contribute what I could to the forces resisting the limitations implicit in systems technology. But the fathers of systems thinking in general, for me, are Bertalanffy, biologist, and Anatol Rappaport and Ross Ashby, psychiatrists, and others of that ilk.

"But coming to your other letter, I wonder whether you intentionally oppose inner discipline and outer discipline as if they were inescapable alternatives? The cohesion of a society seems to me to depend on a discipline partly self-imposed, partly mutually imposed, and partly centrally imposed, and within limits the mix, I think, can vary. On the other hand, some mixes may be much more stable than others.

"My long-gestated book is just now going off to Secker and Warburg. Its latest title is: *Autonomy and Responsibility*. The paper I sent you about 'British Culture' was a summary of part of the argument. But, like you, I am more concerned with the 'education' of the man in the street than with the education of the governors.

"I have in mind two taxi drivers, one in Montreal and one in London. The one in Montreal had a more sophisticated understanding of ecological threats than most of the academics I had been talking to. The one in London, in the last stages of last summer's drought, hoped it would not rain because it obscured his windscreen, although he admitted that he would be sorry if water did not come out of his taps. I do not think the second man was necessarily more stupid than the first. The large-scale issues of pollution and overcrowding were actually present to the experienced driver in Montreal, whilst the failure of the water supply was not yet apparent to the one in London. How far can we expect people to respond to what they have not yet actually experienced, however certain it may be? There is a chapter in this book of mine called: 'The Real and the Actual', which draws this distinction. I am not sure whether it was in the far-away version which you saw a couple of years ago."

"We certainly agree that cohesion in any real society is a mix of inner and outer discipline" Adolph replies, March 5. "But it is important to stress today that excessive outer discipline—autocracy—can be avoided only if inner discipline achieves a quantum leap in all the Western nations. And so long as we cherish a minimum of outer pressure, the kind of mix becomes a major problem. Yes, I always found the chapter on 'The Real and the Actual' very important. Indeed, one major task is to teach people the capacity of anticipation, which is not only an intellectual but also a moral problem. We have to include in our speculation a future beyond our own lifetime—this makes the slogan: 'What has posterity done for me?' a mortal sin.

"Now another word about *system*. In a way it may be a waste of time to quarrel about words. I don't really think so, because there are few realms where it is so necessary to avoid confusion as when it comes to *the one and the many*. Now look, the word 'system' is much older and carried a much wider meaning, almost by now implying 'order', than the one nowadays attached to it by a few 'systems specialists'. One speaks of a deductive system, of a system of philosophy, etc.— all uses that do not fit into the narrow confines of your use. Now when this narrower use was introduced, by Bertalanffy or Ash, the *determinateness* of the system processes stood in the foreground, and rightly so. For biological systems no less than for cybernetic systems one can indeed speak of more or less predetermined motions of the parts.

"I wish they had chosen another word for these phenomena, but I am willing to accept it for what you call the work of systems technologists. But you and I agree that such predeterminateness does not exist in the social realm—or only within so wide a probability interval that what is the merit of systems technology is not applicable. Using the term for these other phenomena is bound to arouse in the reader the impression that the difference is, at best, gradual, whereas in both our views it is 'systemic'. There is perhaps one exception to this, namely when we use the term in an *instrumental* sense. By this I mean that not all factually observed behavior of the social parts is compatible with the stability of the whole. And we might then say that only stabilizing behavior creates a 'system'. But then the term is useless as a *descriptive* tool. And again, I cannot see that a single proposition of your Presidential Address cannot be expounded without use of the weasel word.

"We had a similar discussion about your use of 'dialectics'. I know of Humpty Dumpty's postulate, but once words have acquired a standard meaning they had better be used that way if confusion is to be avoided. All the more so because there are other words—say, feedback organization for one—that can be used without such danger. In substance we are, as I said before, at one.

"Incidentally, you cite Classical Economics against me—it is the very prototype of 'systems technology' because it has the extremum principle of action as predetermined law of motion, as I tried to explain to Norbert Wiener 25 years ago (see also chapter 6 of OEK). So I must cite it against you—after all, this is what I meant when calling classical and neo-classical theory the economics of the hungry rat—Bertalanffy's domain but not yours or mine.

"I just was 85. My Department plans a *'gemütliches Beisammensein'*[6] for Friday. I am glad that nothing solemn is planned."

Geoffrey's letter of 18 March sees things quite differently.

"I am most puzzled about this. I do not in the least regard systems theory at its 'upper end' as deterministic but primarily for the opposite reason. It debunks the inexorable logic of causal chains in favor of interactive fields, and makes it clear that beyond a certain point these cannot be predictive. They can, however, be much more richly descriptive than they were before, especially when they were subject to the pressures of linear determinative thinking.

"For example, the recently demonstrated capacity of my body to recover from injury, adapt to sickness and remain viable, exemplifies adherence to a pattern of order which is built-in but, though relatively determined, is sensitive to some extent to context. The development of my personality is very much less determinate, though I am aware of limitations (and perhaps possibilities) which it has always had and others which it has developed to the point of being actualities now, though they were once only potential.

"This at least is how I see it. I am shaken by the fact that you see it so differently, though I know of course that many systems technologists would. I am comforted only by the fact that if you are right it is probably a good, rather than a bad, thing that I made this utterance in the context of an annual meeting of the Society for General Systems Research. I shall look forward to hearing, and I hope reading, the form in which you finally gave expression to your thoughts about internal and external discipline.

"The editor at Secker & Warburg is abroad until mid-April, but told me when he wrote that the only reading of my book which they had had so far was favorable. I will report progress later. Meantime it is a great relief to have it out of the house. Otherwise all goes well. I begin to go to conferences again and still enjoy my not too restricted home here."

"Our discussion about systems theory is, of course, very funny" Adolph replies March 28. "We are totally in agreement as far as substance is concerned—only you see systems theory, as it was conceived by its originators and presents itself in the literature, as an ally whereas I see it as an enemy. But it is certainly true that you expressed what I should call the deviating view clearly at the end of your lecture.

"Alas, I have nothing new to report about 'discipline'. The reason is that something else has come in between. Bloch's widow asked me for a contribution to a Memorial Volume for Ernst, to be ready by the end of May. I know what I want to write about, but find it very difficult to formulate it—partly because of Bloch's baroque or expressionistic style, which leaves plenty of lacunae in his argument. I see again why it proves impossible to translate him into English. Anyhow, it must be done.

"For quite some time we did not comment on the wider world—probably for reasons of self-preservation. Needless to say, I am deeply distressed about the Near East events, and Begin's attitude in particular. Not that all the changes he resists do not pose serious dangers for Israel, but his manner of argument and negotiation is impossible. Unless he can be dislodged, I see very dark there. And the world economy? If OPEC really refuses to accept dollars as payment for oil I don't know what will happen to the dollar. So far there are hardly any repercussions in our domestic economy, but 'expectations' are bound to raise again the rate of inflation. No one dares so far even to speak of 'controls'—another case of our problem of 'discipline'.

"You seem to have a breathing spell, may it last. I passed my 85th year—the students gave me a quite informal but moving celebration. For the rest, I have not grown in wisdom."

Geoffrey's letter of April 15 encloses a copy of "a curious little paper" called 'Autonomous yet Responsible?'.

"I wrote this very quickly in response to an American friend who asked if I could not express my paper about Western Culture in a 'popular' way. I do not think that what I have written is even as publishable as what I wrote before, but I shall be interested to hear what you think of it. It is another attack on the central problem which absorbs us both.

"No, it is a long time since we talked about the world at large. I have diminished its impact by taking only a weekly paper. I share your desperate feelings about Israel—the more so because I think extreme situations are bound to throw up extreme people. I remember, as you do, the brief euphoria which followed the Treaty of Locarno when it seemed that men of goodwill were in the seats of power. I feel that there were historical reasons why they could not stay there. Belated congratulations on your 85th birthday. Your students must have enjoyed this celebration at least as much as you did."

The meaning of standards

On April 26 1978 Adolph comments upon the two papers which Geoffrey has sent him.

"Let me put down a few quite unsystematic comments on the papers. I need hardly say that I am in full agreement with their general tenor. But I have some difficulties with the details. First, the paper on Autonomy versus Responsibility. As sometimes before I have difficulties in understanding what you mean by 'standards'. Your initial examples make me think that you have certain formal principles in mind, say consistency, reliability etc. Now I am not at all sure that these have nothing to do with 'good or bad', 'right or wrong'. This uncertainty is enhanced by your examples. You and I do not mind whether people are vegetarians or Christians, but I know of some vegetarians who do mind that I eat meat, and on what they claim are ultimate ethical principles (inviolability of life). And I certainly belong to a group about which, for the last 2000 years, the overwelming majority of surrounding people have 'minded' that it is not Christian, and this allegedly on the basis of ultimate 'values', religious or racial. I wonder whether Innozenz IV or Hitler would not have 'minded' less being a mugger than being a Jew. And being a 'reliable' meat eater or Jew would have made the matter worse.

"Now, my difficulties increase when you write: 'the shaping of these standards is what politics is about', to be followed by 'what is shaped (defines) the standards of good and bad, of right and wrong'. I just cannot bring these two statements together. There I must refer to a statement in the other paper. You repeat what you have said often before, that it is wrong to focus on 'man as a goal-seeker rather than a setter and follower of standards'. Now if standards are what I called above 'formal'—consistency, reliability—they certainly cannot exhaust the vectors that determine action. The term 'goal' is misleading because it suggests the aiming at a terminus that can be attained once and for all. What is at stake that we are concerned with are ongoing processes of striving, for the direction of which comparison of 'what is' with our 'standards' is an important 'mode' of behavior, but certainly not its motivation. Rather it seems to me that at this point you have given up the limitation of the term 'standard' as a set of formal criteria and now include substantive 'values' like being a Christian or a Jew, a mugger or a socially-minded citizen. Please enlighten me.[7]

"But now another word on our bone of contention: system. I accept your definition stressing the term 'self-perpetuating', but I maintain that, as a descriptive term, this definition is applicable only to non-human processes. There self-perpetuation is assured by certain laws of nature. On the human level the definition can only have a normative meaning, that is, it describes the conditions under which a group is self-perpetuating, in full awareness that this is a 'standard' by which we can evaluate real social processes and, within the limits of policy-framing, even improve on them.

"What systems theory, as I read it, does is to neglect this fundamental difference between natural and social processes, trying to treat the latter as if they were like the former. I know that you do not do this and fight against the implication of the other conception. Perhaps by making the above distinction between a descriptive and a normative use of the term, our controversy can be settled. But for me this is a decisive issue.

"Otherwise I like the paper very much, especially also what you say in the later parts on the applied social sciences. My entire work on instrumental economics is an attempt to place economics on the level of engineering.

"No, I have not made progress in my major enterprise, and I more and more doubt that I can get it done. I simply cannot find the style appropriate to the topic—what I put down is hopelessly academic. I don't know what is really wrong—I may have come to the end of my tether after all. I wish I could imitate your ostrich policy with regard to the 'news'. Being concerned with the relative short run—the next 20 years—I feel that I must not lose contact with the flow of events. This may well be wrong, and ultimately an evasion."

Exercising judgment

"I am consciously and deliberately taking an unorthodox view about the distinction between what is normative and what is descriptive," replies Geoffrey in May. "I distinguish four kinds of judgment: factual, ethical, aesthetic and instrumental. The first three are Plato's trinity. The fourth is what you have yourself so often distinguished. I describe as exercises of judgment any classifications made in any of these four realms or in any mixture of them. What is abnormal is that I regard them all as more or less normative.

"Of course I realize that the laws of England are different from the laws of nature, but I do not attach such a sharp distinction to this difference as many people do, partly because what we regard as laws of nature we are now content to accept as inter-subjective agreements about the way we shall think about things, and partly because the course of human affairs is mediate and capable of being mediated only to such very different degrees by acts of human will.

"According to this view, all factual and instrumental judgments have a normative element in that the rightness of them depends on standards which are supported only inter-subjectively, whilst many ethical judgments assume a factual judgment, notably the judgment that the matter is within human influence—a judgment which admits of greater or less validity in different circumstances.

"As you know, I have been thinking and writing about the relation of fact and value for a long time, and have been getting more and more radical dissatisfaction with the common polarization between them. The little paper you have is an attempt to erode this common conceptual structure and is clearly inadequate. But anything much better would burst the bounds of a letter. So let me leave it at that until I can do better.

"This also, of course, has a bearing on our controversy of the proper use of the word 'systems'. I would be most unhappy if I had to draw a distinction between natural systems and man-made systems—because all the systems which matter to us most are both. An example is the one which I so frequently use, of the natural water cycle becoming increasingly harnessed to human needs, whilst human needs are equally harnessed to it.

"I hope it may not be too long before I am able to put these thoughts more clearly and cogently. Incidentally, I think that my idea of a standard is quite different from those which you expect, apart from the fact that I regard standards as tacit and indescribable. I have often quoted my favorite examples of this also, notably the criteria of the common law.

"I do not think I deserve to be called an 'ostrich' for absorbing my news in weekly, rather than daily dollops. Few things move so fast that the ordinary citizen needs to review them daily, and I find the weekly *Guardian* good, especially on foreign news. The fact that it contains a chunk from the *Washington Post* and another chunk from *Le Monde* gives it a further international flavour."

Adolph, May 11, tells him that he is quite right in refusing to be called an ostrich.

"It was meant self-ironically, as I thought came out in the context. And the *Guardian* is much better than anything we have here.

"I think that I must wait for your more detailed exposition of the problems of 'standard', 'descriptive' versus 'normative'. Frankly, I have real difficulties in simply understanding what some of your sentences mean. We were at this before, but before we agree to disagree I trust that I can learn what it is with which I disagree. One problem seems to be your understanding of 'normative'. And concerning your systems example, if we are not careful in the way we 'harness' the water cycle to our needs we may well destroy it, whereas if the cycle were left alone it would indeed operate as system's theory states. Of course, nature and human action usually cooperate when action is at stake. But the blessing and curse of human spontaneity requires *specific* behavior based on a norm, in my sense of the word, if the cycle is to persist. No such 'norm' can and needs to be imposed on nature. Well, in the course of time we shall try again."

Writing from Hilltop July 4, he says that work has not been progressing too well. "I am in the third version of my *Liberty* chapter, and constantly discover essential aspects that so far I had overlooked. But of course, the main trouble still is that I don't like what sober evaluation compels me to state as 'prescription'. I am by no means sure that I shall ever complete this piece."

"I can understand your frustrations in trying to assess *The Price of Liberty* which, like other prices, is evidently escalating, but keep at it" replies Geoffrey, July 14. "I am sure there is an answer. I have just written a paper called 'Equality of Responsibility', largely provoked by the seminar at ICI which I had as a result of my paper on the weakness of Western culture. I will send you a copy of the new paper under separate cover. It is awkward in length and shape, largely because of its origin, but it leaves me feeling much more confident than I did that there really is an answer to the question we are both asking. It appears in a very compressed form at the very end of the paper which I am sending you.

"I have had to decline a number of nice invitations abroad (but) have become fairly active here at home, partly with conferences away and partly with visitors here. As regards the book, the Gaither Lecture Fund which paid me to write it tells me that they have funds available to encourage publishers to publish it, and the Chairman has just asked me to send a copy to Jossey-Bass, with whom he has discussed it. So maybe it will find a publisher after all, although I myself am beginning to be dissatisfied with its present shape. I came across and re-read the other day the first version which I sent you and which you criticized. Reading this and our subsequent correspondence has made clearer to me the steps by which the manuscript and I have respectively arrived at our present states. This has been some help, though one cannot turn the clock back and I do not see how to turn it further on except by writing a new book."

Adolph (July 21 1978) well understands Geoffrey's having grown beyond his manuscript, and sees no reason why he shouldn't write another book, except that "this one is so original and enlightening, with all the reservations you may have by now, that it should finally see the light of day". He has received Geoffrey's paper and greatly enjoyed reading it.

"I fully agree with its major propositions as a signpost for what will have to happen if our civilization is to endure. But if I ask myself: what and where are the forces likely to make for such restitution, I have no answer. You may have one, but you remain silent here. I see no evidence whatever for the belief that 'the demands on him for responsibility cannot much longer be ignored', whether I watch Summit meetings or the discussions in our Congress on an Energy Bill, or when our miners strike not against the owners but against their union leaders—I need not go on, though I could fill some pages with examples. All this is well known to you. So forgive me if I ask you bluntly: Is all that you and I and a number of others are doing more than preaching to the fishes?

"What has been stymying me all these months is my inability to discover ways and means to bring about what indeed is, in the end, a change of the individual heart. One reason for our inability to get this across is the fact that, on the surface, matters are 'not so bad'. In other words, the real threats—wars, ecological catastrophes, progressive inflation—I can add to this sample—are all of them 'in the future' and subject to a slow process of accumulation. When the bombs fall on London or the Pacific fleet lies at the bottom of the sea, everyone feels in his bones that the game is up.

"For this reason I have come to the conclusion that these very crises which we would like to avoid by reawakening a sense of universal responsibility may well be the only means of awakening the required sense. Even then, and because of the catastrophic nature of the awakening shock, democratic procedures will not work. Whatever the external constitutional forms may be, *de facto* only an autocratic regime will be able to cope with the situation. Whether such a regime will be accepted—as in Britain in 1940—or will be the signal for revolutionary upheavals, no one can predict. It ultimately does not matter who would win in such a domestic struggle—it would be autocracy from the right or the left, all indications speaking for the first alternative.

"This is the scenario as it appears to me—a scenario that transforms your vision into utopia. I wrote to you before that one factor that paralyzes me is the revulsion from my own conclusions. It may well be a difference of basic temperament between us that prevents me from proposing a 'solution' unless I can see, however vaguely, how to get there. And you can do me no greater favor than to offer me an alternative 'route'. I am most eager to get your answer. In a way I have been fighting the same battle all these years with Ernst Bloch, though of course his utopia was much more utopian."

Dichotomies

Geoffrey (August 9 1978) believes that "the only difference between us is that I do not think in terms of such sharp dichotomies. I do not for a moment hope to 'avert a crisis'. I think we are all in 'crises' now and that they are all getting worse. I have no doubt that most, if not all, will increase their degree by abrupt and calamitous steps. I hope only that persuasive utterance may make the decline more comprehensible, increase however slightly the hope that those who suffer it will learn the right lessons rather than the wrong ones, and mitigate the disasters attendant on learning from experience.

"Nor do I distinguish so sharply between dictatorships and democracy, still less between 'left' and 'right'. Societies at different times allow to different classes of their members different degrees of independence of action, word and thought, and in different fields. Governments play an important part in setting these limits. They have a necessarily ambiguous role in giving a lead to those to whom they should remain ultimately answerable. Sometimes the dominant danger is excess of authority, sometimes its weakness and deficiency. And basically the cultural imperatives which produce consensus or division are only slightly under government control.

"As for left and right—what does it mean now? Was Mustapha Kemal right? Or Salazar? Or Hitler? Why are Fascists and Nazis said to be 'right'? Does it just mean non-Marxist? And what does that mean now? Cast your mind back to classical Rome in, say, BC 200 as Cato saw it, victorious over Carthage and unmenaced from within the Mediterranean area or beyond it, yet already threatened in Cato's view by decadent luxury seeping in from post-classical Greece. Another few centuries and the Roman virtues are a past dream and cultured Romans are awaiting the barbarians' take-over. The outlook must have been almost as bleak as today's. Yet from this shambles arose the feudal order and by 1200-1300 everyone knew his place.

"In England this destroyed itself before the end of the 15th century and a centralized autocratic, bureaucratic power took over and achieved a lot before it bred the revolution which destroyed it in the mid-1600s and by the end of the century had substituted a constitutional monarchy controlled by the landed gentry. The controlling class widened with the accumulation of wealth outside land, but the underlying 'order' remained powerful even when social mobility increased. Another 200 years and the widening of the suffrage, universal education, secularization and so on has eroded the old order, but not made a new one fit for carrying on the old enterprise of living together, more demanding because more interdependent, yet less acceptable because of the new expectations of individual autonomy.

"Over this huge span freedom to do one's own thing, including freedom to starve and to die, has ebbed and flowed in at least three dimensions—its overall area, its particular content and its beneficiaries. Taken in reverse order, the pecking order has varied and so has the number in the top class. The Trade Union Congress has replaced the barons of Runymede. The content has varied. A man's religion is regarded as wholly his own affair but the way he treats his children is of intense public concern. The total area has widened and the area ordered by cultural imperatives has correspondingly shrunk.

"You and I think it has shrunk so much as to render Western societies ungovernable. This has happened before. We are right to fight it because cultural imperatives are easily destroyed and only slowly rebuilt. We cannot be sure that they will ever be rebuilt. But for those whose only public impact is persuasive utterance, it is important to say the right thing at the right time, and often influential too. It is a time to shout that liberty and still more equality are not values whose dominance is independent of time and circumstance but are only one element and today the less important one in the struggle for order and differentiation.

"The brief unification of Britain in 1940-45 was not a dictatorship of either right or left. Responsibility was hugely devolved but the common need suspended individual feuds. There was no anti-war movement such as there was to be later over Vietnam. It was the last manifestation of that spontaneous consensus which so impressed you 40 years ago. It could be repeated only by a crisis which eliminated unemployment, an achievement never yet achieved except by war. But even today there are areas of common policy shared by all parties and I expect, even hope, that this will spread a safer form of dictatorship than the more common one-party type, though not yet shown to be possible over some critical areas.

"Freedom and order is a spectrum of complementarity in which, as you once so lucidly showed, freedom is bought by accepting the inner and outer limitations of an order within which it can be enjoyed. These limitations change, widening in some respects, narrowing in others—wider or narrower over-all only insofar as one attaches more importance to one area than another. Of course they may become polarities, opposite oscillations of an unstable system in which experience of either breeds support for the other. And I'm sure we are all headed for a reversal of the swing, putting order first. This will in time breed its own reversal, but we need to say what needs to be said now.

"And what of the corporative state? Do unions and businesses need the weight of formal political responsibility? Even informal political responsibility is making a difference over here; a lot of learning is going on. 'Ignorant armies clash by night'. Only history will show whether they learned anything in the process. But they might, and you and I might contribute some mite to that learning though no-one will ever know, least of all you or me. Does any of this make any sense?"

"Yes" replies Adolph, August 13, "what you are saying makes perfect sense, and is in some way more consistent with our role of affecting the world through 'persuasive utterances' than is what I am after. And yet I find it difficult to adopt your attitude of Olympian serenity, finding solace in well-chosen historical analogies, and in blunting the edges of what to me are indeed still 'sharp dichotomies'. I mentioned in my last letter differences of temperament as a possible cause. I shall mention another, substantive reason later on. But perhaps what separates us is that you have Britain both in your bones and before your eyes, whereas I have several German catastrophes in my bones and growing American anomie before my eyes.

"It may be that I exaggerate the difference between our two countries—I mean now Britain and the US. After all, daily life here still moves in customary channels whereas it is possible today for a Briton publicly accused of murder to try re-election to Parliament. Anyhow, the main concern of both of us is to find a balance between Freedom and Order in accord with our complex modern societies. You have described in your last paper, and several times before, the attitudes of Government, Business and Labor, and also of the professional critics of society, the intellectuals, that are required for establishing such a balance, and we are in full agreement about your vision. With one difference—that my interest centers on the social and psychological processes that are likely to *create* such attitudes. You think that 'making the decline more comprehensible' will teach the potential sufferers the 'right lesson' and will mitigate the disasters. I have, very reluctantly, come to the conclusion that the only effective teachers are the disasters themselves.

The teaching capacity of disasters

"I do not know what kind of disaster will have this productive function. Surveying the actual scene in this country, two come to mind: (1) the likely fall of the dollar to a level that will bring on drastic import controls with the consequence of a reduction in the standard of living; (2) progressive inflation to the point when saving ceases and the accumulated savings will be mobilized for current expenditure. Then measures of domestic control will become feasible that today are 'unthinkable'. There I am guided by my German experience in 1923. It seems quite possible that both disasters will occur jointly. Whether even this combination will be grave enough to break through the wall of individual and group egoism that stands in the way of 'public consent', no-one can know. A stronger medicine may be necessary—I pray that it will not be atomic war.

"Now in the handling of such disasters the difference between Democracy and Dictatorship, and between Right and Left, may well decide the long-term future. I am indeed convinced that democracy understood as the conventional parliamentary game cannot cope with disastrous shocks. But democracy has a weapon in its arsenal that may well be effective. To understand this we must beware of an ambiguity in the term 'dictatorship'. To use historical examples, there was Cincinnatus[8] and there were Hitler and Stalin. Churchill during the war was vested with the power of 'commissary dictatorship', as the technical term has it, and though he did not voluntarily go back to his plough (as Cincinnatus did) but was sent back to it, the entire procedure conformed to democratic principles.

"It is my hope that, in the hour of need, a man will be found in both our countries capable of fulfilling this function. It is important to realize that, even under these most auspicious conditions, it is not the dictator that creates consent. His activity rests on the existence of consent, and the turn from anomie to order can only be the realization on the part of a large majority of ordinary people that the hour has struck—the hitting home of the disaster itself.

"Again, let us pray for such a course of events—it is by no means assured. The alternative is some sort of Stalin or Salazar—dictators in the conventional sense of the word, as used today. Neither do they go home when the crisis is over, nor can they be sent away so long as they are successful. They too rest ultimately on the consent of the majority—they manufacture it by means that are all but 'spontaneous'. Now don't you think that the difference between a 'democratic' and an 'autocratic' dictator—Churchill and Stalin—is fundamental for our future?

"Moreover, under the conditions described, the distinction between 'Right' and 'Left' may become equally cardinal, certainly in this country. Our Right is out to dissolve the Welfare State and to abolish public controls to the utmost— type Milton Friedman. The consequence may well be the dictatorship of the 'military-industrial complex'. There is at this time no parallel on the Left in this country, which is totally disorganized and, leaving out a few uninfluential intellectuals, without ideology.

"I am aware that in Britain the alignment of forces differs, but in a way that makes the distinction between Right and Left even more relevant. In the UK the

Conservatives have retained some remnant of the true conservatism of a Burke or Tocqueville, with its emphasis on 'order', though marred by traditional class distinction. And this brings me to the main point of distinction between Right and Left—the attitude towards Equality. I differ from you in believing that, with the inescapable limitations to economic growth, the issue of redistribution of income, and especially wealth, will gain importance. Our commissary dictator had better take note of this—the range of consent may well depend on a fair solution of this issue.

"Now, you may say: if catastrophe rather than the printed word is seen as 'teacher', why do I not sit back and wait for the 'redeeming' event? I have often asked myself that question. My answer goes in a direction you are unlikely to follow me. Ultimately I see in all our troubles the birth pangs of a new civilization at a higher stage of human emancipation. As you know, I mean by this the taming by deliberate action of some of the impersonal forces and domineering human masters that have kept mankind in bondage throughout the millennia. The child 'may' be born, but the dangers are so great that it may all end in final disaster. But I think that the better alternative is still open. And this seems to me worthwhile stating in public in the face of so many dogmatic doomsday prophets. You see: something of the Utopian spirit of my late friend Bloch is alive in me—or it is the prophetic tradition to which I can trace my origin ..."

It is not until September 14 1978 that Geoffrey replies to this letter. "I cannot believe that you mean what you so clearly say. Even with your passion for dichotomies, you cannot really believe that people learn *either* from teachers *or* from experience. Of course no large-scale change will occur quickly unless and until widely shared change in experience makes it impossible to go on as before. This is what you call learning from disasters. The most that 'teachers' can do before the event is to prepare minds so that they are more likely to interpret these experiences more correctly, and to respond to them more effectively when they occur. That is what I call 'learning the right lessons rather than the wrong ones' and thus 'mitigating the disasters'. Neither of us hopes to avert the disasters. Neither of us would go on writing and thinking if we did not hope that it might contribute something to responding to them when they come. So what are we disagreeing about?

"You may find it hard to understand how I can feel so aloof from so dark a prospect, but you have yourself suggested some good reasons and I can supply many more. Temperamentally I have always found it easier to await inevitable horrors which I could do nothing about than to deal with even much less threatening ones which required or allowed anticipatory action by me. Also, I have not actually experienced, as you have done, some of these horrors. Probably more important than either, I have less vitality now, less mental verve and spring, a doubt whether I have any more to say, a greater concern for personal relations and individual lives as against the socio-cultural background in which they grow, a sense of biological and psychological withdrawal from a scene in which I have almost finished playing a part of which I am not proud. In any case, it doesn't matter. How easily or uneasily we respectively support the spectacle of unfolding disaster should make no difference either to our understanding of it or to our responses to it.

"As for democracy and dictatorship, I think our countries will develop the governments which they respectively learn to deserve. And here again, all we can do is to contribute our microscopic forces to the understanding which may make our respective countries more tolerant of the common constraints and commitments which they will have to develop, more ready to pay 'the price of liberty'. Although personalities do count for a lot, I think that corporate power will continue to play a greater part, meaning by 'corporate power' organized pressure groups in the widest sense.

"An article in this week's *Guardian* described the terrible proliferation of lobbying in Washington, due partly it seems to the restriction of gifts by individuals to candidates' election expenses and the corresponding growth of more dangerous organizations for pressure and patronage. We have the same problem in a different form with the political power of the unions. Of course, dictators have always exercised their power, not just by personal charisma but by controlling organized power centers, usually the armed forces or an action-organized political party or both, and using this power to prevent the emergence of rival centers.

"I find it hard to picture a state in which pluralism meant multiple power to negate without responsibility for the result, distributed not between individuals but between organized and largely functional pressure groups with no dominant common culture of commitment and constraint. But this is the way our countries are moving now, and the movement will only be stopped by the disasters which it will generate.

"As for left and right, the distinction is of course more blurred here than with you. Do you mean rich and poor? This distinction here is right within the trade union movement. Do you mean pro- or anti-government intervention? Here a huge ambivalence affects both rich and poor. There is cleavage between the 'social democrat' on the one hand, and the extremes of left and right on the other, about the viability of any large-scale control. Hence the growing demand for more autonomy at the cost of more diversity—not quite the same thing as more liberty at the cost of less equality but a closely related urge. And behind it all, for those who can see it, the heightened importance of equality as an aspiration in a society of static or abating wealth, where more for A means less for B. (Did you really mean that you don't agree that this last tendency exists?)

"And behind all this, two radical inconsistencies. First, attitudes to 'employment'—viewed as *the* major distributable good by governments, by the unemployed and increasingly by the unions, but passionately not by economists and businessmen. Secondly, the growing irreconcilable clash between two ways of distributing wealth—(1) as wages to an individual irrespective of his personal status, and (2) as social entitlement based on his family circumstances. No clash while (2) is minimal, but insoluble as (2) climbs to deal not only with the disadvantaged but with the unemployed.

"Even (1) has its internal inconsistences. Staff are graded and ascend with time at least to the top of their grade. Manual workers, at least in Europe and America, get the rate for the job irrespective of age and circumstance. In Japan, I read, every employee's wage rises by regular instalments over 25 years so that at 45 he is getting more than three times as much for the same job as he got at 20—apart, of course, from any change in scale which may happen in the meantime.

"And all these cultural diversities are buttressed by their own sense of equity. Even the power to break your contract by a lightning strike has become as sacred a human right as the right to life and liberty. It is hard to deal with such a silly shambles or even think of it with compassion rather than disgust. And yet we are all in it and all helping to make and mar it, and it has at least the dignity of tragedy.

"I was with friends in Dorset on Thursday, so I heard and saw our Prime Minister, for whom I have a warm regard, tell the nation that he would continue to govern until the Parliament they had elected expired with time or withdrew its confidence by a vote—a very sensible decision, I thought. The power to dissolve parliament at any tactically convenient moment is an odd and I think doubtfully useful power anyway. I feel much safer with a government which can't put across anything it chooses or is forced by its supporters to do, and yet which declines to go until one or more of the many oppositions dares to dismiss it and take the responsibility of offering to do better. All the constituents of our Labour Party are learning difficult lessons which they couldn't learn if they didn't have the responsibility of office. Long may they stay there, say I—so long as they don't have an absolute majority. Of course they can't lead our 'cultural revolution' until the new scale of disasters begin. But the Tories couldn't either.

"This autumn we shall be slaughtering some of our best herds of dairy cattle because it wouldn't pay to pasteurize their perfectly clean milk. We spent hundreds of millions extirpating the tubercle bacillus from British herds. The French didn't. And being in the EEC we must all move at the pace of the slowest. I had better stop this sour outflow, or at least try to turn it into one of the papers I ought to be writing. I'm sorry it's not more cheerful. It will probably persuade you that my 'Olympian detachment' is not a sign of euphoria."

It is, in fact, a sign of Geoffrey's deteriorating physical condition. A handwritten note September 26 is very sombre in tone.

"You will now have returned and found my rather disgruntled letter. Apart from the different moods in which we face the prospect of various disasters (some imaginable and predictable, some not) I am in considerable personal difficulty in that my limited physical resources are now cutting back my intellectual ones. I have only a little more that I think I can usefully say, and I am doubtful whether the organism will manage to say it. I am trying to write a sequel to the paper about Western Culture but so far the 'back room' has not been able to respond.

"Even if it did, it would not answer your most pressing question. I think only history can answer that—perhaps not even history. Who knows, even after the event, who contributed what, for good or ill or both, to the endless unrolling of events? But I would like to help tidy up the confused concept of the ethical dimension and to restore respectability to the concept of ethical judgment. I too greatly value our joint pursuit of the same quarry. My focus is the mutual relations between awareness—morality—ethos—institutions—events. I think I said something true and important at the end of that last paper when I said that unstable systems might pass into oscillation or ossification or dissolution, and that another name for the last is cultural vacuum. I think I have something more to say about that ..."

Institutional reforms and mass psychology

Adolph's September 29 letter is in reply to Geoffrey's earlier note: "I take it that we are nearer to each other than the words reveal. We both know that any improvement of the situation is conditional on certain institutional reforms—possibly more of them here than in Britain, though both our countries are in urgent need of having labor disputes settled by compulsory arbitration, and probably require also much stricter control of monopolies. These are just examples. At the same time we know that, without a profound change in mass psychology no institutional changes can be achieved, and even if they were achieved, they could not work. Though the institutional and psychological factors are in a feedback relation, the spell can be broken only if first something happens psychologically.

"Now my main question is: what can that be? There perhaps exists some difference in emphasis between us. You are more confident than I that exhortation and 'social learning in the small' will make a major impact. But when you write that 'the movement will only be stopped by the disasters which it will generate' we come close together. In other words, we both seem to agree that the disasters, which everyone tries to avoid by 'tricks', though probably very bad to stand through, are yet the only remedy that will affect the key factor: mass attitude toward the general interest.

"Morever, I am convinced that such disasters can be dealt with, not with our habitual democratic processes, but only in some authoritarian manner, analagous to what happened in the war. So I see the process toward betterment as a two-stage process—first, the emergency stage during which the necessary institutional changes can be carried out, possibly by a freely accepted autocratic regime, and secondly a gradual relaxation of these controls in the direction of decentralization. I am fully aware of the present movement against government, etc. Alas, it is done for the wrong reasons—I have still to read anywhere that such a change must be met be heightened public responsibility of persons and groups. And of course the demand is ill-timed—what we need for institutional reforms are stronger, not weaker, governments. All this is central to what I am trying to do, and I am grateful that you continue our dialogue about it."

For Geoffrey, writing October 7, "one clue to our apparent misunderstanding is to be found towards the end of your second paragraph, when you suppose that I am more confident than you that exhortation and so on will make a major impact. I do not think I have any confidence in this at all. I have no idea whatever how much impact it will make, least of all how much impact any contribution of mine will make. I only know that (a) communication is an important means by which cultural norms are changed; and (b) it is, anyway, the only contribution I can make.

"Another point on your last paragraph, in which you refer to our 'habitual democratic processes'. Without actually denying that we still have habitual democratic processes, I am very conscious that they are changing rapidly and that they have already changed too much for me to understand them. One of the changes, and a sinister one, is the rise in importance of the pressure group as compared with the individual. Thus, I do not think with confidence of any 'return to normality' following whatever disasters may be in store. I think the situation will be permanently changed.

"I am also conscious that this period of emergency will not necessarily be a period of dictatorship, still less need it be perceived as such. When a single objective dominates, as in war, politics tend to evaporate and your world of spontaneous consensus tends to return. Power in England was highly devolved as well as highly centralized during the last war, but it did not have to be exercised to coerce people into sharing a common purpose or to silence those who did not, so the political possibilities of the emergency period seem to me to range over a spectrum which is not easily described in our usual political terms.

"I have just had two very interesting letters from senior people in ICI's Personnel Department. They both see the future of unemployment linked with a radical change in the conception as well as the organization of paid work. The new assumptions which they postulate as possible would call for a change in a number of economic assumptions. I will write more about this later. Meantime I remember that you once pointed out to me that it was economically unorthodox to think of employment as a distributable good. Since governments, voters, unemployed workers and even (with a qualification) trade unions all concur in assuming that it is a distributable good, is it not time to bring the economic assumptions into line?"

A brief note on October 16 encloses a page from the weekly *Guardian*, "which will show you that my gloomy prognoses are not confined to me." He is still in correspondence with the two ICI people, "both of whom seem to me eerily unconscious of the impending cultural vacuum and its implications. Perhaps they are right and I am wrong. Let's hope so. They are much nearer to contemporary British industry than I am. I think my correspondence with them has at least released the log jam, which will enable me to write my promised paper for *Futures*, but I am not at all sure that this will produce any convincing answer to the question which haunts both you and me about how to get from here to there." He sends Adolph a copy of his letter of the same date to one of his ICI correspondents, parts of which are quoted below:

> Briefly, you seem to me to ignore the essential novelty of 'work'—a regular pay cheque at regular intervals, paid holidays, paid sickness, increasing security of job tenure and a pension at the end. This, the receiving end of 'work', is not I think being widely rejected. On the contrary, it is usually prized as a treasure when not already accepted as a natural right. And it is absolutely, uniquely new. The hunter and food gatherer did not know it. The farmer did not know it. The industrial worker did not know it until he won it by struggle in my lifetime. It looks like the nearest thing to security that unpropertied men have ever known. But there are two snags in it.
>
> First, these promised slices come out of a cake of uncertain size. The uncertainties of life are still there; but they have been pushed into the stratosphere and it is still almost universally assumed that they will stay there whatever we do.
>
> Secondly, the distribution of the cake has become an ethical, not a factual, issue. How far should a man's share be decided by (a) what he owns, (b) what job he holds, (c) what wealth he creates, (d) his family circumstances and (e) his political and industrial muscle. Failing any agreement on a, b, c and d, dominance will pass to e.
>
> But that is to behave like a hunter in a 'post-industrial' world. And everyone knows that the price of human economic development has been to increase the mutuality of relations between the would-be subsisting human and the environment which supports him. This environment is increasingly a man-made system ... Man the hunter could almost afford to be a mere predator (though he might suffer if he killed female game in the breeding season). Man the farmer learned to feed his land if it was to feed him—and not to eat his seed corn. Man the industrialist, having used up the empty space and much of the irreplaceable resources, has produced the Welfare State, structural unemployment and reactions like Proposition 13 and what the Ford workers are saying about supporting their brothers in Leyland.
>
> Universal mutual predation is not a viable way to distribute the product of an interdependent human world. It is today a marked trend, but not a 'natural stream of events' which we can afford to take as a datum. But which alternative cultural structures would serve? That's why half the world has gone Marxist in 60 years. Compared with this, the problem of the employed, even the problem of the unemployed, seems to me relatively tractable. And few of our 1,500,000 unemployed would agree that they are 'rejecting work'. They know, as you and I do, that work is rejecting them.

What baffles me in your paper is your apparent sense of global and national security. I agree with nearly all your suggestions, often warmly. Some will help the employment, some the unemployment, situation. They will increase interest in the job, perhaps even responsibility for the job. But so long as we lack means to settle who gets how much for what, I cannot see the beginnings of responsibility, trust or a sense of belonging remotely equal to the needs of today, let alone tomorrow.

Adolph comments on October 26: "The reason for my delay is that I wanted to finish a first draft of my chapter on 'Liberty Tomorrow and Afterwards', just to find out where I stand. I have taken your warning very much to heart, that I should not let my 'passion for dichotomies' run away with me. If you should ever see what I am struggling with, which would certainly be a second draft if not a third, you will, I hope, admit that my bark in a letter is worse than my bite in writing responsible text. And I certainly believe with you that people learn from both teachers and experience, though in many cases it may require experience to make them understand what the teacher talks about. So there is really no dichotomy between ourselves on that score.

"Speaking further about the 'deep doubts about the viability of large-scale control', I share those doubts so long as popular opinion insists on maintaining what goes today by 'liberty' of individuals and, we again agree, of pressure groups. Therefore the plan to fight inflation which our President announced last night is stillborn before it is even formulated. And contrary to the view of my leftist friends, I hold mandatory controls equally unworkable for the same reason. We are being taught the hard way that all collective power rests on consent—a consent that requires the substitution of long-term interests for short-term gains—a substitution that would go a long way to restoring what you call responsibility, because in the long run our respective interests are, though not identical, yet inseparable from what sustains the community at large.

"I would like to understand more clearly what you mean by viewing employment as a distributable good, an idea to which, you say, economists object. Does this mean that employment rather than efficient output should become the criterion? Reading Peter Jenkins' articles, is not raising productivity the prime necessity, at least for Britain? Or have I misunderstood what you have in mind?

"I strongly feel with you when you speak of a growing concern for personal relations, combined with a sense of biological and psychological withdrawal. How could it be otherwise at our age?"

In the September-October 1978 issue of *Challenge* Dr. Robert Heilbroner paints an affectionate and admiring 'Portrait' of Adolph. Quoting Dr. Kenneth Boulding's comment, in reviewing *On Economic Knowledge* in 1965, that 'Adolph Lowe, professor emeritus of economics at the New School for Social Research, is one of the few people in the world today who deserve the title of economic philosopher', he says: "Fortunately, at 85 Lowe is more vital, keen, amusing and provocative than most men half his age. He receives a stream of visitors who range from scholars of international repute to students who seek his advice on endless matters, sometimes even on economics. He is still the severest friend and the warmest critic I have ever had."

Productivity and employment

Geoffrey tells Adolph November 9 that he has finished his paper on 'Responsibility'—the sequel to the one of last December—and that he should receive a separate copy within a few days.

"I had a funny experience the other day. A letter from a stranger in Australia set me rereading material that I wrote in 1938/39 about a responsible society. This was produced in connection with a movement which one of my partners and I initiated in the City, in the days between Munich and Dunkirk.[9] It was probably just before we met, and you very likely never saw any of these papers. I am not sure that any are worth sending to you, but it was strange to read myself saying 30 years ago just what I am trying to say now.

"The relation between employment and efficient output seems to me to depend on how one measures efficiency. There are at least four obvious measures of productivity: (1) production per man-hour; (2) production per man-year; (3) production per unit of the workforce per year; and (4) production per unit of population per year. Since everyone consumes, whether they produce or not, the last seems much the most sensible, but it is seldom used.

"If two men in a year can produce 100 units of value, whilst 3 men in a year can produce 105 units, it is obviously more efficient to employ 3 if the alternative is for the third to remain idle and share the products of the other two. In the second case, 3 men share 105 units. In the first they share only 100. This, of course, is the argument which Schumacher used to the Indian Government when persuading it to measure agricultural productivity as productivity per acre rather than as productivity per man. Given a surplus of men but not a surplus of acres, it would obviously pay to flood the land with otherwise idle men up to the point at which the addition of another would add absolutely nothing to the productivity of the acre.

"The same argument seems to me to apply to Britain, and indeed to all other countries which suffer what looks like permanent unemployment. There is, of course, a lot more to say about this and about the question of distribution which it raises, as well as about the present and future place of work in the culture of western societies, but I certainly am questioning the value of the first measure of productivity whenever there is significant unemployment. And so, of course, are the government and unemployed, and the voters and even, to some extent, the trade unions. What about them?

"This alone, of course, supplies no precise clue on how to deal with unemployment. My view on this is that one should start with the school leavers who have not yet got jobs, and consider locally what useful work can be found for these people in these places. The people concerned are not a cross-sample of humanity. They are the least successful minority of each school-leaving cohort. They are also the least mobile because they are still living at home and cannot afford to live elsewhere. Some of them may already be unemployable, but the remainder need specific local efforts. The result will be, I think, the growth of a new sector of the economy, small at first but humanly very important from the beginning and perhaps growing very rapidly more so."

Adolph writes November 18 that he has received Geoffrey's paper. "This is an excellent document, and all I can add is my enthusiastic agreement. You have clarified many difficult issues. I am especially happy about your definition of responsibility as proper responsiveness to the 'requirements' of the situation. So much so that I would like to take it over. But how can I quote you? Once the paper is published, as I expect it will be soon, this problem will solve itself. I arrived at the same notion of freedom, namely not to be without constraints but to substitute one's own choice of constraints for the imposed constraints of outside forces. And I am glad that you stress the 'equality' aspect of the present stage of Western civilization which, of course, demands equality of responsibility first of all.

"There are many more statements that fall in with my own convictions. Perhaps I still see the 'breakthrough' of recent steps of emancipation as somewhat more positive than it appears in your draft. What is wrong is not those steps as such, but the lack of the self-imposed restraints that alone assure their benefits without involving us in the dangers that accompany them. Of course, the question of how this change in popular attitude can be brought about remains. And I still think that only disaster—strong enough to hit the average person but not so strong as to threaten the foundations of civilization—can be the trigger. I am fully aware that the result may be something else than a new 'conformity', namely autocratic imposition of order—in the worst case even '1984'. But—and there we are again in full agreement—when the choice is between true anomie and tyranny, the latter will win out.

"I am still dissatisfied with my own writing, but I hope that your paper will help in some redrafting. Anyhow, I am only too happy to see you at the very top of your creative activity in spite of some pessimistic rumblings you let me hear recently." He has had some reassuring signs recently of his 'instrumental analysis' finding finally some echo. "So far the response was mainly British, that is, from England and, of all places, Australia. Too many vested interests in traditional thinking and lecture notes will have to be overcome.

"By the way, for more than one reason I am happy about Simon's Nobel Prize. He was one of the first to contest the 'maximization' principle as the general behavioral maxim in Economics. Contrary to people like Samuelson or Friedman, he is a very modest man and little known to the wider public. So there was real consternation here when he was chosen ... Our attempt to stem the dollar tide is laudable, but I wonder whether it can succeed unless 'responsibility' takes over or is imposed after all by mandatory controls—though even those will work only when responsibly accepted and administered."

Geoffrey tells him (November 27 1978) that 'Equality of Responsibility' is to be published in *Futures* in February 1979.

"You probably remember that Köhler published a book shortly before the war called *The Place of Values in a World of Fact*. It is ages since I read it, but I am almost sure that he also made much use of the concept of requiredness. I am rather ill-placed here for referring to a book and checking up things like that, but I will ask the library to get it, though it will be too late to include any reference that would be appropriate in next February's publication.

"I am delighted to hear your opinion of Simon. I have had two brief engagements with him by correspondence, one of which was accompanied by a meeting with him in Pittsburg. I found him most kind and helpful and undogmatic, even on the point on which we continue to differ, namely the usefulness of chess as an analogy for solving the problems of political life.

"I have written yet another paper as a sequel to the one you have commended.[10] It is intended to be presented at an International Conference of the Society for General Systems Research, to be held in London next August. It is all about using the actual school and the actual local authority where each child works as subject matter for studying the inherent requiredness of living in organizations. I have sent it to two school teachers I know, and if it survives their criticism you shall have a copy."

Three days after writing this letter, Geoffrey receives, belatedly, another letter from Adolph, dated November 19, which had crossed his earlier letter.

"I reply at once to answer your clarification of what you mean by productivity. For once, my economists are better than you think. They have been discussing your problem since the late 1890s under the heading of marginal productivity. Now I think that the traditional measure—output per man-hour—makes good sense and is indispensable if one wants to know whether the level of technology or the intensity of effort have changed.

"What you have in mind is of real importance in agriculture because, by and large, the capital factor—land—which is to be combined with different quantities of labor, is non-specific. Indeed, it is easily possible to put more men on a given acre. Alas, considering the highly developed specificity of industrial equipment, there it is possible only in rare cases. Were we to put an additional man on a linotype machine, output might well fall to zero because the guy would only 'be in the way'. Retail stores are another case where such 'addition' of labor is feasible within limits.

"In other words, to carry through your scheme on the large scale, one would have to alter first the equipment—certainly not a 'productive' procedure. For this reason the way our governments are seeking is 'public works', road building etc.—again cases with non-specific capital. What you suggest for the idle young seems to fall in the same category. What one might consider is public control of the introduction of new labor-saving equipment. I have been advocating this for decades, but I need not tell you what the response of business is to such ideas. They will be part of the total remodelling of our incentive system—after the disaster!"

For Geoffrey, November 30, Adolph's letter is perplexing: "I am left most confused. Of course output per man hour is indispensable *if* you want to know whether the level of technology or the intensity of effort has changed. But these are not the only or the most important things one wants to know if one's concern is with unemployment or with distribution. You say you yourself have been advocating for years the public control of new labor-saving equipment, presumably with the object of preserving jobs. If you did so, productivity per man hour would be less than it would otherwise have been, though production, at least in the undertaking so inhibited, would be no less.

"We are already doing this to some extent by obliging employers to pay redundancy pay to employees when they lay off. The principle could be extended and made more selective so that the savings otherwise to be expected of the proposed labor-saving machinery would be even more offset than they are now. Note that this method defers but does not necessarily inhibit permanently the introduction of the new technology if, but only if, it can be introduced piecemeal. There is no penalty on not replacing a man who dies or retires.

"There are countless ways of favoring labor-intensive industries—including, as you mention, public works, if road building and such are still labor-intensive—an ascertainable fact which I don't know but don't assume when I see a modern building contractor's plant. All of them would decrease productivity per man hour, reduce unemployment, and increase or hold constant DNP. But all would result in someone earning less than he otherwise would.

"I think the whole thing is undiscussable except in the framework of the two great questions on p.3 of my letter of 15 September: (1) How far is employment to be regarded as a distributable good, and (2) How far are we prepared to rely on means and *principles* other than employment to distribute DNP? The answer to (1) depends largely on the answer to (2). If personal employment is to remain the main form of distributing income (as economists assume) then employment must be regarded as a distributable good (as economists deny) because nearly everyone still wants the opportunity to earn by working more than they would get by not working, and such opportunities are currently not available to 6-7% of our labor force—indeed to more, since some whole-time workers also receive supplementary benefit. (About a tenth of British households, including some with wholetime workers, receive supplementary benefits, related of course to household as distinct from individual needs.)

"Even if the prophets of the communications revolution are only half right, we shall continue to lose jobs, especially jobs which 'ordinary' people can do. The last I heard of was a machine to read labels on goods bought in a supermarket, total each purchase, and let each purchaser pass when he has paid, thus dispensing with cashiers (though hopefully adding a few security guards).

"The old workhouses required work in exchange for subsistence. Prisons also require work, though I think they pay union rates for at least some of the jobs. The workhouses were damned past recovery by deliberately making work less attractive and less rewarding than corresponding work outside. Our alternative philosophy is the social wage or negative income tax—not the same but the philosophy is similar. Everyone has an equal birthright. What he chooses to add and is able to add to this is his own affair. I don't know the literature or the arithmetic, but we are all practicing this philosopy now. The communist countries impose an obligation to work, provide the opportunities partly by feather-bedding, and use their control of employment as an instrument of persecution. It is not an attractive alternative. But what we are all actually doing seems to me doomed because it requires from the employed contributors more than they seem willing to give unless unemployment is kept lower than we yet know how to keep it. My only solution is that everyone who is fit for employment but not otherwise employed should spend so many hours a day working a hand-driven generator to put power into the grid!"

Adolph's brief reply to both of Geoffrey's letters is dated December 6. "I cannot see why you should feel confused by my last letter. We basically agree as well about the facts, that is, what goes on, as about what is desirable. I drew your attention to the fact that, for once, economists since the time of Ricardo are aware of the fact of technological displacement, though they were, and are, over-optimistic about how to handle it. Have a look into my *Path* (pp. 250-255) where you will find the conflicting arguments and my answer to them.

"What we actually do is to combine employment as the major factor of distribution with making purchasing power independent of employment—anyhow since unemployment compensation has become an 'entitlement'. What we should do, but what meets all objections directed against interference with 'free' enterprise, is public control of labor-displacing innovations. (There are others, so-called product innovations as opposed to process innovations, which rather attract labor through their secondary effects, e.g. the automobile). Control would indeed need to be gradual in the place of sudden and bunched innovations. Alas, you are right that most 'public works' have become capital-intensive. Your idea with the hand-driven generator is a good one, at least as a symbol of what should be done.

The thrust of technological change

"Do you know about the OECD report prepared by Christopher Freedman, according to which even contemporary hard core unemployment is the consequence of accelerated automation, and that the impact in the early '80s will be on 'the entire manufacturing sector of the industrial world'? So far the effect is mainly non-absorption of the new influx into the labor market. Anyhow, apart from the atom bomb, the future effects of cybernetics is my nightmare, because it will in the end reduce not 6-8% but 60-80% of the populations to the status of state pensioners, apart from the socio-psychological consequences of the 'relief' from work.

"For the rest, I envy your productivity—I am still struggling. I know what I want to say, but fail to find the right form. By the way, I think that Köhler, who indeed makes 'requiredness' a central concept, understands it in a transhistorical sense following Husserl. This is not your idea, if I understand you correctly?"

Geoffrey replies (January 9 1979) that he is still confused: "Is the concept of a 'wage fund' still valid? Is it still valid to assume that technological change is driven by some dynamic of its own, presumably the effort to make profits or stay in business rather than by the need to get rid of human employees by any means which in turn is related to their increasing expensiveness and unreliability?

"I did not know of the OECD report, but I have heard other people beside you express alarm at the prospect of greatly increased unemployment due to the next wave of computerization, and I am as concerned and confused as you about the appropriate reactions to this trend."

"I am fully aware that what I call 'minor catastrophes'—thus excluding an atomic war—are by no means a safe cure of the ruling anomie", writes Adolph, January 20. "But I see no other, especially because at least our present looks so cheerful that no-one believes what awaits us. You are dead right: even if we economists could devise perfect solutions for the economic ills, it would be futile. The field of battle is power politics with total concentration on short-term advantages. With us, business monopolies are worse culprits than organized labor—a relative scale of evil. We others are reduced to the role of Jeremiahs, which fits me badly.

"I am at the moment busy with something that permits me to speak out to some extent. You may remember that more than a year ago I was interviewed for a broadcast over the Berlin Radio. They have now sent me the original transcript of 110 pages, to be edited for publication in a collective volume. The informal technique of question and answer makes it possible to say many things that do not fit into the streamlined form of a book. Perhaps this may help me in my bigger enterprise."

A letter from Geoffrey dated February 4 1979 deals with a strike situation in Britain.

"Well, we seem to be having a minor catastrophe—if that means anything less than an atomic war—but it is not clear to me how its therapeutic effect is to be achieved. Not that I see corruption or blackmail in high places, or even necessarily stupidity and cowardice. It is that an understandable course of legislation and acquiescence has produced what even its opposite would probably have been unable to stop—a web of uncontrollable, militant unions almost without any effective international organization. The TUC and even the individual union HQs have little if any more control of their members than the government has.

"And the government, having at least a little more control in the public than in the private sector, has now let the two radically diverge by allowing the truck drivers to get their demands of 15-20%. It has been a queer, hushed-up affair—not a policeman in sight of a picket line, not even a newspaper story about intimidation and injury. Election tactics?—or long-term strategy?—or just appreciated impotence? I don't know. The question now is where the public sector strike will leave us by election time. But then another wave of negotiation is due in the private sector—miners, power workers. It is already February. I do not look forward at all to a Thatcher government. If Callaghan and Co. can do no better while they are in power, what would happen to them in opposition?

"Well, we shall see. *Le Monde*, in a leader reprinted in our weekly *Guardian* and entitled *Le Mal anglais*, asks: 'What has happened to this proud nation which ... the left wing Labour leader Aneurin Bevan saw as a precious island which once had to thank heaven for having preserved it as an example of humanity?' What indeed. A German-type inflation seems the most likely of impending mini-catastrophes, but it is not clear to me that people would learn much even from that. A total ban on picketing and a huge limitation of the right to strike seem the minimal first steps; and I can't see these this side of civil war.

"In a paper I wrote years ago I listed nine mutually inconsistent ethical reasons accepted by both sides in current wage negotiations. The least valid but fastest-growing was the logic of the protection racket— that men should be paid not for what they do but for the harm they abstain from doing. Our unions aren't quite protection rackets yet but that's the way it's moving. A Labour MP talks of free collective vandalism and urges everyone to cross picket lines if they want to—landmarks, these, in Labour language. But he is careful not to admit what a picket line now is.

"I think Michael Polanyi[11] was right when he said that so long as a people believed in and revered its institutions its morality remained personal, concerned with the proper performance of roles and interpersonal obligations. But once the institutions were challenged the forms changed; sinners became victims or patients and the only heroes were revolutionaries. He called it moral inversion. He may have under-rated the extent of the change on the individual as well as the society; it is disaster for both—I was born in the first and have lived to see the second, and the contrast is overwhelming.

"I forget what he had to say about religion in this context, but clearly the individual needs some foothold outside or rather transcending the State as for the time being embodied. The European dichotomy between church and state since Charlemagne has probably been very useful, and I remember it vividly in its family and domestic form in the years pre-1914. Even in the 1930s the trade unions were more deeply rooted in the non-conformist chapels than in Marx. Well, that's all over."

The preservation of civilization

At the end of January 1979 Adolph had sent Geoffrey a paper he had written for a memorial volume for his friend and colleague, Hans Jonas. The paper was published in 1978 under the title 'Prometheus Unbound? A New World in the Making'.[12] Some of the ideas in the paper were to find their way into the first chapter of the book Adolph had been struggling with for almost three years. Examining the cataclysmic changes affecting world society since World War I, and especially since World War II, he points out that, to some of those who have grasped the deeper meaning of these changes, the headlong rush into new knowledge and revolutionary action means the dissolution of the ties which have held together society through past millennia:

> To them the prospect is one of self-destruction in atomic wars, ecological catastrophes and, the ultimate penalty inflicted on such a Promethean rebellion, the madness of universal anomie ... The recent quantum jump of emancipation will prove compatible with the preservation of civilized life only if we can reap its potential benefits without falling prey to the multiple dangers which this transformation of nature and socio-political conditions poses. This, however, implies that strict limits must be set to the use of our new freedoms, substituting new constraints for the discarded ones ... From now on the preservation of civilization is conditional on insight into the long-term consequences of our actions and omissions and on the adoption of a moral principle which guides our choices toward the constructive ... Given the slow-working process of rational persuasion, our best hope may lie in a succession of small calamities which may teach a more convincing lesson than the preaching of Doomsday prophets.[13]

Geoffrey writes February 21 to thank him for this "beautiful bit of work. I do not much like the importance which Jonas attaches to survival; and I am at the moment, as you may imagine, more than usually doubtful about the extent to which a workable system of constraints and commitments can be developed by a large society once it has lost its traditional ones. I am glad to be reminded of Niebuhr's distinction between moral man and immoral society. Perhaps I had better dig that book out from the library and look at it again. I have some more radical comments on this paper but they are still too latent to express." (In fact, he seems to have handwritten a lengthy PS to the letter—though not on the copy—in which he expresses a number of reservations.)

Adolph replies March 2 1979: "You seem to have missed one important aspect of my little paper, namely the question mark in the title. In other words, practically all your reservations are shared by me, especially the almost unsurmountable difficulty of re-establishing a system of constraints and commitments. And I do not mince words about what the alternative will be: autocratically enforced conformity.

"On the other hand, I wish I could share your skepticism as to the significance of the postulate of 'survival'. Perhaps one had to live on the spot through the Cuba crisis of '62, revealing Kennedy's unpardonable recklessness, to fully grasp the practicality of this command. Of course, there too the question arises: how to assure its acceptance. But the first step is the acknowledgment of the principle and I see everywhere, especially also in the discussions of political philosophers, an attempt to evade the issue.

"I quite agree with you that, at this juncture, national rather than international stabilization is in the foreground, even if it is an open question to what extent the former can be achieved without the latter. At the same time, I wonder whether one should speak of an 'endemic' hostility of different populations, meaning nations. Such hostility existed between smaller units before the rise of the national state. And though not all traces of this have disappeared—your Welsh and Scottish irredenta, or the antagonisms between North and South Germany—it is hardly a major impediment today to domestic national stabilization. It is a distant hope that something of this may develop internationally. But I should not think that it is the 'nature of man' that stands in the way.

"To be honest, I expected your opposition to direct itself against what I call the dialectics of the present stage of emancipation, that is, my conviction that there is a lot of 'good' in this development, even if the chances of its winning out against the 'bad' are dim. I would be very happy if I could assume that you also acknowledge the double edge of our situation.

"All this is, of course, of little interest when we think of the practical issues of the day. When it comes to this, my outlook is possibly even more sombre than yours. Anyhow, it looks as if we had not to wait much longer for 'small catastrophes'—the SALT Agreement is practically dead, though Carter wants to carry it out through Presidential Order, which may open a constitutional crisis on top of all else. Economically we are moving toward mandatory controls—I wonder whether they will not be sabotaged."

He writes again March 13 in answer to another 'explosion' from Geoffrey.

"But why explode? We are together in practically everything you mention. Of course, the question mark in my title is rhetorical. And I have dissociated myself unequivocally from the anarchist dream of Man's innate sociality that would automatically create an identity between what is aspired and what is required. This, however, does not on principle exclude the possibility that a spirit of conformity, fostered by institutional structures and spiritual forces, could one day inspire groups larger than the present nation state. If you had told a medieval burgher—my historical paradigm for the 'gentleman'—that one day such a spirit would dominate life, not in communities of some thousands of souls, but in a nation of 40 million, he would hardly have believed his ears.

"This has nothing to do with the fantasy of world community whose members do the right thing because of rational insight—the original Marxian dream, to be fulfilled when all corrupting institutions have been removed. We are agreed that the more technological progress (in which I include not only material but social 'engineering') and critical thought overcome the hitherto autonomous impersonal forces in nature and society, the tighter the 'bounds' that must be accepted if order and not anarchy is to arise.

"The one point where we do not yet seem to agree concerns my emphasis on the difference between 'objective', meaning institutional factors, and 'subjective' factors of rationality and morality. Certainly one cannot function without the other, but there is a widespread belief that 'organization tricks'—a more effective Charter of the UN, a more subtle fiscal and monetary policy along Keynesian lines—are our salvation. The trivial fact that no institution is more efficient than the spirit in which it is being operated must anew be hammered in. Give me a nation in which the interests of others are generally part of the interest of everyone, and I will solve all our political and economic problems. (I chose this formulation in view of Rawl's *Theory of Justice*, which has become the Bible of American political philosophers. There he stresses that benign neglect of the interests of others (include: public interest) is all we can demand from the 'just' person.) It is for this reason that I stress the subjective factor, as you do when you speak of National Ethos etc. as the 'great internalizer'.

"I fear that, under the name of freedom, the dissolution of all past internalizers of the West has gone too far for 'enlightenment' to have a chance. Therefore my desperate expedient of 'minor catastrophes', where I agree with you that even their effectiveness is dubious. They could work only if there is enough *erbgut* (inherited response) left that can be revived. They cannot create the right spirit. In all this, the clarification of what freedom can mean in our situation is so essential because it is, compared with the last two centuries, that quality of Western life that is most in need of readjustment and least recognized as such."

Geoffrey, replying April 4, agrees that "indeed, there is little between us, and probably less every time we write. The experience of this winter has made me more doubtful than I was of the power of a mini-catastrophe, at least in this country, to awaken the sense of community you speak of.

"I have just been reviewing Hayek's last book, *The Political Order of a Free People*. It is uncanny in 1979 to hear these views being expounded. Fortunately there is more in his book than a repetition of his arguments about *laissez-faire*. He insists rather surprisingly that social coherence has an autonomous value independent both of biological urges and of rational considerations, and he wants the rules of rightness which they dictate to be safeguarded better than they are in the American Constitution, let alone ours. We might differ from him if we sat down with him to write these rules of rightness but I like his outright assertion, though there is no sovereign right to do anything outside the constraints which the rules of right must impose. I will enclose a copy of my review.[14]

"I am sorry to read what you write about Rawl's *Theory of Justice* and its reception in America. I rather thought that was the way it was. I was also dismayed to hear that our Anthony Crosland, in one of the latest papers he wrote before he died, took as a basic assumption that social justice was out of the question except in a society where everyone was getting more net disposable income every year. Something more than current ideas of freedom is clearly needed as 'the great internalizer'.

"I wrote what I thought was an outrageously Blimpish paper, in view of the audience, called 'Ethics, Patriotism and Homelessness'. After the talk I tried it on the *New Society*, which to my surprise accepted it."

Adolph, April 23, is much less happy about Hayek. "You are indeed a generous reviewer! I agree with you that it is a step forward on the part of H. to proclaim the need for constitutionally safeguarded 'rules of rightness' though, as you say, much will depend on their content. But more important: such a 'legalistic' approach is at best half the solution to the problem. What creates social coherence are non-rational beliefs and feelings, which cannot be legislated. In their absence there is not even hope that the rules of rightness will be observed in the spirit—you cannot put a whole nation into jail.

"I spent much time on the correction of the galleys of my German interview, which amounts now to 50 printed pages. It says in a quite informal manner almost all I have to say, and which I find so difficult to translate into normal prose. I too am by no means certain that 'mini-catastrophes' will solve the problem of attitudes—our nuclear mishap might have provided an answer if it had led to mass evacuation.[15] Looking forward to your 'Blimpish' paper!"

Political structures

"I wonder whether you would really prefer to live under the US Constitution" asks Adolph May 16, "once you consider that, in two years, we have not been able to get an energy legislation or now even a standby rationing authority for the President, a demand that has been rejected even by the majority of his own party? I realize the problems the British Constitution poses. But at least you get things done—for better or worse. So far the indications are that the new Government will move cautiously. Of course, the test case will be their treatment of the unions. By the way, your longing for Proportional Representation makes you overlook that you might have gotten some more liberals, but most likely a dozen other parties. No, this is the worst electoral system for bodies that must decide. It is different if they only have to advise. Among the many causes for the downfall of Weimar, PR is not the least important.

"The plan of those Americans to publish a selection of your writings seems to me a grand idea.[16] It will get you going also in new directions. And no 'executor' could do this as well as you yourself. My interview should appear in June under the bad title *Die Zerstörung einer Zukuft* (The Destruction of the Future). It is a collective volume, so I cannot interfere with the title. Anyhow, I by no means feel that my involuntary emigration destroyed my future, though it certainly did change it considerably. Alas, there will be no English translation; I cannot imagine that there would be an English-speaking market for it. But I trust that you will have no difficulty with my conversational German.

"I knew Bateson[17] quite well when he taught at the School—he was still married to Margaret Mead, who sat in at his lectures, interrupting and correcting him. We are rapidly approaching a national crisis over the SALT Treaty. As it looks at present, it would be a miracle if the Senate were to accept it. Of course, we are in the middle of the election campaign of 1980—also one of the dubious features of our Constitution. I am as desperate about our set-up as you are about yours. But what is the alternative?"

Geoffrey's letter of May 26 contains no answers, and Adolph's reply June 4 continues his comments about the situation in the United States.

"Our sort of anomie shows in the total destruction of the ancient 'separation of powers'—meaning that the power of President and Congress are no longer complementary but fiercely competitive. This means on the part of Congress that all Presidential initiative—energy, inflation, reorganization of government, not to speak of foreign policy (SALT above all)—is paralyzed by refusal to act on the part of Congress. Since Congress cannot be dissolved, nor the President be voted out of office before the appointed term, still one-and-a-half years ahead, our petrol situation, our wage and price structure, are in total disarray. And there is no probability whatever that a radical swing of the electorate—which is anyhow doubtful—would make the slightest difference. Our type of syndicalism has conquered all strata of the nation.

"On top of this, there is spreading mistrust that any official information speaks the truth, not to mention the stench of corruption. The resulting cynicism is fully understandable, but further impedes any change for the better. Our unions bear their share in all this, but they are in many ways victims rather than profiteers. And this all the more so as our 'syndicalism' is a rebellion of the rank and file against the leadership, which itself has altogether behaved quite responsibly. At the same time both output and employment keep up quite well—the obvious consequence of the inflationary expectations of the public—which most of my colleagues confuse with 'basic stability'.

"I agree with the Pardoe article, though he missed an important point when stressing the significance of the Keynesian model in situations of underutilization. Keynes made it unmistakably clear that his policy will be successful only if Labor during the recovery renounces wage demands, so that the additional purchasing power can mobilize additional factors of production. Otherwise, with rising wages, the spending is dispersed in rising incomes per person rather than in constant incomes of more persons. On the other hand, I certainly agree with his conclusion that adjustment to a falling rate of growth is a most difficult problem in a modern system with immobile resources and long-term commitments. Chapter 18 of my Growth book has dealt with this extensively though, alas, in cryptic technical language.

"Now, your papers. I can only express my admiration for the shorter one on Patriotism. It is a real model, also in the simplicity of its language, for which I have so far been struggling in vain. I have two little reservations: (1) I understand that you concentrate on the sins of Labor. But when you—rightly—say that the reward for technological progress should be rising *real* incomes through falling prices, the sins of the other side—monopoly, administered prices, etc.—come most forcefully to mind. (2) Even if Justice and Equality are not the ultimate goal, I believe that, rightly understood, they have become preconditions for a social structure representing humanity. Once the mystique has been removed from injustice as the work of the Lord it has become a principle on which social reconstruction must build."

The future of morality

He writes again July 14 in reply to Geoffrey's of June 16.

"I have finally read 'The Future of Morality' and find it very good indeed. As I expected, it is quite in accord with my own thinking, and you will detect many an allusion if and when my final text materializes. Today only two comments: twice—quoting Bevan and once more later—you speak of 'humanity'. I know what you mean, and yet I feel that this too cannot be totally dissociated from the social-historical context. It meant something different in Athens from what it meant in Victorian England. And the fact that we have reached a stage where political morality extends beyond national borders makes it again mean something else.

"How I agree with you that the alternatives—'individual is a mere cell' and 'he is an entity free to make his own relations'—are deadly! It occurred to me that this controversy, and it is probably the most fundamental one among those carried on today, is a revival of the medieval controversy about 'universals'— are they a 'reality' or a mere conceptual abstraction? The great Abelard, better known for his affair with Héloise, gave the striking answer: the community of disciples is neither a 13th entity besides the 12 disciples, nor the 'sum' of the 12; it is the 12 when they are assembled in the spirit of Christ. I need not enlarge upon how well this fits into your own exposition.

"I have not yet taken up the second paper, but shall do so in due time. I trust that you enjoyed your visitors—I am expecting quite a number myself, among them Gräfin Dönhoff, the remarkable editor of the remarkable German weekly *Die Zeit*. She was a student of mine in Frankfurt, and we have renewed our friendship. I am afraid she will have little good to say about my old country—except economically. By the way, so far we have not strictly controlled money supply in this country. Whether it will be possible in Britain we shall see. The entire structural change toward the Welfare State hinges there. It will be one of my topics."

Geoffrey replies July 30 that Adolph's point about 'humanity' is very important.

"There may be transcultural human values (though not, of course, a-cultural) and if so humanity must be one and perhaps the only one. I think there is a vector which defines the direction as the more human, as against the more human in any particular situation. But because it is context-bound it will always come out differently, even though the nature of the criterion can be expressed in general terms. Bevan was indeed expressing a view of humanity which was strongly characterized by his historical position in space and time. This no doubt is why the distinction between 'absolute' and 'relative', like the distinction between 'object' and 'subject', is not satisfactory or comprehensive. I must be more explicit about this—if I can. Thank you for your reference to Abelard's neat illustration of the meaning of a community.

"I am glad you should have such an interesting visitor as the Editor of *Die Zeit*. I wish I could be present to hear what she has to say. I was very surprised some time ago when a young American friend, who had spent a couple of years in Germany with her husband (he had been posted to a German subsidiary of his company), came over here to find a job and somewhere to live because she said she could not bear the cultural atmosphere. This was not because she had not tried to enter into it. She had learned German and evidently mixed a lot with Germans. I found it hard to identify clearly what it was which had so greatly put her off, but it was evidently something very real to her.

"I successfully let off my talk about 'Stability and Quality' to the Open University Summer School. I think this is the other paper to which you refer. I hope soon to have a collection of papers sufficiently coherent to put together in a book. But these days I count no chickens until they are definitely hatched."

The Veblen-Commons Award

Adolph, August 25, says that he has managed to write the section on Inflation, which he regards as paradigmatic for the weaknesses of what its opponents complain about as the superpower of the Welfare State.

"And I was just about to continue with my Liberty chapter when I was notified that I am to receive at Christmas the Veblen Prize. You must know that our profession here gives two prizes—the Clark Medal for 'good' boys, who accept the ruling neo-classical framework, and the Veblen Prize for 'bad' boys, who doubt the fruitfulness of orthodoxy and work along different lines.

"Among the former recipients of that Prize are Myrdal and Galbraith—so I am quite satisfied with this classification of my work. But it means that I have to write an acceptance speech, in which I shall compare my work with the general trend of 'evolutionary economics', as Veblen called his undertaking. I don't know whether you have a clear idea of his work. In a way he is equivalent to an American Marx, insofar as he even advocated a revolution, but one to be led by the 'engineers' who represent the 'spirit of workmanship' in contrast with the ruling spirit of monetary profit. Considering my own emphasis on the impor- tance of the 'functional intelligentsia' as planners in the widest sense, there is even some affinity of thought between us. Well, you will see the piece in due time.

"What you wrote about your American friend who could not adjust to the German atmosphere remains a ticklish problem. I have found among my younger colleagues half a dozen people whom I would count among the finest minds and hearts I know. But I am well aware of the others, and they abound in business."

"I was delighted this morning to receive a copy of your interview on Salvation through Small Catastrophes" writes Geoffrey, September 27. "I began to read it before I finished dressing and nearly stuck in that position for some hours. But I managed to stop and lay it aside at least until this evening. I find your German remarkably easy to read, and the tale you have to tell is fascinating." And again, September 30: "I have read your wonderful Interview. Now I must read it again. Imperfect German leads me to miss or guess at meanings here and there, rather than interrupt and turn to the dictionary. But I have got and enjoyed nearly all. (It is most racily written—was it really a tape-recorded dialogue?) Are you thinking of writing a piece about the price of self-actualization? Is this as hostile to spontaneous conformity as the German concept of inner freedom? Are they the same?

"I feel more doubtful than I did about the value of small calamities. Why should we learn the right lessons? We conformed spontaneously in the old days, not to save our lives but to avoid damaging a sense of solidarity which we valued. Empire, security and the rest had helped to build up a sense of something worth belonging to. *Civis Britannicus* had the same overtones as *Civis Romanus*. A different appeal from: 'We'll all sink if you don't'.

"How subtle it is! I have in my room a book lent me by a fellow resident, in which is bound up the forms issued in 1798 'by authority' (it doesn't say whose) to every 'hundred'[18] in the South of England, commending certain measures as appropriate in the event of a French invasion. Each 'hundred' is invited to have a meeting and decide whether they agree to cooperate. If they don't, so be it— it's a free country. The only penalty is no compensation for war damage by forces of either side. But if they do, then there is a lot of work to be done. Find pounds for cattle well inland, appoint drovers, choose routes which won't block the turnpikes for the troops, choose people to stay behind, fill up forms A to F with the names of these volunteers ...

"Spontaneous consensus didn't come down from heaven; but it could go down the drain. Perhaps it has. I'll send you if I can find it a *Guardian* interview on why Tony Benn doesn't believe in Social Democracy any more. I'm not quite sure who does. Who would or should, without the spontaneous conformity to make it work? What's the good of a political philosopy which only works when everyone is getting richer? (I don't really understand the social democracy which Peter Jenkins finds in Germany but not here. Can you enlighten me?)

"Will you give me the reference of the book in which your paper appears so that I can quote it, along with *The Price of Liberty*, in something I have written? How nice of you to refer to me among the members of the Moot, and so kindly. I was a latecomer. Do you remember our walk before breakfast that morning at Jordans?

"You have a wonderful perspective. You say it was relatively parochial, i.e. national-culture-centered, for your first 40 years, but compared with mine it was universal. I managed to remain wholly unconscious politically until Munich, when I was 44! And even now I'm only a picker up of pebbles.

"I have been looking a little, this weekend, at marvellous photographs of the Pope's Irish visit. What other figure could do that in Poland and Ireland? What of America? What do you think of the role of the Catholic Church? Welcome in a world which contains B.F. Skinner and counts Maslow as a great humanitarian?"

Adolph confesses October 4 that he is very tired and hardly able to work.

"I wrote my acceptance speech for the prize in Atlanta at the end of December, otherwise I simply rest in every free minute. Well, this too will pass. To my personal worries has been added the horror of our foreign policy. This Cuba matter was the folly of the century, and for domestic reasons it continues to be dragged in. We are even sending a military mission to China to prepare for a conventional war with the Soviet Union.

"It is difficult to say whose Government is worse. In your case the radicalization of the Labour Party has now been added, making their return to power practically impossible. And what the hell do people like Benn mean by Socialism? I do not mention the dollar—quite hopeless, because all effective means would be very painful in the short run, and we are already in the midst of the election campaign. If you think back to our meeting at Brig—a century might have passed since then. And certainly the 'small catastrophes' that have occurred since have not contributed to our salvation!"

"Yes," replies Geoffrey October 15 1979, two days after his 85th birthday, "there are times when politics become overwhelming. ('Mankind you dismay me'). Perhaps we expect too much. But that brings me to your Interview. Here is a first batch of scrappy comments:

1. I was of course fascinated by the bit of personal history with which it began. How could such news (the surrender of passports) come out quietly 48 hours before the deadline? A sympathetic editor? An accident? How lucky for me and many others that you were so ready to go. But the approach to that frontier passage must be something you will always remember.

2. Spontaneous conformity—not fallen from heaven. No indeed. But how teasing your account of two cultures over seven centuries, potted in a few hundred words. Was the 'Inner Freedom' claimed by your intellectual young before the first war the same, basically, as that claimed by Western youth in, say, the '60s and typed by me as individual autonomy? And was it an intellectuals' characteristic or a wider one? I am very interested in your awareness that the influence of the intellectuals varies—from the nugatory to the overwhelming. And why?—because of the then current state of the ordinary man's awareness? And have we still a class of ordinary man with the character and influence of the burghers?

3. Instrumental analysis: I am still bothered by (a) the assumption that we (1) choose ends (2) choose means and (3) use (2) to achieve (1), because of the implication that ends are singular or compatible and also attainable. I expect you would say that you describe only one round of an iterative process whereby the most desirable and attainable end (or set of ends) becomes visible through discarding the others as their implications are realized. But, as you know, I have had occasion to criticize this type of rationality, which I associate with Herbert Simon, and I am not quite sure how far if at all we disagree. But, more importantly, (b) you seem to assume that the means are known and present, once the end is defined. I thought economists were at present in an unparalleled state of doubt about how to achieve such economic ends as stable money and sufficiently high employment. Many people over here seem to accept increasing unemployment as an indefinite trend, to be lived with and perhaps turned to some good account. Are you really so confident that you know how to implement any wishes that seem good to the governors of the new realm of Freedom?

4.   And this leads to what you have to say about socialism. Not on the agenda? Whose agenda? I think of Yugoslavia and Tanzania and Sweden as a half-way house, working until the other day, perhaps still. I think I agree that it would take a catastrophe to make UK or USA into real 'socialist' states. But are we talking of alternative states or of a spectrum? How near was Callaghan's Britain to a socialist state? Was Attlee's nearer?

"I am left with two pairs of antitheses—rightly so stated (for clarity) even if you regard them as ends of a spectrum. First, spontaneous conformity v. coerced conformity. Second, control of wages, prices and investment versus leaving them to 'the market' (and other private manipulative techniques). And I am not clear how closely they are connected or whither either leads.

"I was 'conditioned' to my spontaneous conformity (such as it was). And Cuba? And China? And what of America's response to the need to make its immigrants, at least of the second generation, feel 'American'? Isn't the manufacture of spontaneous consensus the biggest growth industry in the world?

"Of course there may be qualitative differences in the target. Consensus on 'avoiding extremes' will, if successful, produce something other than Ayatollah Khomeini seems to be after. But isn't it a specific quality of a given consensus rather than a product of consensus as such? It may be an unusual quality in that, without it, a consensus breaker might expect to be visited with wrath proportionate to the completeness of the consensus he had violated. (Offset, on second thoughts, by the fact that in a confident consensus his deviance might seem less threatening, even though more shocking.)

"And on 'control'—we now have thirty years of experience (excluding the war experience) of control in varying degrees and cultures—Western European, individual states and now EEC also; USSR, its developed satellites and the combined system which they make, perhaps others—case histories varying in method, in intensity and doubtless in outcome. Can you say, however roughly, which instrumental methods have proved adequate in what circumstances, or even what cultural change would be needed to make a society in which what instrumental methods would be effective?

"Well, enough for now. My book is only a collection of papers, all of which I think you have seen, except the last which is so inconclusive that I shan't bother you to read it! Its conclusion, not clearly stated, is that (without a degree of spontaneous consensus not now in sight) majority democratic rule no longer suffices to govern societies of any complexity, and that no imaginable degree of devolution will make it work. So what?"

"Indeed this is a tape-recorded interview" says Adolph, October 21, "subsequently slightly edited by myself. But I tried hard not to reduce its 'lightness'. Altogether the reception has so far been good, but you are the first 'foreigner' to react and therefore of special importance. Alas, I agree about your doubt in the value of small calamities. Probably the shock would have to be profound to have any beneficial effect. And this could come only from war—now a self-defeating proposition, apart from all other objections.

"Social democracy appears to me *in theory* still as the only promising political organization capable of handling our problems, even if imperfectly. But again you are right. It rests on a minimum of conformity which apparently has so far been present in Germany while things went well. The rest is about to come with growing unrest among labor. As I said in the interview, I greatly doubt that there the foundations are strong enough after those destructive centuries of history climaxed by Hitler.

"I am grateful to you for sending me the Jenkins article. But it is not only labor who is the villain. What we learn about the behavior of our oil companies over the last decade shows that irresponsibility is evenly divided. On the other hand, I simply do not see what form 'socialism' can take today—quite apart from the fact that it would be even more in need of spontaneous conformity. No, the alternative, I fear, is a new autocracy introduced with democratic slogans.

"The vastness of the country will make this difficult here. And yet, the man in the street will in the end passively accept it if it succeeds in solving some of the problems, above all the unbloody but relentless class struggle—struggle about the division of the social product—that now goes by the name of inflation. The contesting strata are new ones: big business and big labor against small business and unorganized labor plus the fixed income strata. The worst for the losers is not reduction in their real incomes, but the dwindling of their assets. What this means for social instability can be learnt from the German experience in the '20s.

"Oh yes, the Pope. Most impressive personally, but his message is understandably provoking rising protest from the 'liberal' wing of Catholicism. He is at the moment more popular with non-Catholics, who are not hurt by his conservatism."

Spontaneous conformity

Geoffrey writes (November 13) that he has been thinking a lot about spon.con. and that it seems useful to distinguish three levels:

"The basis for level 1 is commitment to *membership* of something; most typically a patria; perhaps a class or an organized class (the trade union movement) when this becomes strong enough to challenge or supersede the patria as the dominant loyalty.

"The basis for level 2 is commitment to the *institutions* of a society, especially those for containing conflict. When this breaks we have civil war. We had our last in the 17th century. Level 1 went into abeyance but did not dissolve. (Happily the division was not territorial so no question of secession arose.)

"The basis for level 3 is commitment to a *policy*. The last English example was the multiparty support for the Beveridge legislation in 1946-50. Strong consensus at level 3 reinforces level 1 and level 2. Strong divergence at level 3 reveals the strength or weakness of levels 1 and 2 and will in time erode the strongest. So developments at level 3 are continually reinforcing or sapping levels 2 and 1. For all the support for the Beveridge plan, consensus on policy was not enough to bring Labour back to power in 1951.

"Now consider the war. External threat always boosts level 1. The replacement of Chamberlain by Churchill undoubtedly fortified level 2. But even so the change in micro-economic behavior represented by food rationing might not have been successful if it had not been seen to be both necessary and fair. The necessity sprang from the fact of the blockade. The fairness sprang from the good judgment of Woolton and his colleagues. So there wasn't even a significant black market.

"Now consider our experience over the past ten years. Three rival economic policies compete for our allegiance. The social democrats of both parties have tried to get agreement on statutory or voluntary wages policy, a concept highly repugnant to the habits, and even the basic purposes, of the trade unions which have become the rival foci of loyalty. The policies have not even been manifestly fair, as were the rationing policies of the war, because it has been impossible to constrain either prices or other forms of income with equal rigor. The policies have also been assailed by two rivals—on the right Thatcherism, responding to dismay at the growth of the public sector; on the left socialism (backed by the Cambridge economists), calling for control of imports and investments and more control of industrial policy. These acute differences at level 3 have contributed to the decay of level 2, which has also been fuelled by the growing acceptability of minority pressures of all kinds. And all this has further eroded level 1.

"This is of course an incomplete summary but it will serve to explain my puzzlement over a sentence at the foot of your first page where you diagnose the evil as vain hope of *institutional* reforms, in antithesis to increased spon.con. Apart from the 'hen and egg' point, you don't mention policy. Where spon.con. is weak, is not agreed (and ultimately successful) policy a necessary focus for it? And *per contra* is not perceived weakness of policy a major solvent of spon.con.?

"That's why I asked whether you can state your macro-economic policy in terms so understandable to the man in the street that he will see the need for change in his micro-economic behavior and act accordingly, as he did in the war. I don't underestimate the value of spon.con. in implementing a policy—or at least in putting up with it—even where it is neither welcome nor understood; still less do I underestimate the need for trust in both leaders and institutions. But even the most modest democrats today expect to see the point, at least in a general way, of any policy they are asked to support, especially if it hurts them. And today, at any rate over here, they see the experts in total disagreement and thus destroying each others' credibility as competent 'instrumentalists'.

"It may be that we need a bipartisan (or rather pan-partisan) policy for internal economic behavior, as we have always needed it for external political behavior. But are you saying either that spon.con. can of itself generate effective as well as agreed policies, or that it can survive indefinitely if it doesn't? It seems to me now that not any calamity, whether large or small, will of itself suffice. It must be one which carries on its face a clear lesson for micro-economic behavior. And here that at present is lacking. Is this not so also in the USA?

"If there were two or more policies which would be likely to secure the desired result, we might be fiercely divided which to pursue. But there is none. We know what we want—stable money, full employment and rising real incomes for all. Many people know we can't have all three but none of the three competing theorists dare say so. Worst of all, the social democrats insult us by assuming that no policy will be acceptable to anyone, however rich, whom it leaves poorer. How can spon. con. emerge or survive in such circumstances?

"Hazel Henderson is an unorthodox writer on economic matters in the tradition of Fritz Schumacher, an influential spokesman, I believe, for the counter-culture. She recently published a volume of essays, *Creating Alternative Futures* (Berkeley Windhover Books 1978). But even she clings to the 18th century belief that what is good for all in general must 'ultimately' be good for each in particular. She is as far as anyone from accepting the idea of unequal burdens willingly borne and unequal benefits seen to be enjoyed.

"I have just been reading a history of the Coal Miners' Organizations from the earliest times until 1910. It is interesting and sobering to see how issues which have come to the fore in the present internal disputes of the Labour Party have been boiling away and intermittently boiling over for decades past—notably the relative advantages of political and industrial action, and the extent to which wages should be tied to prices. But more of that another time. This conflict is I think of the greatest possible importance, and I have no idea what the outcome will be and little idea even of what I would hope it would be."

The meaning of social democracy

But Adolph is sick and in no state to write a reasonable answer. In spite of this, he manages to send, November 11, a "brief word" with regard to two points in Geoffrey's letter.

"First, what do I mean by SD—Socialism—autocracy? We must be careful not to be trapped by conventional definitions. By SD I mean a democratically ruled Welfare State, based on a controlled market economy, primarily indirect controls. By Socialism I mean what Marx and later Marxists meant—please refer to the Interview. This is what I strike off the present agenda in the West (and also in the East!) as totally utopian. On the other hand, all Eastern regimes which go by the name of socialism are, in my terminologies, autocracies of a more or less draconic kind. Largely public ownership of the means of production—comprehensive direct planning—elimination of what we in the West mean by constitutional government—establishing not consensus but acceptance by coercion. If the political and economic result tends toward egalitarianism, we might speak of 'socialist autocracy'—the reverse can be named 'fascist autocracy'.

"This leads at once to your second question: should we not distinguish between agreement as to the desirable state of affairs and agreement as to how the outcome should be decided? Certainly, and in fact we have always done so. When people speak of 'formal' democracy—now usually in a negative manner—they speak of the latter. Obviously this is a necessary condition of a democratic regime. Alas, in our present upheaval it is not enough ...

"Speaking of inflation, if I am right that it has become the major tool in the class struggle, it cannot be overcome unless we have consensus about the ensuing 'shares'. It is absence of such consensus and thus escape into surreptitious robbing of certain groups that perpetuates inflation. This is the reason for my fear that only autocracy, that is coercion, will solve the problem.

"What do I mean by coercion? Ultimately the police and the army. We with our mercenary army composed 40% of disaffected blacks have laid the groundwork for this. Believe me that I find this no less horrible than you do. But I force myself to face the facts. At the same time I am desperately searching for a 'spontaneous' way of establishing consent, or at least acceptance. I have not found one.

"But one misunderstanding must be removed: I never meant to say that spon.con. could take the place of institutions. What I oppose is the blind trust in institutions and institutional reform without regard to the attitude of the public that alone can make those institutions work. Indeed, I think that I could devise a scheme of policies that would stop inflation—wage, price and profit control combined with a compact between capital and labor; taxes to mop up floating purchasing power; blocking of savings except in emergencies—just to give you a general idea. But all this is pure illusion so long as the consent of all strata of the public is absent. This makes spon.con. the key problem. Certainly what policy is effective (when supported by consent) must be found out on grounds other than spon.con. Much more needs to be said—another time. I am misusing your patience, but I know that you don't want it otherwise."

"Yes" replies Geoffrey, December 7, "I can imagine that you could produce a policy to control inflation and the rest of our ills which would work if everyone agreed on it; and I have no doubt that I personally should agree with it. In a world of old-fashioned spon.con. most people would go along with such proposals, even if they were painful, if the leaders were agreed on them, because in such a society people expect the leaders to know best. But in our society (1) people expect to be able to understand the rationale of their leaders' decisions, especially when they are painful, and (2) in this particular instance even the leaders don't agree.

"I am not saying that more agreement on policy will take the place of spon.con., or even that there can be agreement on policy without spon.con. I am rather emphasizing the opposite, namely that basic disagreement on policy cannot fail to erode spon.con. and may even produce civil war, even though the latent spon.con. may resurface later, as in my example of the English Civil War. Don't bother to write about this now.

"For the last day or two I have been engaged in a truly fearful exercise. My filing cabinets are full of files of paper generated by my 1975 talks at Berkeley and the subsequent unsuccessful book. The concept of the book originally looked clear and simple, but every version made it more complicated and more indigestible, and I now accept the fact that the final result does not deserve to be published. I have been trying to see first why it went so wrong, and secondly whether there is anything to be saved from its wreckage, especially from the earlier parts. So far I have answered the first question but not the second.

"In a sense I have already answered the second question to some extent in the various papers which I have written in the last two or three years. These have now found a publisher in California who claims to have worldwide outlets but has not yet given me any details of his outlets in England. I shall probably let him have the book nevertheless, as I would be glad to get these papers into book form though they are still half-baked. The book is called *Responsibility—its Sources and Limits*, but it does not live up to its title.[19] In the course of my mammoth turnout of papers I found a complete xeroxed book by Niebuhr called *The Responsible Self* which a friend in Washington sent me years ago. I wish I had found it before completing my book. It seems to me very good and I find his thinking very congenial ... more of that later on."

Adolph's next letter, December 16, announces that he has sent Geoffrey the first five chapters of his book.

"I sent it with much misgiving and hesitation. I simply have lost the judgment, and much rely on your honest verdict. It is not a question of details, but of the drift of the argument at large. As you will see, it breaks up at the decisive moment—simply because I am still unsure when it comes to moving from history and analysis of the present to—shall I say: therapy? Well, you will see. There is no hurry in this.

"You will be very busy with making your new book ready—what I know of those papers makes me quite confident that the book will find its readership, even if this may not be a 'majority'. Perhaps you can, after all, include parts of the earlier manuscript?

"To your brief comments on popular agreement with policy, I will only say: this is true so long as the democratic façade is maintained. And it is a major reason why I am more and more doubtful that it will be maintained. A turn to autocracy will overcome the present disagreements on policy, though I do not say that the 'victor' will have the best solution."

Cultural consensus

Geoffrey replies Christmas Eve, 1979: "Your five chapters arrived by the same post, and I read them at a sitting. I think they are wonderful. The historical perspective is precious and is illuminated by your personal experience, as well as by your knowledge and reading. There is a vast amount packed into this small compass. I shall read it again, which will be easy because it is admirably written. My only comments are these:

"First, you are not very explicit about what the spontaneous consensus 'consenses on'. You do not seem as ready as I should be to regard the generation of spontaneous consensus as the not always welcome function of any culture— a word you only use, I think, once.

"In countries where the vendetta is still practiced, cultural consensus forces a man to kill a stranger, and supports both him and the man who later kills him or his kinsman as having done what everyone agrees to be required. Duelling was similarly supported for long in England, even though against the law. In much of the world today, no-one would give evidence against a member of his family or tribe except in a family or tribal forum, even in the most outrageous case of aggravated murder. In England today trade union consensus against strike-breaking is so strong that until last month hundreds of thousands of steel workers and transport workers looked on for a year while a whole new port remained idle, because their respective unions could not agree which of them 'owned' fifty new jobs which the port had created. All these are equally examples of tacit agreement on what is and is not 'done' in given circumstances.

"They also show that the areas so governed vary in size. I think you are right in stressing that in England, for a happy period, this area was as large as a modern nation state, thus showing that this is not impossible (or has not always been impossible), despite size and class division. But I would be happier if you put it into its cultural context. For you the puzzle is to reconcile the individual and his collective nexus. For me it is to reconcile the number and variety of collectivities which compete to enable, to constrain, and even to create him.

"Secondly, I think you go too far in saying that men are not social but associable creatures. Again, it is because you do not distinguish between the social and the cultural. We call deer, wolves and apes social creatures because (a) each generation depends on the previous one for its nurture, and (b) in varying degrees the herd, pack or tribe depend on cooperation for subsistence. These relations are mediated partly by innate responses and partly by social learning. We too are social animals in this sense, as they are, though we differ, as they do, from ants and bees.

"But we, far more than they, are also acculturable and none of us is ever found or could ever be found unformed by one or more specific human cultures. I am whatever I am partly because I am English. And England is fractionally different (for ill I fear as well as good) because I have been part of it for 85 years. It would make no sense to ask what I would be like if I had not been English, because there was no 'I' until two English people started the process which bears my name and of which I later became partly and intermittently conscious. Becoming conscious of my heritage, I can work to preserve, transmit, alter or even destroy it. But I did not antedate it nor can I escape it. And all this, as it seems to me, would still be true if my life had suffered the transitions that yours has. Your exceptional understanding of the differences and historic developments of culture is, of course, partly due to your traumatic experiences, and we are the better for it. But does it really make you feel culture-free, rather than unusually culture-enriched?

"On the other hand, I don't quarrel with you for a moment in concentrating on those cultural imperatives which hold together the 160 nation states of the world, despite the competition of both internal and transnational loyalties, because these are increasingly needed (and increasingly lacking) to sustain the present organization of human life on earth. Nor do I question that current Western culture has opposed to this an atomized materialist society, which has deformed and exalted the concept of liberty into what I regard as little better than a contemptible nonsense.

"You know the authorities far better than I; but have many of them sustained the concept of liberty independent of any sense of responsibility to God or man? And by responsibility to man I mean, of course, far more than allowing them, at least in principle, an equal right to undirected license? Until after the first war a large slice of English people, I always supposed it was a majority, regarded themselves as personally responsible to a personal God for all their acts and omissions—responsible not in the sense that they expected reward or punishment but that they expected themselves to measure up to internalized standards identified with God's will.

"Christmas Eve—warm, misty and pleasant. My book on Responsibility will take care of part of the abandoned book and most of the rest might go into a book which I've been asked to write by IIASA (International Institute for Applied Systems Analysis) in Vienna. You will regret, perhaps I do, my adherence to this systems milieu (though I am delighted to find in your own book an unusual number of references to stability!)." He adds two postscripts in a letter mailed three days later:

"1. You speak of the family as the basic social unit. Is it not more correct to speak of the tribe? Most tribes, I know, are united by much real, as well as mythical kinship. But it is only the group of families, not the family, which is capable even in theory of supporting itself indefinitely through time. And it is consequently only the tribe which is a serviceable transmitter of culture. Perhaps again we encounter the subtle difference between the social and the cultural.

"2. The (Richard Neibuhr) book is evidently xeroxed from a printed book, so the name can be no mistake. Who was Richard Niebuhr? Did Reinhold Niebuhr have a brother or son? Did he change his Christian name? It's good, it might well have been written by him. But the account of his professional life on the blurb doesn't quite cover all I remember of Reinhold. Can you enlighten me?

"The world slowly and partially returns to life. Next week we await a steel strike, which seems likely to be the end of our steel industry and our motor industry. On the other hand our wild Rhodesian adventure has not yet collapsed, so we may still just hope that we may be able to lower our flag, raise our top hats, and leave the Shona and the Matabele to sort out their pecking order in their own way. This, if achieved, will show that statecraft still has possibilities among both black and white. If not achieved, it will still have been a daring effort. All good wishes for this terrible-looking New Year."

Notes

1. The new version of *The Price of Liberty* was published in 1988 under the title *Has Freedom a Future?*
2. *Op. cit.*
3. It was to be reprinted in 1983 by Harper and Row, London.
4. A completely rewritten and revised version was published in 1983 under the title: *Human Systems are Different*, Harper and Row, London.
5. Economic miracle.
6. A happy get-together.
7. The argument can be seen in Vickers, *Responsibility—Its Sources and Limits*, Intersystems Publications, 1980, in which this paper was incorporated.
8. Cincinnatus—Lucius Quinctius, early Roman general famous for his frugal simplicity. Appointed dictator in 458 BC, he defeated the Aequi in a brief campaign then resumed life as a yeoman farmer.
9. The Association for Service and Reconstruction.
10. 'Education for Systems Thinking', published in G. Vickers, *Policymaking, Communication and Social Learning*, Transaction Publishers, USA, 1987. Previously published under the title 'Systems Analysis, a Tool Subject or Judgment Demystified', in *Policy Sciences* No. 14, 1981.
11. Hungarian scientist and social philosopher, noted author on freedom of scientific thought, philosophy of science and social science. Fellow at Merton College, Oxford.
12. S.F. Spicker (ed.), *Organism, Medicine and Metaphysics*, 1-10. D. Reidel Publishing Company, Dordrecht, Holland.

13 . His words were to strike home with the atomic disaster at Chernobyl, in the Soviet Union, a few years later.

14 . Hayek, F.A. *Law, Legislation and Liberty*, Vol. 3: *The Political Order of a Free People*. Routledge & Kegan Paul, London, 1979.

15 . The incident at the Three-Mile Island nuclear plant.

16 . This was published posthumously, as *Policymaking, Communication and Social Learning* (Transaction).

17 . Gregory Bateson.

18 . Ancient sub-division of a county, common in England and Ireland and still used in the State of Delaware.

19 . Published 1980 by Intersystems Publications, in the Systems Inquiry Series, USA.

6

The Eighties

As the new decade began health problems mounted and life became very difficult, but the exchange of views which had come to mean so much to the two men continued. January 6, 1980, Adolph writes to Geoffrey about the latter's evaluation of his text:

"You cannot imagine how essential it is for me that you seem to accept the whole. It sounds ridiculous, but I have been slaving on those less than 100 pages longer than on my two books, with the result that I am quite uncertain whether there is something worthwhile in it or not. This relief of mine about your response has nothing to do with your critical comments, of which the first—what spon.con. 'consenses on'—is only too well taken. I was aware of this defect all through—it vitiates also *The Price of Liberty*—but simply could not find an answer. Frankly, your pointing to 'culture' as the lacking element may be true, but culture appears to me as vague a concept in this context as what I have said. Could you be explicit and tell me in what way 'culture' can fill the gap?

"It is different with your other two objections. I still think that all higher animals, and especially Man, are 'socialized' creatures for whom social learning is essential. This does distinguish us—and the higher animals—from ants and bees. The role of the Family is a moot point, especially if you consider the *Grossfamilie* of the nomads. The point is not essential for me. But the role of responsibility in the notion of Liberty is essential, and I am afraid it became progressively negative during much of the 19th century."

Geoffrey returns to the discussion on Adolph's paper in his letter of January 21, saying that he will read Adolph's paper again and see if there is anything more he can add:

"I can, I think, now shed some light (or what seems light to me) on the point which you raise and which I raised about the focus of consensus. May not the preservation of consensus be itself something which needs to focus and can focus dominant consensus, and may not this make a great difference to the way in which the resolution and containment of differences proceeds? When in an earlier paper I referred to common culture as being a focal value which helped to explain consensus, I think this is what I had in mind.

"I do not know whether you are familiar with the procedure of the Society of Friends. In business meetings they start from the assumption that there exists waiting to be found a course of action which everyone will agree to be the best—not merely a compromise, still less one which gets a majority of votes. The search for this 'sense of the meeting' often takes a long time, and is expected to do so. If it becomes so acrimonious as to blur the assumed goal of all parties to find the right answer, proceedings are suspended and silence reigns until people have recovered the mental attitude which they know to be necessary to the exercise. In the end, mortals just as fallible and hot-headed as other mortals do reach an agreement which not only settles the matter under dispute but, even more importantly, confirms everyone in the faith that they will be able to do so next time.

"I once read a book by a Quaker who analyzed in detail a few of the most contentious case histories which he could find in the records of his meetings over the last few decades. It was very interesting and encouraging—and amusing. I am not saying that a population of 50 million could settle all its problems that way. I am only using it as an example of the way consensus can be created and preserved simply by being valued.

"I am not questioning for a moment that humans are social animals. I am saying that they are also acculturable animals. I think this accounts both for the uniquely complex and diverse relations within each human society, and probably also for the equally unique hostility between them."

"I had better wait to resume our discussion about consent and the social nature of men until I am back in a more productive mood", writes Adolph, February 20. "Only this: when I wrote that men are 'socialized' rather than 'social' animals, I meant exactly what you seem to have in mind, namely that their 'socially useful' behavior must not be taken for granted, as is the case with ants and bees. Since we both point to the process of 'acculturation' that really 'socializes' man, we seem to be on the same wavelength after all.

"As I wrote earlier, recent events make me doubt the 'social' effect of 'minor catastrophes', though I wonder how the American people would have responded if a Roosevelt or a Churchill had used the international provocations for a serious appeal for sacrifice, combined with an adequate policy. Perhaps a potentially promising opportunity has been missed in the turmoil of electioneering.

"But while the voices multiply that tell us that we can muddle through with our present evasiveness, I very much doubt that the inner dynamics of inflation will permit us this easy way out. With double digit inflation, the demand for 'indexing' will spread, which will progressively narrow the basis that makes inflation effective as taxation. And this means that the rate of increase of inflation is bound to rise rapidly, with an uncertain inflection point where the currency will be repudiated. With us, progressive mobilization of savings for current consumption veils the actual state of affairs, by creating the impression of a 'booming' economy. What happens to the savings rate in Britain?"

Adolph writes again March 25 to say that he has been busy trying to streamline presentation without altering substance, as well as to answer Geoffrey's question: what did the 'conformants' conform about?

"In due time you will see the revised version and will tell me whether it is an improvement. Of course, the test of everything will be chapter 6, when I must say to what extent the historically quite exceptional English model can help us today. All would be easier if I could stay with the writing. But many administrative chores interfere with this, quite apart from the reduction of my creative energies. Frankly I do not feel up to a real answer even now—it would have to be very extensive. So let me just jot down a few cursory answers to some of your questions.

"Yes, Keynes had in mind a balanced budget over the period of a cycle. Alas, by 'bracketing' practically all the monopolies and arguing on the assumptions of competition, he excluded an important factor creating bottlenecks. Moreover, his concern was how to get out of depression—the threat of an inflation is mentioned only in passing. Concerning the wisdom of governmental borrowing, you must be aware that the source of these funds is mainly the Central Bank which indeed prints the money. There are some other sources, as Eurodollars floating around to the amount of $700 billions!

"Now why should the Treasury pay interest to the Bank of England? Because—this is the ancient idea—only this will prevent the Government from being irresponsible in its credit demands—a political, not an economic brake. If we can—could—trust Governments, this burden could be shed. As it is, it will be transformed into new credits! Will the balloon blow up? Yes, if runaway inflation—the final state—gets under way, which destroys the current monetary system in its entirety. Before that stage there are social strata—mainly fixed income recipients—who, by having their real purchasing power reduced by rising prices, pay the bill. But this will come to an end—possibly by general 'indexing', which leads to an astronomical spiralling of prices.

"I don't know whether these cryptic remarks are in any way helpful. But your distrust of the situation is fully justified. Your papers will prove very helpful when I redraft my section on inflation, and also for the next chapter. For the rest, we are going through the worst possible election campaign, with no candidate commanding real respect. And nothing is done to fight our 20% inflation. But we are heading here for a combined subway and bus strike which will make the city more bankrupt, quite apart from the results of the final settlement."

Third World Debt and the Overdeveloped Society

Geoffrey is glad to receive these clarifications. On April 8 he writes that, in his innocence, he did not realize that most of the increase in indebtedness was simply the result of printing money.

"I wonder how this applies to the international scene? The *Times* a day or two ago, analyzing the Brandt Report, produced the most lurid figures showing the extent to which the international indebtedness of Third World countries has increased over the last few years. I do not understand how this has happened because I would not have thought that the central banks of those countries could have expanded their currency to that extent without wholly destroying their credibility and therefore the rate at which their domestically created money could be turned into an international indebtedness.

"I have just come back from an arduous conference in Yorkshire of about thirty rather high-level technologists, mostly from the R&D departments of our big corporations. I was supposed to talk to them about current changes in values, and I knew it would be very difficult to hit the right note with an audience like that, especially after dinner. In the event it went very well, though it left me very tired.

"I cannot remember whether I sent you a copy of the first draft which I prepared before the meeting. I am going to rewrite it extensively and make a new paper of it, probably to be called 'The Overdeveloped Society'. They were shocked and intrigued when I pointed out that hunting societies and agricultural societies could become overdeveloped, and there was no reason that I could see why the same fate should not befall industrial societies. The main difference, I suggested, was that over-expanded earlier societies could always slim down by the process of emigration or colonization, whereas now the whole place is full up there is nowhere for anyone to go.

"I wonder whether this argument will seem nonsense to you? In any case don't bother to come back until you see a draft of the paper. I have been favorably impressed by a book called *The Seventh Year* by W. Jackson Davis, who is a Professor of Biology at the Santa Cruz Campus of the University of California. He seemed to have some interesting thoughts about the economic implications of scarcer supplies of energy and resources. I do not know whether it would bear on any of your thinking, or what you would think of it.

"Is the unusual experience of tacit consensus all that unusual, except in the Western world of the last two centuries? (And even there, are Sweden, Switzerland and Austria equally good examples of it?) In earlier societies, including feudal societies, it must have been almost the rule."

Adolph, May 1, had only just received Geoffrey's letter of February 26, which had arrived by seamail.

"One brief comment on our earlier discussion of public debts. The Third World, as you rightly remark, cannot act like the industrial nations by expanding their own currency. Their debts are 'real', that is, they borrow from abroad, among other creditors from OPEC. Their unavoidable failure to repay must have grave repercussions on the banking systems of their lenders.

"You are certainly right that, preceding the liberal era in the West, tacit consensus held society together. Of course it was usually 'enforced' consensus under autocratic regimes. But the element of spontaneity must not be over-looked, e.g. in the small-scale units that characterized medieval society. It is there that religion played its significant social role—a role that Mannheim hoped could be revived in modern society. You may remember that I spoke about this in my interview with the German journalist.

"Of all the useless speculation, one about a socially binding religious revival seems to me the idlest. All we have so far seen in this country of so-called religious revivals tended to extreme individualism—evangelism, that is with-drawal from the world in analogy with what Luther achieved in Germany. And it is interesting that in ancient Athens, as I indicate in my draft, spontaneous conformity and the communal controls that guarded it were apparently created by secular forces—shame and the fear of one's neighbor's disapproval.

"I can imagine how you feel about our recent imitation of your Suez adventure. One must be glad that it miscarried—it could not have succeeded without loss of Iranian lives, pushing them finally in the arms of the Russians. Our new Secretary of State is an intelligent and decent man. Whether he will be able to tame our wild Pole will have to be seen. We have a President who conducts foreign policy as if it were the response to the behavior of club members—he is offended, hurt, and reacts emotionally. We are really helpless and totally at a loss for whom to vote in November. Of course, some international disaster may solve this problem for us. At this moment I learn through the radio that you have now also a problem with Iranian hostages!

"In the meantime our inflation rate moves on. This may well prove in the end the specific disaster that will arouse the public. Whether it will be an integrating force, or lead to violent division, heaven knows. You are heading for a similar course with the Government's libertarianism. Again think back to our meeting in '73—is this the same world? Or how could we all be so blind?

"While writing this the news arrives of Sweden's strikes and lockouts. You had rightly mentioned Sweden—besides Switzerland and Austria—as a mod-ern case of spontaneous conformity. But these recent events make it clear that material interests are the predominant 'cement', and not some deeper consensus. I doubt whether matters are different in Austria. They may be so in Switzerland with its century-old tradition of three linguistic groups living together. I am always questioning my German visitors on this issue. No-one is confident that the apparent unity would survive a deeper economic crisis. Of course they, like the Swiss, were lucky in being able to conceal the rising unemployment of recent years by just sending home a large part of the *Gästarbeiter*[1]."

"Creativity has not yet emerged" writes Adolph from Hilltop, June 25. "I am rereading some old drafts, going back to the middle sixties, which deal with some of the problems that have been haunting me all these years—the dialectics of emancipation and the burden of freedom, though from different angles. Perhaps this will spark something.

"What you write mainly puzzles me. First, I always thought that hunting-farming-craftmanship developed more or less simultaneously in different regions—not in a linear 'progression' owing to the exhaustion of an earlier activity. However that may be, I cannot make sense of 'unemployment', not to say 'inflation', as valid for primitive ages. It was largely lack of manpower—growing difficulties in slave hunting—that brought the economies of Greece and late Rome down. And what does inflation mean in a non-monetarized economy? There are stories of 'debasement' of coinage on the part of ancient rulers. But the first real inflation leading to a general price rise occurred to my knowledge with the discovery of the transatlantic gold and silver mines in the 16th century.

"I confess that I am getting more and more skeptical about 'monistic' explanations of the course of history, as I do about 'perfectionist' programs of solving the world's ills. From what you indicate you seem to feel the same. Incidentally, was expansion not constrained by the 'political ownership' of territory as far back as the ancient empires—a situation which the discovery of the 'New World' changed for a little while? Does our century really differ in this respect from, say, the 17th century?

"The growing self-assertion of the European countries is all to the good—certainly so long as we have two Secretaries of State. And as to economic policy, no sooner does our strict monetary policy show some effect on the price level than we change gears and promise tax reductions that can only stimulate further inflationary expectations. And finally it looks as if Reagan cannot be beaten any more. And it does not look any better where you are. Yes, it would mean much to me if you were here—our hours together in front of the Simplon tunnel stand out in my memory."

Unemployment, populations and nationhood

Geoffrey replies July 15 with what he considers an interesting example of early unemployment.

"The BBC put on a few weeks ago a documentary film about a small independent state called, I think, Zankyar, high in the Himalayas. Life in this place seems to have gone on unchanged for at least nine hundred years. The winters are awful but in the summer the high well-watered valley bears good crops and supports a larger population than is needed for its cultivation.

"In consequence a third of the male population, and I think an even larger proportion of the women, spend their lives as Buddhist monks and nuns supported by the farming community, which takes a third of its product to their support. This serves, among other things, as one of their population controls, which apparently has worked well for many centuries and is completely accepted. Only the eldest son inherits a farm holding, and he is required by custom to retire so soon as his son attains the age of twenty and is deemed fit to take over. The narrator said that at the height of the monastic period in Europe a somewhat similar proportion of the population was to be found in monasteries, and although, of course, some of them were also engaged in producing food they must have constituted a significant safety valve for agricultural workers for whom land was not available. Of course, this is a far cry from the economy of the Roman Empire at its fullest.

"It must be a historic fact, must it not, that the human race subsisted on hunting and food gathering for a long time before any serious farming began, although I realize of course that there was a long period of overlap when still migratory peoples burned areas of forest, planted harvests in the ashes and moved on after a year or two to do the same elsewhere. There does seem to me to be something persuasive in the suggestion that better weapons first improved hunting and allowed some small increase of population, but then reduced game to an extent which still better weapons could only make worse, and thus made settled agriculture an imperative.

"You are right, of course, that apart from the most recent areas of colonization, primarily North America, the whole surface of the planet has been in the ownership of some political organization for a long time. Nonetheless, I feel that there has been a change in the last two hundred years, with the dismemberment of more than eight empires and the establishment of one hundred and sixty sovereign states of most varied sizes and powers, coupled with the extreme sanctity which has come to be attached to political boundaries because of the fear that small wars may escalate into big ones. It is interesting that even new African states have preferred to sanctify their often quite irrational boundaries rather than risk trying to tidy them up. Perhaps part of the difference is that the barriers have become so impermeable. It becomes increasingly difficult for any human being to settle anywhere outside his own country, and even multinationals find an increasing barrier both of restriction and of risk in most places.

"I am much struck by the fact that, ever since the end of the Napoleonic wars, British policy at least seems to have been animated by the conviction that free men could only live in a free country, and we took an active part, at least informally, in liberating the constituents of other empires (Spain, Turkey, Austria, Hungary) even while we were building up our own. This faith, coupled with the passionate effort to define aggression (which was a major preoccupation of the League of Nations, and was only settled a decade or two ago in the United

Nations by the reluctant admission that aggression was too ambiguous a word to be defined) seems to underly a great deal of today's troubles.

"But I am not clear enough in my head to pursue this much further. I am grateful to you for pointing out that I shall have to do so rather than simply assert that the surface of the earth has for the first time become fully owned by this variety of states. The novelty, I suppose, consists more in the variety in size and character of the states concerned. You remember that the old League of Nations was supposed to be a league of like-minded states, which reminds one of the confidence which then existed that the like-minded states were agreed on the way to combine freedom and order and that this was the only way and would soon come to be adopted by everybody.

"These are only casual thoughts—a poor substitute for a long conversation at Hilltop such as we had at Brig so many years ago. I promise you a more considered utterance later. I am at the moment greatly obsessed with a talk I have to give at an Open University Summer School at the end of this week and which seems very reluctant to set into an appropriate form.

"To revert for a moment to the question of unemployment—whatever ways a population adapts to provide itself with the necessities of life there must, it seems to me, be a limit to the size of the population which can be permanently maintained in the particular habitat and also a limit to the number of people who may be actively engaged in generating its product. I see no reason why the two numbers should be the same.

"Where the number of producers needed is more than the area can support as consumers, the situation is obviously unstable and will probably breed acute inequality in the distribution of even what is produced. Where the balance is the other way, there is a surplus of leisure available which can, in theory, either be spread or be concentrated on an activity which is not materially productive, such as the monasteries of Zankyar and medieval Europe. Of course, these activities are not wholly unproductive, apart from whatever good they may do to the souls of the participants. They copy books, keep alive the traditional wisdom and maintain the rituals which help to hold the society together.

"We, of course, have wholly lost the idea of an objective sufficiency for all because everyone is supposed to want more and more, just as we have also lost the idea of an objective insufficiency for anybody, since we now determine the poverty line, not by reference to the biological everyday need but by reference to the average income of the society. I am, of course, comparing today not with periods like the later part of the Roman Empire but with very simple communities. Nonetheless, these simple communities are not very far behind us in time. Some are contemporary, like the Kingdom of Zankyar. Even in our lifetime, the concept of poverty was based on objective insufficiency rather than on relativities; or rather it has become so in a few countries of the West, most of which seem already to be jibbing at it.

"May it not be that a formidable simplification is on the way in which the product available to a Western country, at all events to one like Britain rather than USA, will fall below contemporary standards of what is enough, but will not be expansible by any form of activity to which the unemployed can be put? I did not mean to start again. I hope your creative springs are again flowing."

"For most of us, a person is unemployed if he seeks employment but cannot get it" comments Adolph, July 23. "Within the limits of my historical knowledge this happened on a large scale in the late Middle Ages, when the serfs—who were only too much 'employed' on the land—began to run away into the craft towns, hoping to find there under the guild rules both freedom and employment. Considering the primitive technology of the time, the 'labor market' was limited and we have there the beginning of the modern proletariat.

"The problem attained large dimensions with the industrial revolution, which on the one hand greatly extended the range of employment but also put a premium on technological advances that 'saved' labor—reason being to counteract the rising wages of the employed. But there is nothing 'natural' about this—it was the consequence of the system we call capitalism and its distribution of ownership in the means of production. Moreover, the domination of private surplus obscured the fact that—soon—the unemployed had to be cared for by public subsistence. That is, the true 'costs' of unemployment were disregarded— on a large scale the same problem which we now discuss under the heading of ecology, when a firm spoils the water or the air without so far having been held to paying for these social costs.

"The simplest way of counteracting the predominant use of a labor-saving technology is to have the displacing firm pay the maintenance costs of the unemployed. I am sure that, with further automation, we shall get there, that is, place the costs where the profits arise.

"Now, the problem you raise is a serious one: is there a limit to the size of population which can be permanently maintained in a particular habitat? We certainly could not maintain the total population of Europe in the habitat of Britain. However, it is very difficult to define the limit. Belgium with more than 400 persons per square mile has one of the highest standards. Again, technology is decisive, as is division of labor among different 'habitats'. As I already stated—your second question—it is technology that limits the number of people who may be actively engaged in generating a nation's product.

"Ultimately the limit is given by the relationship of the size of population to the size of available resources. Since I expect a redistribution of the world's resources in favor of the non-Western world, I agree with you that the present Western standard is unlikely to be maintained. And Britain may well be the 'leader' in this regress because of its technological conservatism. I am not arguing against this—life may be better in a world that shuns technological 'optimization'. Only British labor wants to eat its cake and have it, which will indeed end with their eating a smaller cake. Just on the side: the territorial barriers have been impermeable only since the end of World War I."

Conservation and the true costs of production

"I am in the middle of writing a review article on the Brandt Report[2] combined with another publication called *World Conservation Strategy*, which impresses me greatly," replies Geoffrey, August 5. "What do you think of the Brandt Report? I am surprised at the unquestioned set of Western economic assumptions on which it is based. When I have done my report I think I will let you see it, in the hope that you will find time to warn me of anything you regard as grievous error. The authors ought to know what they are talking about much better than I do.

"I am very interested that you regard unemployment as 'unnatural' and one of the consequences of capitalism. I see no reason why the amount of work waiting to be done should necessarily occupy all the people available to do it, either in our own economy or among the Australian aborigines. A food gatherer who hunts all day and finds nothing seems to me to be in much the same boat as an unemployed man who spends the day looking for work. At the other end of the scale, if world steel production exceeds world demand, some steel workers are going to be out of a job, whether the means of production are privately or publicly owned. This is, of course, a major industrial issue here at the present time.

"I entirely take the point that, where producing something causes ecological damage, the cost of making good the damage should be added to the cost of the product. This cannot always be done, but it often could be, at least in theory. If in practice the result was to put the product out of business, in competition with other countries which were not pursuing the same policy, what would you do? To apply the same principle to firms which make employees redundant, not because they cannot sell their product but because they invest in labor-saving machinery, goes a lot further and I am very interested that you advocate it. It would, of course, slow up still further the rate of technological change, but that I would regard as a great advantage provided it did not destroy even more employment than the alternative.

"Economically it seems to me it would be rather less difficult if it did not have an international dimension. One of the things that surprises me in the Brandt Report is its unquestioned assumption that more and more economic interdependence is desirable as well as necessary, internationally as well as nationally. There is a lot more which I would like to discuss if only we could talk instead of writing letters.

"My talk at the Summer School went well, even if the audience rated it more highly than I did. I must make a text of it, but the absurd thing is that I am swamped with work. I have been asked to write a book for the Open University. I have this review article about Brandt on the stocks, and another review article of something I ought to read, though I do not want to. I have two or three talks waiting to be made into papers, unless they go into the Open University book instead. And like you, I find that the wheels move rather slowly and stop too soon. Never mind. We can't expect to be maintaining the output of twenty or thirty years ago."

August 14 he sends Adolph a copy of his review of the Brandt Report and asks for his comments. "I find it embarrassing to criticize a body with so much knowledge and experience as the Brandt Commission, and it would be very welcome to know how this strikes you." Adolph's response arrives by return mail, August 22.

"My reaction to the review could not be more enthusiastic. Among the many admirable papers you wrote in the course of years there are few that make their points both as strongly and as fairly as does this one. It is much more than a review—it is a measured declaration of faith based, to my way of thinking, on irrefutable facts and thoughts. And for a strange reason I feel that I can speak 'with authority'—I have not read either report. I have been trying to get the Brandt Report from the UN—they are out of stock, and the libraries accessible to me are still 'cataloguing' it. Of the other report I learnt for the first time in your paper.

"So I can go only by what you have said, knowing of some of the people involved, and being not quite unfamiliar with the issues I venture to say that your review is as objective as can be. There just appeared in the September issue of the *Scientific American* an article by Leontieff, 'The World Economy of the Year 2000'—interesting because of the statistical material, but equally biased by Western conceptions and the complete disregard of what confronts the developed nations.

"I have nothing to propose by way of change, except perhaps with regard to the ecological consequences of universal industrialization, which make it simply impossible to expand Western industry much further while the rest of the world industrializes also (carbon dioxide, heat). Considering the rapid proliferation of atom bombs, the 'shift' from North to South is unlikely to proceed peacefully—whatever we may think of the function of some 'catastrophe' for the solution of our domestic problems I cannot see how catastrophe can be avoided in the international arena—with unpredictable consequences but hardly favorable ones. Incidentally I also agree that some sort of regional autarky is more promising than more international interdependence. As I try to show in my next chapter, this is even compatible with, and even indicated by, the new technology that progressively obliterates the inequalities in resources and skill which nature and history created.

"On your letter today, only this. True, imputing the social costs of unemployment on those who create it will create a problem in international competition. But this is true of any such assessment, say, of the costs arising from 'cleaning up' the environment. The answer is simple: nations who do not assess these costs commit dumping in the proper sense of the word—selling abroad below real costs—and a proportionate tariff against such imports is legitimate.

"Your 'food gatherer who hunts all day and finds nothing' is at par with an unemployed man who in vain looks for work—because both lack at the end of the day the means to satisfy their needs. But your food gatherer was, if anything, 'overemployed'. And the reason of his failure is due to natural and technological conditions, whereas the plight of the other fellow, who was employed by walking the streets, is due to corrigible social arrangements. And it is not true that, if world steel production exceeds world demand, steel workers 'must' be out of work, except under a system of private enterprise. In a socialist system they can be kept on part-time work, receiving the same—possibly reduced—wages as other workers, because the balance between receipts and costs is necessary only for the system as a whole, not for an individual enterprise. This reminds me of a discussion I had with Michael Polanyi during the '30s—*Manchester School*, Vol. VII, No. 2, 1936—alas, I have only one copy left. If you can get hold of this, it might help clarify the difference in 'mechanism' between the two systems."

Adolph's article entitled 'What is Evolutionary Economics? Remarks upon Receipt of the Veblen-Commons Award' was published in June 1980.[3] In this he explains the background to his work on instrumental analysis as outlined in his *On Economic Knowledge* and *The Path of Economic Growth*, and the need for such analysis in dealing with the problems of what he calls the 'post-liberal present'. In bestowing the award on behalf of the Association for Evolutionary Economics, Dr.Robert Heilbroner said that the Association honored a 'true pioneer' in that discipline—a 'worldly philosopher' in whose view 'the proper role of economic theory is not only the positive task of anticipating the macro and micro failures that may disrupt society but also the normative task of prescribing the remedies that will ensure a proper degree of micro interlock and a satisfactory path of macro motion. Thus theory is important to Lowe because it is the key to social control ... But if Lowe is an interventionist, it has always been in the name of preserving, not of undermining, the values of social freedom.'

Adolph sends the reprint of his paper to Geoffrey September 11.

"I have just finished a short piece on inflation, which you will see in due course. I also finished chapter 6 of the larger draft but do not like it. Never was I so much in two minds about a project. You will be amused to hear that my German interview, which you liked, is on the desk of Helmut Schmidt. The intermediary is my friend and former student, Gräfin Döhnoff, editor of *Die Zeit*."

A special birthday gift

"Some of your American friends tell me that October 13 is a special birthday" Adolph writes, October 2 1980, "and indeed at our age every successive birthday is a special event. So I am happy to join them in wishing you not only one but a series of good years, meaning years lived in fair health and undiminished capacity of thinking and expressing it in that special idiom that you master so impressively.

"In a way I find it funny that I should write such a letter. After all, we are in as close contact as the distance of 3,000 miles permits. It is somehow a miracle that, of all our friends in the Moot, it is you and I who not only have survived but in our own manner carry on what was born then and there. I have not given up hope that we shall meet again eye-to-eye ... it makes a difference, as your past visits here and our day in Brig has taught us. In the meantime I wish for myself that our friendship may stay alive as it has by now over more than 40 years."

"How in the world did you know I had a birthday coming along?" writes Geoffrey, October 8, five days before he is to be 86. "I wonder whether you and I are the only two survivors of the Moot which met at Jordans during those months of the war. I remember very well walking with you before breakfast one morning. It is a great thing that the 3,000 miles which divide us have made so relatively little difference—though I too would immensely welcome another meeting—preferably of the Brig pattern." The mystery of the source of the 'birthday news' is solved in Geoffrey's letter of November 5. "Bayard Catron[4] rang me on my birthday and told me of the forthcoming *Festschrift*, which amazed and delighted me. I cannot believe that I am in the category that rates a *Festschrift*. It was particularly welcome to hear that you may be contributing to it."

Economics—science or profession?

"I have to thank you for two letters," Adolph had written October 23, "the first of which is a very lucid interpretation of the purpose of my work. Indeed, under the ruling conditions of 'irregularity' of economic behavior the traditional cause-effect analysis, originally borrowed from classical mechanics, is inapplicable. I draw the consequence that economics cannot be an explanatory or predictive science, but must be turned into an engineering science, which is what you mean by the term 'profession'. The limiting 'laws' stem first of all from the known engineering rules, the term used in the technological sense, which themselves are based on the laws of nature, than from psychology—alas, still an unsafe foundation—which bestows on the resulting means-ends relations at best a high degree of probability. What does not exist are 'economic laws'.

"Now the illusion that there are such laws dates from an historical 'accident'. Scientific—classical—economics was developed in an era in which the natural and social environment made 'maximizing' receipts and 'minimizing' costs a condition for survival. Under these conditions, the mechanical model could be applied with fair results of explanation and even of prediction. The error of orthodox economics is its lack of historical insight, and its transfer of that model to an historical situation—late capitalism—in which the environmental conditions have made the behavioral axiom inapplicable.

"I don't want to enlarge on this—you know that my books are devoted to this critique and to the elaboration of what I called above an engineering model. What I want to add is that even this model may well be obsolete under new historical conditions. I think that I sent you years ago the report on the two conferences that were held about my *On Economic Knowledge* in 1968, entitled 'Economic Means and Social Ends'. There, on pp. 185-188 I spoke about this. One possibility is that our insight into psychological processes may one day reveal regularities underlying what we at present see as behavioral disorder. The other possibility is that spontaneous forces may develop that will bring about an ordering of the behavioral field. In either case, sufficient regularity of economic processes may ensue that would permit us to 'explain' and even 'predict' after all. As all this would be in the context of historical and not mechanical processes, the probability of any conclusion would still be lower than in the 'sciences' proper. But all this is speculation intended only to avoid dogmatism. In the world in which we live, the engineering model is the only useful one!"

"The distinction which I draw between a professional and an academic is more radical that the one which you admit" replies Geoffrey in his November 5 letter. "I do not regard engineering as a science, even an applied science, but as a profession, although the expertise on which it draws is more largely provided by various sciences than is that of most professions. Similarly, I regard a doctor as something quite different from a biologist, although he has to know a lot of biology.

"I have written about this elsewhere and I won't expand this letter by riding my hobby horse, but I don't think it is an accident that the great professional schools have so often been at loggerheads with the academic disciplines in universities since medieval times, and I deeply deplore the current tendency to subsume the professions under the heading of applied sciences. The divisions between the fields are quite different. Recently the school of planning at MIT wanted to enrol an economist (who) insisted that he must be a member of the economics department seconded to the school of planning. But when the time came for him to be given tenure he did not get it because only the department of economics could give him the tenure and he had not been working in the department.

"All the social sciences in my view, or nearly all of them, are cursed by the same difficulty of being less able or less willing than their colleagues in the natural sciences to distinguish between the academic function of accumulating reliable knowledge and the professional function of acting competently in some defined area. I would be sorry to see economics give up the role of a science in order to become a profession. Where would the profession gets its science from?

"Of course, the professions have often contributed to the sciences. Doctors, as I have often observed, discovered viruses because they were pathogens. Biologists then explored the new area and produced a science of virology, including many viruses which are not pathogens at all. The academic leader in even the most exact science seems to me just as remote from the professional who uses some of the academic findings to pursue his professional role as does any other scientist, however exact or inexact his field of study may be.

"You probably will not agree with this, and I am not inviting you to prolong the discussion of it (unless you can briefly show me where I am wrong). But if economics is to be regarded as a profession, I shall be particularly sorry to see it compared with engineering, which seems to me to be at the other end of the scale when measured by the precision and exactitude of the laws on which it can rely.

"No, Catron has not yet sent me the papers, and I imagine that he will not do so until they are complete, but I should of course be delighted to see yours."

Adolph writes November 13 to say he is sending his contribution to the *Festschrift* by separate mail.

"Concerning your 'worthiness' to receive a *Festschrift*, you will have to put up with a view on the part of the contributors opposite to yours. If ever a pioneering mind has deserved this form of public acknowledgment, it is yours, and we all feel proud to be taking part in it.

"As to our dispute about the role of economics, I feel guilty of having misled you by my use of the term 'engineering'. What I meant was that—in contrast with tradition which, in analogy with the physical sciences, has treated economics as a cause-effect procedure based on alleged laws of motion, on the basis of which the past is to be explained and the future is to be discovered—I see it mainly as a means-end analysis in the service of 'imposing order' (your term). Such means-ends analysis is certainly part of the scientific enterprise, though heuristics—the ancient term for it—has been badly neglected since the rise of the hypothetico-deductive method applicable to the physical sciences.

"I have described the appropriate method in great detail in my *On Economic Knowledge*, and have demonstrated its concrete application in my *Path of Economic Growth*. Now the engineering aspect enters at a second stage when, as is to be expected, the findings of the first stage—instrumental analysis—differ from what the real world presents us with, namely disorder in varying degrees. There, controls enter—my term for 'imposing'—to approximate the real world to 'order'. But such 'ordering' is not just a meta-scientific step—it is the condition for making a 'means-ends' analysis empirically valid. I have even gone further by claiming that, once such ordering has been successful, we have an economic world that is again treatable with the traditional cause-effect method, because the behavioral findings of instrumental analysis can now be used as a verifiable law of motion.

"This is what in OEK I have called the 'three-pronged structure' of Political Economics—a 'resolutive' discovery of the goal-adequate structures and forces; a 'compositive' prediction of what will happen if the goal-adequate forces are activated; the linking together of these two theoretical stages by an intermediate practical stage in which political controls try to adjust the actual forces to the goal-adequate ones.

"I re-read your Chapter 8 in *Rocking Boat*, and I do not see any basic con-tradictions. It seems to postulate—of course in a much wider context—what I have been trying to carry out in economics. I leave it at that—another issue that can be fully clarified only in the give and take of a direct talk."

Responsibility, and the education of leaders

On December 1 he writes to thank Geoffrey for his *Responsibility—its Sources and Limits*, and subsequently comments on the book in his letter of January 12 1981.

"Yes indeed, the Inflation paper is my contribution to your *Festschrift*. I hope that Catron's plan to publish the *Festschrift* will succeed—it is not easy to place anything but bestsellers these days with American publishers. I plan to include large sections of the paper in my manuscript—obviously this is a major test case of 'spontaneous conformity'.

"But now let me thank you again for your little book on Responsibility. Though I knew some of the chapters from earlier drafts, there is enough new meat to satisfy a big appetite. Especially important for me is the section on 'Education in Systems Thinking'. I realize now why this is so central to you, and how you avoid the pitfalls of rigidity that mar most attempts at applying this conceptual setting to social problems. What you say there will help me greatly when I get to my chapter on 'The New Methodology'. I hope that I shall be able to clarify there the relationship between systems analysis and instrumental analysis. They actually complement each other, because in the human sphere all systems bear a normative character, even when hidden in traditions and routines.

"World population: I thought it was more than 4 billions by now, which would only strengthen your argument. Mrs. Thatcher and Mr. Reagan are about to meet, and I pray that she will not influence him too much. It is quite strange how common sense has come to the fore since the election. There is a clear attempt to create some middle ground. In fact, the Republicans practice a virtue which

I always thought was a British heritage but no longer seems so. The impending elections in Israel may symbolize a wider return to sanity.

"I was told the other day that the New School plans an Adolph Lowe Institute for Economic Research, devoted to new theoretical approaches that should be helpful for planning. I am naturally pleased, but only too well aware of the difficulty of avoiding another ivory tower enterprise."

Geoffrey, writing January 20, is "delighted that you found something in my little book on Responsibility. The paper on 'Education in Systems Thinking' excited some interest at the conference at which I gave it, and has since been reprinted in various places, but so far as I know no-one is acting on it except insofar as they always were. How far this is I do not know. I hesitated to produce the paper because of my lack of practical knowledge of current educational curricula in England and USA, but was encouraged to let it loose by an American teacher who liked it.

"Thank you for the correction about world population. I will check the Brandt Report figure. I am also much encouraged by your finding that 'common sense has come to the fore since the election'. We, as you know, are in the early stages of a most interesting debate which may result in the formation of a Social Democratic Party grouped round Roy Jenkins, now back from EEC, and including some of the real social democrats in the Labour Party. But, as you know, all fusions of this kind cause enormous trouble and it is too early to tell whether the manifest tendency towards polarization has been checked.

"I am simply delighted to hear that an Institute is to be named after you. I cannot imagine a more satisfactory or more appropriate honor."

Unfortunately he has addressed the envelope wrongly and the letter is returned to him. It finally reaches Adolph with Geoffrey's letter of May 13. Meanwhile Adolph writes again March 7.

"A long interval of silence. I have not even thanked you for your moving letter to Catron—an ample reward for all those who contributed to the *Festschrift*, though they certainly did not expect one. On my side the silence had for once a good reason: suddenly in early February the ice broke. One morning I sat down at the typewriter and within three weeks I re-wrote chapter 6. I am in no position to judge the result. It is now in Heilbroner's hands, and he will not mince words.

"As you know, I was lying fallow for practically the whole of 1980. If I knew what brought about the change I would know more about the 'creative process'—it is all a mystery. I am now starting on the chapter about the new bureaucracy and its education. Then a chapter about the new scientific approach is to follow, where I hope to 'marry' instrumental analysis with systems analysis. And then the last chapter dealing with the new ethical criteria. As you see, there is still a long way to go, but my general feeling has much improved. Let us hope that this will last.

"Our 'pollution' is located in Washington. Your lady did her best to confirm our man's obsessions with putting the clock back. I have come to the conclusion that most likely his policies will bring about that catastrophe which may be catalytic. But there is a nasty spirit of 'revivalism', which exposes all opponents as traitors."

His letter crosses one of the same date from Geoffrey, to which Adolph replies 21 March.

"I can see that your political mood is no more cheerful than mine. You are right: the title of the book might well be 'The Price of Order'. As it stands at present it is: *The Dilemma of Freedom.* I just wrote at the end of chapter 6, which has been such a chore for many months, that the post-absolutist principle 'Government should be one of Law and not of Men' can no longer be upheld. Once we succeed in overcoming the 'tyranny' of impersonal mechanisms, there are no safe 'checks and balances' that could restrain the masters of planning against their will. This is the problem with Brezhnev and his likes, after the fear of Hell has gone. At the same time this makes both the rational and the moral education of our leaders and their functionaries the most urgent issue of our age. I have some—utopian—ideas how to go about it; the topic of chapter 7."

Again, Adolph's letter has crossed with one dated March 23 from Geoffrey, who is delighted to hear that his silence has been due to inspiration and not to calamity.

"Your comments on the political scene are as I would expect. We have often discussed whether a 'mini-catastrophe' would trigger the change we need, but this view is now complicated by the query whether the catastrophe will indeed be so very 'mini'.

"I am still rather flat, and my book remains in a trough. I hope to get it going again very soon. I hope, more dubiously, that there may be something in it that I have not said before. It sounds to me as if you were working up to a conclusion more fruitful than mine.

"A Canadian friend the other day sent me the prospectus of a Japanese School of Government and Management (The Matsushita School). It is the most refreshing and astonishing document. Ethical education gets prominent attention. Philosophy, including classical philosopy of the West as well as the East, is highly stressed. It is assumed that the chief job for the future leaders of Japan is to study, understand and be proud of what Japan has been hitherto, and to work out what it needs to be in the future if its great traditions are to be carried forward. Do you know any Western school of government which puts that kind of thing in its prospectus?" He replies to Adolph's March 21 letter on April 1st.

"I am puzzled at what you write about the 'principle' that government should be one of law and not of men. It seems to me that we need to distinguish sharply between the legislative and the executive functions of government. Even the laws, of course, are made by men. But they are of greater or less generality of application and usually apply to the men who make them. The executive function, on the other hand, is surely a necessary expression of human initiative. Roman roads and viaducts, and equally Roman bread and circuses, which we are increasingly imitating, were executive acts no less than the building of a motorway; and so of course were all external acts such as the making of wars and treaties. Surely no-one ever expected these to be other than the initiatives of particular men? How the men were chosen before the event, and how they were held to account after the event, makes up much of the history of politics, but the need for men in top executive positions has surely been there since the earliest hunting tribes.

"I agree, of course, that the enormous increase in the need for executive action adds to the importance and difficulty of the executive side, but has it not always been there? And of course I agree with what you say about the moral as well as the rational education of leaders (and equally of the led).

Printing money

"At the end of last week I quite suddenly began to think and write and walk again, and I hope for another period of activity. When you have time, would you sometime tell me the answer to a most naive question which I should be able to answer for myself. When the government prints new money, does the amount appear in the total figure of government borrowing for the year, in addition to what it borrows from people at home and abroad who already have money or credit to dispose of? If not, where does it appear? I know such a question will disclose phenomenal ignorance, but I am afraid it is widespread, though I should not still be sharing it. I have now got back to the book, though I am by no means sure that it will suit the Open University or for that matter anyone else—except me."

"Many thanks for both your letters and the interesting clipping about the wonderful achievement of economics as a science" replies Adolph April 10. "What impressed me most is the acclaim the author gives to the work of my late friend Marschak. He arrived in Germany early in 1919 as a refugee from Bolshevism and was sent to me by a mutual friend. I helped him into the academic career by later bringing him to Kiel as my deputy in the Institute of World Economics. He was for a time Head of the Oxford Institute of Statistics, but left before the war for the States, where he really became the intellectual father of all those Nobelists. Alas, he died before the honor was bestowed on him.

"Substantively, the writer of the article confuses two quite distinct fields of Econometrics—the one that builds predictive models, so far a total failure and, in my opinion, for good so. The other covers indeed several specifications of instrumental analysis—you will find a brief reference to that work in OEK, pp. 261-3. But, like Molière's Jourdain, they do not know that they speak prose ...

"Concerning the difference between governments of law and of men, you must see this in the context of displacing the absolutist regimes by constitutional governments. What you say about the crucial role of men is, of course, quite true. Still, there is a difference between Henry VIII or Louis XIV and the lawful limitations to which even a Churchill and a de Gaulle were subjected. And no doubt we are moving again in the direction of less restrained executives, and there is no alternative to this within the given world.

"Certainly if the government 'creates' money this must appear somewhere. In fact, it usually does appear under borrowing, because the present technique is a loan from the Central Bank which actually 'creates' the money. It is only this type of borrowing which is inflationary. So long as government borrows from the private sector, it reduces the borrowing capacity of others. This will raise the rate of interest as a consequence of the competition between the public and the private sector, but it will not increase the total volume of spending—at least, so long as the sums lent come from current savings and not from liquidation of assets."

Geoffrey's brief note of May 13 encloses his letter to Adolph of January 20, which had been incorrectly addressed and returned to him. He writes again May 19:

"Thank you for your comments about the economic article. What puzzles me, as you know, is that whereas there may be some economic troubles where we understand the situation sufficiently to design a preferable alternative, if only people were sufficiently governable to do what is required, there seem to me to be others where we cannot plan an effective instrumental reply. Is there, for example, any known effective instrument of reply to the need to provide reasonably full employment—apart from making work more labor-intensive and sharing the wages as well as the work? An alternative presumably would be to educate people for a possible life of total unemployment. But at present nobody would consider either of these goals to be acceptable, and would therefore be uninterested in any form of instrumental solution designed to attain them.

"Thank you for confirming my understanding about the appearance of new money in the government's borrowing requirement. Am I right in thinking that it is unable to decide in advance how much of this borrowing requirement will have to be satisfied by the printing of new money and how much by the genuine borrowing of money and credit which is already in circulation? In discussions of the public sector borrowing requirement I have never seen much emphasis placed on the difference between the two sources of governmental revenue, and yet they seem to be absolutely crucial. I would have thought that all estimates, however rough, would have distinguished that part which was expected to be produced by printing money. Of course, I suppose there is the further complication that even printing money may not be inflationary since more money may actually be required (using money in the broadest sense), but I don't want to involve you further in my elementary economic education.

"I am in the middle of a critical chapter which may be similar to your critical chapter. I have found light on the ethical problem from a curious source. An American friend lately sent me Ruth Benedict's book *The Chrysanthemums and the Sword*—the analysis which she made of Japanese culture during the war to help the American Armed Forces to understand the mentality of the people they were fighting, and also to help the government in its early stages of operation when the war was over. I am particularly interested in what she has to say about the ethics of China and the way the Japanese distorted these when they imported them in order to preserve their ideas of rigid hierarchy. I won't develop this further in a letter, but it seems to me that the Chinese ethic was far better adapted to combining 'autonomy' with a common source of authority to which everyone could appeal.

"I am sorry that you find your political atmosphere oppressive. So do I. But one can always hope that we, or our successors, will climb out of the dialectical trough into a world of sufficient assurance and consensus on the other side."

"Can you think of any other civilized country" asks Adolph, June 14, "where a letter addressed as yours was would not be delivered, considering the amount of mail I get every day? But it is obviously more convenient for the Post Office to send the letter back 3000 miles. By the way, the financing of the planned Institute has run into difficulty. The main capital was to come from the German *Volkswagenstiftung*, who now drastically curtail their donations in view of the bad situation in Germany.

"I am happy to know that you keep the standard flying—I still do not know how to 'control our controllers', present and future. So forgive me if I answer your questions quite briefly. Establishing full employment? By what I call 'domestic colonization', that is, by restoring our 'infrastructure' in the widest sense of the word. Of course, this is up against the resistance of our two governments and those who put them into power. You are right in complaining about the obscurity of the addition to money supply due to printing. But the real danger is a mass liquidation of savings, amounting here to more than half a trillion dollars, if inflation continues, as it will.

"You are probably right in what you say about Chinese ethics, at least of the Confucian type. This may have been an effective 'control of the controllers'. But what will it help us? The Middle East plus Poland makes one despair. What will the French election bring? Mitterrand gave a most impressive interview to the *New York Times*—more insight into the state of the world than all Reagans, Thatchers and Schmidts taken together."

"My book for the Open University goes slowly along, but my output is limited" writes Geoffrey, June 24, "and other things which I welcome in themselves are filling my plate a little more full than I would wish it to be. This is nonetheless something to be thankful for at our age. I am grieved to hear that there is a hitch in the setting up of your Institute.

"As usual, you have said a lot in a short space. As regards reducing unemployment by increasing investment in the infrastructure, I fully see the point. But am I right in thinking that, if it was done on the scale you envisage, it would significantly alter the share of the total cake which cuts into investment as distinct from personal consumption? Would this not mean that the workforce, although more fully employed, would have to put up with little if any increase in real personal income, or more probably a reduction of it, in order to avoid inflation? It has always seemed to me very odd that governments should measure their prosperity by GNP while all their citizens measure it in net personal income and take for granted, or regard as a cost to be grudged, the increasingly elaborate infrastructure which keeps them alive. Nonetheless, they do, and it will be difficult for Western consumers to learn to regard and improve infrastructure as part of their wages."

"The turn of world events depresses me deeply" writes Adolph from Hilltop, July 11. "What goes on in England is only too symptomatic. Following 'Thatcherism' here, we shall see similar reactions in due course. But the worst is US foreign policy. I have a faint hope that the growing 'peace movement' in Europe, especially Holland and more and more in Germany, can serve as a lever for the respective governments to compel our government to undertake negotiations with the USSR seriously. More and more talk about a limited atomic war that 'can be won'. The newest idea is to imitate the Israelis by destroying the atomic installations behind the curtain with conventional bombers, that is, without an atomic attack but by doing so to lay waste and poison large stretches of land. If one could only see some center of power capable of reversing this trend.

"You answered your question about the effect of public works on consumption very well. So long as there are idle resources, consumption can in principle increase with investment. But to have the proper effect on employment, money wages must not rise—otherwise the effect is spoiled by improving the lot of some without adding to the total employed work force. Keynes was quite clear about this. He expected the pressure of the unemployed to achieve this effect, as if we had 'free competition' in the labor market. Another instance where absence of solidarity ruins an otherwise sound policy. We are always led back to this— the idea that lowering taxes 'will' increase savings belongs here too. Instead the behavior patterns of the liberal era are uncritically assumed to hold. In a way, alas, they do hold, but with totally disruptive effects. I wish I could write more cheerfully, or could think that my gloom is exclusively based on my physique."

Indexing credit—and debt

"Congratulations on the completion of the first part of the Open University book!" writes Adolph, August 2. "How many parts will there be? I have decided to lay my manuscript aside for the time being, and to do something radically different.

"Yes, you are right, a rise in the basic tax rate is an indispensable condition for stopping inflation. Another is the indexing of credit taking, so as to annul the chance of profiteering by borrowing today and paying back in devalued money. Such a measure would considerably reduce demand for funds, reducing it to the proper level of credit used for productive purposes. I proposed this years ago to members of Congress and colleagues, but hardly received an answer. Someone with 'authority' should take over the idea—I have not found him so far.

"I regard the case of Israel as practically hopeless. It will end with another Masada, only this time with the use of the atom bomb, with unforeseeable consequences for all of us."

"I am sure you are right to give your book a rest" Geoffrey writes, August 10. "I am much obsessed by mine, but encouraged by the fact that, re-reading what is done—the first two-thirds—I actually liked it, though I can't think anyone else will.

"Queer that both Thatcher and Reagan can get away with lowered basic rate and lowered (promised) inflation. For me the Thatcher government lost all credibility from the day it announced that 3-point cut in basic rate. If you want to reduce the money supply when you are borrowing some 10 billion annually, it seems a rather obvious remedy. Oh well! Yes, I see the logic of indexing credit repayments. But it's a more open-ended liability than a rise in basic rate, and I can imagine getting the second through much more easily than the first.

"It's good to be in touch. I never cease to be astonished as well as grateful at the support of so many friends—mostly transatlantic! But ... you are my only pre-war friend that counts. Indeed, I know scarcely anyone whom I first met before I was 60! Well, we'll go on supporting each other, even if we can't put the world to rights."

"I have become a member of your EXIT society" replies Adolph, August 21. "I should like to be master over my fate if it should happen that no-one should depend on my being alive any more. It is interesting that no such group exists here, and no publisher would dare to publish the Scottish pamphlet which, I know, has also aroused controversy over there.

"I go through a strange experience. For months I was totally frustrated with the book. Three weeks ago I decided to put my lecture notes on the economic theory of value on paper. What shall I say? I have more than 7000 words on paper—partly new ideas, and working on it is a real pleasure. One reason is that this is a problem where, if you postulate your premises, definite conclusions can be drawn—so different from the 'morass' of socio-political analysis. Of course, I am aware of the very different level of abstraction. Whether there will in the end be a 'spill-over' to the book I do not know at this stage. But I feel at least reassured that my troubles are not exclusively due to senility.

"Just one more word about indexing debts. It would from the outset reduce the demand for loans and thus depress interest rates—quite rightly considered as a condition for revival. In contrast, fighting inflation by high interest rates is a medicine that in the end may reduce inflation, but at the same time will choke investment—the experience in both our countries.

"The insensitivity of our government shows again in the handling of the Air Controllers' strike. They were right in locking them out to begin with. But the time has come for a face-saving compromise. *One* serious accident, which may not even be due to control failure, will arouse public opinion, and rightly so. And who can doubt that the airways *are* less safe under present conditions? So I am afraid the worst is still to come."

"About indexing debt" writes Geoffrey, September 7, "my trouble is that I find it difficult to imagine a situation in which a debtor would dare to take on a liability so open-ended. The indexes of inflation which we produce look very tidy, but they must contain large variations between what is happening to different individuals. A man taking on an indexed debt would need to be sure that, whatever else happened, the profit he made on the money would at least keep pace with the inflation of currency while he was using it. I suppose this would be so if he spent the money on, say, investment in machinery, because the machinery which he bought would have a price which would go up year by year and would be ascertainable so that he could write his capital assets up as well as down. But unless he is really sure that the operation is going to be funded, and will produce assets the value of which can be written up at a rate enormously comparable to the rate at which his debt is going up, it seems to me that he would be taking an unacceptable risk. Perhaps the proposal has a wider application than I realize. In any case, it does not look as if it is going to happen."

The four instabilities

His letter to Adolph of September 16 1981 is a cry for help.

"I am in trouble! The end of my book is in sight, but the prospect of completing it seems remote. I begin to wonder whether it is any use except as a conversation with myself. The main object of the book is to explain to technologists how much they contribute to the world's economic problems and how little they contribute to solutions. This has led me to an even more full and stunning comprehension of how complicated and obscure economics is than I had before.

"I am just completing the second of two chapters about the inherent instability of the relations between each of the world's populations and (1) its physical milieu and (2) its human milieu. The first is difficult though familiar. The second is a morass.

"For the second I have chosen four instabilities: (1) war, (2) international development, (3) inflation and (4) unemployment. I want to write something which will make the facts of economic life clearer to ordinary people, especially technologists, without being vulnerable to valid economic criticism. And I doubt if I know enough economics to do so. Of course it assumes your principle that economists are instrumental agents, carrying out other people's policies. But it raises two questions (equally familiar, I am sure, to you), namely:

1. What are the limits to what economists can do, under *any* conditions, to use money and credit in producing and (far more) distributing goods and services?

2. How far are these conditions further restricted by the ignorance and misconceptions of would-be consumers who are also both producers and electors?

"My secretary will soon have finished typing two chapters—'Instabilities in relation to the Physical Milieu' and 'Instabilities in the Human Milieu'. I will send you copies. If you could find time to glance at them and send me any comments, however caustic, I would be eternally grateful. The first is straightforward. Technology doesn't 'cause' war, but it makes it worse, generates the arms race and the military-industrial complex and all that.

"International development is much worse. What do you think of the Brandt Report? How can an international distributive system based simply on reciprocal exchange enrich those who want more than they have to offer, and could reverse the process only if their suppliers equipped them to be successful competitors? Are international credits even supposed to be repayable—even out of further credits—when each leaves a legacy of service charges of 10-15%?

"Inflation is all right in theory but here I find myself in historical ignorance. Did our national debt increase during the 19th century? I thought we were the world's creditor. Didn't Keynes expect that deficit financing in slumps would be offset by credit budgets in booms? Has it ever been? Did not industrialization at the turn of the century make goods actually cheaper?

"And so to unemployment, the only one where I feel my description can't be far off, though it offers of course no solution. The book leads up to a final chapter which tries to answer the question—what is the least that everyone would have to understand and agree on to avoid a progressive free-for-all battle in which the battling parties would get ever smaller and more violent, and the cake they were battling over even smaller because of their battles?

"I reject the idea that we are all in the same boat. Inhabitants of relatively undespoiled continents like America, or some of them, should manage to survive a bit better than, say, Indians although their culture is worse than any in its assumption that if you have enough money you're bound to have enough food. But the main puzzle is the limitation of money both as a bridge over time gaps and as a stimulator of production. Very few consumable goods can be stored for any length of time, except at great cost. Money has been the storage mechanism and as such it is breaking down.

"While I am at it, let me add one elementary query which increasingly bothers me. If I have any spare money to invest, my broker does not buy *new* shares and subscribe to *new* loans. He buys from someone else securities already invested. The seller may spend the proceeds on drink or horses. My claim to be 'investing' money seems wholly groundless. The only conceivable effect on the investee is that, if his securities appreciate on the market, he may or may not be able to borrow more cheaply next time. What does all this activity amount to? What if anything do the net profits and losses represent in terms of goods and services generated? Yet there are people who live by doing nothing but that.

"Of course, underlying both questions in different ways is the question to which you often revert—distribution. For hunters and subsistence farmers distribution (if any) was a function of production (if any) which bore no assured relation to effort. Today distribution (of goods and services) bears little relation to production but confidently assumes relation to effort (except for writers and a few similar types!) We hunt jobs. And when we catch them we form them."

Geoffrey writes again September 20, having just received the *Festschrift* paper by Adolph.

"The *Festschrift* is a great boost, and I look forward to reading it all. But I seized first on your paper, which is a masterpiece of lucidity and cogency. I hope the *Festschrift* finds a publisher. If it doesn't I expect your paper will find a wider circulation elsewhere. It certainly needs to be universally digested.

"It is no criticism that you don't answer the question 'So what?' more fully. But it does leave in my mind one economic question on which you must have views. Granted that our total demands must not exceed the total of the cake. But we don't know how big the cake will be and to some extent it is a function of what we assume it will be. Here we bump into the oddity that while, in times of stable currency, you and I can save money in cash, we collectively can't. Of course, I realize that the money I save is in a bank or building society or investment where it is doing work (except for the obscurity mentioned in my last letter about issued securities changing hands). But is this a sufficient answer?

"In my law firm we distributed sums on account of profits as money came in; and annually when the accounts were audited we credited partners' balances to their capital accounts (with or without a final cash distribution). We also distributed 25% of profits in bonus to staff. But these distributions took place after we knew the size of the cake, maybe 4-5 months after the end of the year in which the cake had been accumulating. Can you do that on a national scale? Especially when the cake or at least its consumer-constituent is shrinking?

"I wait to see whether our new political party will come out in favor of a steep rise in basic rate of income tax. Am I right in thinking that until someone does there's no hope for anyone? (If the year turned out better than expected one could allow a rebate next year!). I hope to post you next week two sections of my book on inflation and unemployment. I can improve them after reading your paper." He adds a long postscript.

"One other question. Callaghan in his last year urged our unions to keep their wage demands to 5%. They wouldn't; so we had our winter of discontent and the Thatcher backlash. But if they had done, should we be all right?

"With competition there are always as many losers as gainers, even if the pie grows. Once competition becomes an unacceptable form of distribution, radical things happen both at personal and at national level. Personally, everyone wants a job-based income. Nationally, each politico-fiscal unit, unless currently 'competitive', wants protection—except where it can arrange those 'complementary' exchanges which were the essence of the early trading world and the colonial world. Or except where it is constrained by some form of regional economic pressure, of which COMECON is the most extreme (and the most successful?).

"The folk who have been cast for the role of (passive) regulators of the system—low-skilled individuals and weak or dependent (but now not so dependent) states—are declining that role. How much respected doctrine has in consequence become mere doubletalk? What counts today is natural productivity per head of population in each politico-fiscal unit. And even that doesn't yet count with individuals when the cake is shrinking."

The limits of economic policy

Adolph's letter of September 23 is in answer to Geoffrey's previous letter of September 16.

"I had better postpone a detailed answer until I have seen your chapters. But I will respond to a few more general questions.

"First, economists—or rather governments following their advice—can in principle do *any* thing except what defies simple arithmetic, such as distributing more than is produced, or cutting taxes while increasing expenditures and at the same time balancing the budget—the promise our present government has given.

"By this I mean that technical procedures can be thought up which, when followed through, will achieve the goal. However, these procedures require that the public either applauds or acquiesces or can be forced. I need not go into details in showing that, and why these conditions are fulfilled only in rare cases. In other words, the limits of economic policy are not in the realm of techniques, but in the socio-cultural set-up which, as we know, can be changed, if at all, only slowly.

"While this is true of of developed countries, it is doubly true of the underdeveloped ones, which lack private incentive, efficient bureaucracies, etc.—you know all this. For this reason, proposals like the Brandt Report are totally utopian, as you have shown so well in your critique, with which I heartily agreed at the time. On the other hand, the recommendation to develop through private enterprise, as our Secretary of State just proclaimed at the UN, is equally utopian. Again, all socio-political and cultural preconditions are absent. The much advertized progress in Korea and Taiwan is based on huge US subventions, given for reasons of foreign policy. This will not, and even cannot, be repeated all over the globe.

"You are quite right: we are *not* all in the same boat. With the unwillingness of the West to act as the Samaritan, and the inability of the majority of the Third World to make proper use of big support, I frankly do not see any 'harmonious solution'. I expect most of them to end up with military dictatorships, armed with atom bombs and ready to start real terrorism on the large scale.

"Secondly, Public Debt and Inflation: don't fall prey to the popular bogy that a large public debt ruins a country. If it is based on genuine borrowing—not printing money—it transfers private purchasing power into public hands, contracting private demand to the same extent as it expands public demand. And the interest payment is an internal affair, where one part of the population—the taxpayers—enrich another part—the creditors. I do not know what the situation was in Britain during the 19th century—I guess that public debt played a minor role. But, more important, at least in the US, the ratio of the debt to GNP has fallen during the last two decades.

"It was not so much Keynes as some of his followers who propagated the idea that during upswings a budget surplus would compensate for the deficit during recessions. It did happen here even during the '70s, but is in no way important in view of the earlier argument.

"Thirdly, public spending of money is benign only in situations of idle resources, so long as both wages and profits are kept stable. Even then there are problems where immobilities prevent a simple adjustment. But outside this 'scenario' spending is inflationary, as I tried to show again in the piece in your *Festschrift*.

"Fourthly, the stock market. You are right that there is no assurance that, in the first instance, your savings will be invested in new stock. But if it goes into old stock, it drives the price of the old stock up, thus reducing the profit. This gives a premium to new stock, whose prices have not been driven up. But more important, the role of the stock exchange in financing new investment is quite minor, probably less than 10% in the US. New investment comes mainly from retained profits of corporations. And private savings are mainly channelled into mortgage and similar investments. I leave it at that for the moment."

Geoffrey writes his third September 1981 letter to Adolph on the 26th. It is as if he senses that his life is drawing to a close, and that not much time is left to him in which to test his ideas under the particularly fruitful conditions provided by this correspondence with his old friend, whose state of health is also precarious. He is about to mail his chapter.

"The last 2-3 pages need omitting or heavy editing, which I am deferring. The part up to there is as I mean it to be, but I have lived alone with this so long that I no longer have any idea whether I am merely articulating what everyone else knows (including even my primary audience of technologists) or missing vital elements or making elementary blunders—or even providing a useful mental spring-cleaning. You will tell me.

"The book is now substantially finished, except for its very last chapter, and for any revulsions which I may feel after I have read it through this weekend. I am delighted to hear you are through your Value paper and back on the other one. The key snags seem to me to be that:
1. the basic problem is distribution, even (or especially) where there is also shortage;
2. distribution is an ethical problem, not an automatic by-product of any imaginable form of market, though markets can be one of its mechanisms;
3. ethics resist radical or abrupt change.

"How I wish we could have a long talk! Yes, I see that high interest rates include a premium for depreciation. The fact remains that the lender, not the borrower, carries the ultimate marginal risk. The *Times* the other day had a piece about some indexed loans actually being made. As I write, our own interest structure seems to have collapsed. Do I exaggerate in my analogy with the Cheshire cat's grin?"

Adolph replies briefly September 28 to say that he will be only too happy to look at Geoffrey's economic chapter. "Be assured that I shall give it priority over everything that is not just 'life-important'!" He is delighted that Geoffrey's book is making such good progress.

"One more word about indexing credit. You don't seem to be aware that every debtor already bears the risk you speak of, in the amount of interest he is being charged. Take our 20% level. At least half of it, if not more, represents a risk premium for the bank to protect it against inflation. If the debt were indexed, interest would fall to half if not less, this risk being gone. I need not explain the stimulating effect of such a reduction, not to say that by crowding out speculators through indexing, demand for credit would fall, itself an anti-inflationary effect. I am trying to propagate the idea among banking people. Yes, Keynes' volume on *Essays in Biography* is a gem. The part on Newton is especially interesting."

"You are the most generous of teachers" writes Geoffrey, September 29. "Now two things on your most lucid letter. First, is it not possible, and would it not be desirable, for a government to show in its figures how much of its borrowing was real and how much new, printed by its central bank and shown as a debt? I can see that one can't distinguish between new credit and old, but can't one and shouldn't one distinguish increases in the (cash) money supply?

And secondly, isn't this vast market in securities significant? *'Two billions wiped off the security market yesterday'*. What of the credits which banks had given against these very securities? And are not most of a country's savings sterilized if they go into increased market prices of existing investments? The offset you mention seems minor.

"But you have enough queries from me. This week the Open University is deciding on the basis of the first half of my book whether they want it for their course. I am not much enamored of it, but I am enjoying a rest and near finality. I have (knowingly and unavoidably) worked harder and more obsessively than my organism can take. It's a relaxation to turn to unanswered letters."

Inflation and OPEC

"I am happy that the *Festschrift* finally reached you" says Adolph in a long letter written October 4. "I wrote to Catron three weeks ago enquiring whether it will be published, and asking for the one paper which seems to deal with my own work. So far no answer. Knowing what goes on in present-day book publishing, I fear that the moment is not very opportune for this venture. Here practically all houses—except university presses—have been taken over by big business and their only yardstick is profit. *Festschriften* on the other hand are usually not best-sellers. Concerning my own contribution, I had originally planned to use it in the book. But now when the shape of the book is in doubt, I don't know what will happen to that part. Anyhow, if it is of some use to you its main purpose has been fulfilled.

"I pick out from your letter the question of the 'unknown size of the cake'. With stable prices the size of the cake—quantity times average price—equals total incomes. With inflation the adjustment comes only ex-post, and for this reason induces the well-known 'spiral'. We *can* collectively save as much as we want, so long as the savings are invested; that is, so long as the resources that might have been devoted to producing consumer goods are directed to producing capital goods of any form. But of course, and this was one of Keynes's 'Columbus eggs', there is no necessary mechanism for this diversion; therefore public investment may have to fill the gap.

"I don't know whether a wage rise of only 5% would not already have been too much at the time of Callaghan it would have depended on the rise in productivity. The Austrians have so far succeeded because they have a functioning 'social compact', which kept wages within the bounds of productivity and prices down to the actual level of costs plus customary profits. Though on the surface all went quite peacefully, their laws had teeth in case of misbehavior. All this falls obviously in the realm of socio-political psychology—'conformity'—rather than of economic 'mechanisms'. Not that it is for that reason less essential. What you say about raising the basic rate of the income tax falls in the same category. Will it be accepted?

"But now to the manuscript: a most impressive document, with the basic trend of which I fully agree. First a word about the section on unemployment. I find it truly admirable—I wish I had written it. There are only two minor points:

1. Even with growing demand of the public sector, the size of consumer income need not fall if productivity rises accordingly. This is not just a classroom statement; per capita in USA has been rising, partly with the help of transfer payments, up to quite recently. Of course, there is another reason why consumer incomes may fall; fall in the rate of growth owing to international developments. But you should tune down the verb 'is falling' and state the conditions.

2. Your concept of GNP is not the conventional one. Conventionally it consists of the sum of goods and services produced during a certain period, including replacement of worn-out real capital. Public borrowing has no place there, because we deal with 'real' magnitudes. Otherwise no comment except congratulations. Perhaps the danger of technological unemployment might be stressed even more in view of the 'micro-electronic revolution', which threatens to displace most services which so far were the receptacle of industrial displacement.

"Now we come to *inflation*. There, I am afraid, I have fundamental objections. They begin with your definition of inflation on page 134. I do not know of anyone who defined it as 'worsening of the relation between economic effort and its reward'. This would make inflation a problem of a disparity between 'real' factors, whereas it is in common agreement a monetary problem that arises only once money appears as an intermediary between real exchanges. The popular definition—too much money chasing too few goods—hits the nail on the head.

"In other words, inflation as such has nothing to do with 'decreasing returns of our efforts'—a phenomenon that makes us poorer. Inflation is—in parts (oil cartel)—a futile attempt to compensate for this. As such, if there were no 'frictions' affecting incentives and thus productivity, inflation would not make us in the aggregate poorer, as taxation does not make us poorer. It redistributes real income, making buyers and creditors poorer and sellers and debtors richer. All the aims that inflationary processes pursue can be pursued without inflation, namely by taxation, which means that, as a rule, other strata will be penalized in favor of those—governments, welfare clients etc., when they wage war—who are destitute.

"I have described in my paper what the proper economic response to the oil cartel would have been. This is the way in which 'normally' any increase in the gap between 'effort' and 'reward' has been treated in 'compcustomitive capitalism'. And on the following page I indicate the reasons why the restraints of the past do not operate any more. You say yourself that the 'money effect' on prices is quite different from the relation of effort to output.

"By the way, there can be inflation even under the gold standard, as Sweden proved during the first war. An exporter of important war material, she received gold as payment and, following the rules of the gold standard, she expanded her domestic circulation of money accordingly. In other words, even under a strict gold standard the 'judgment' of the monetary authorities cannot be dispensed with. What you call 'rigidities' I would call the political weakness of democratic governments which do not dare to tax for the expenditures you mention. There we hit again at the socio-political barriers of our age, which apparently are much more 'rigid' in the big nations than in the small, like Sweden or Austria. There a 'social compact' between government, business and labor has been feasible.

"All is minor if you can bring yourself to simply dropping the idea of a discrepancy between effort and output and treat the problem as a monetary one exclusively. Well, I am eager to have your response."

Geoffrey has not yet received this letter when he writes October 14, the day after his 87th birthday.

"I have been thinking out what I was trying to say about inflation. First of all, for everyone here (except, I suppose, professional economists) rising prices mean inflation and vice versa. Even those who know that prices sometimes rise and fall for other reasons have been taught, and taught by Friedman/Thatcher, that the only and sufficient control is the money supply. I want to rub in what I express as two but should have expressed as three independent sources of variation.

1. The relation between *effort* and *supply*. Long before there were markets or even barter the hunter or fisher might work all day for nothing or catch more than he needed in half an hour. This uncertainty still subsists to some extent in fishing, whaling, agriculture, mining.

2. The relation between *supply* and *demand*. Once effective markets came into being, surpluses became valuable and specialization worth while. But a new and additional source of variation came with it. The farmer or fisherman with a bumper take was often worse off than if he had a smaller one, i.e. when everyone else had surpluses too. The manufacturer who made plastic dolls in Hong Kong and magically turned them into Argentine beef steaks was even worse off. You can't eat plastic dolls.

"All this is true of market variations even if the money mechanism on which markets depend works perfectly, i.e. reflects no more uncertainty than is inherent in the two already mentioned. (It can't reflect less except—perhaps a big exception—by providing a medium for storing wealth in flexible and convenient form.) But it may introduce a third set of uncertainties of its own in ...

3. the relation between *money supply* and *price*. If Sweden in 1914-1918 takes all that payment in gold, its prices will rise. Ditto (wasn't it?) 400 years before when Spanish galleons flooded Spain with gold from the New World. Since the medium of exchange was itself a commodity with a market price it had its own fluctuations, indeed far greater ones, because of its far-reaching effects.

"Now consider the British context in which I write. We are irrevocably past stage 1. We rely on imports to pay even for food. T.H. Huxley in the 1890s wrote a sombre essay observing that no Englishman however rich was safe from starvation. Our survival depended on preserving (1) our technological superiority and (2) our social coherence. We are on the wrong side in stage 2. We no longer compete sufficiently effectively. The only way we can become compititive (apart from a wave of inventiveness) is to cut our costs. And the only cost theoretically under our control is labor cost and that is set in the belief in an up-and-up. We could begin to learn better only if we believed absolutely that relation No. 3 was optimal and under control. But we don't, and most of us doubt whether it is even theoretically controllable by one country or even by any probable consortium of countries. "Now add one further relation ...

4.   the relation between *money supply, product supply* and *price*. Ever since Keynes (if not Douglas' social credit theories years before) we have learned to regard money supply in a fourth way, additional to its three traditional ways, namely as a stimulus to production (indirectly in the private, directly in the public sector). How then can anyone restore its credibility as an automatic regulator—or as a regulator at all—if there is no accepted measure to distinguish too much from too little?

"Finally, consider one relation which has impressed me deeply for 25 years, the relation between *developed* and *undeveloped countries*. 25 years ago I would have been amazed if I had been told that by now the terms of trade between the two would not have shifted infinitely further in favor of the undeveloped countries. They have much of the raw material and masses of cheap labor; the multinationals are tailor-made for setting them to work. And the end of the colonial era gives them unlimited leverage before their wage rates even begin to catch up on ours, even if ours were not rising at a pace which most of them would envy. Don't we need a Brandt Commission to plan the survival of Britain—if indeed anyone except the British is interested?

"Consider in particular the most dramatic recent change in the terms of trade between the two worlds, the OPEC price rise. This, I take it, was a variant of my type 2 instability. There was admittedly no real physical shortage but the producers created one. Banks created more credit to enable public and private sectors to buy their oil requirements. All prices rose by at least the increased energy price included in each. Economies in use followed. But overall the world pays much more for its oil and needs more money to pay with. Was the increase in money supply inflationary?

"The words inflation and deflation imply that there is some intermediate state which is neither. Is there? Can it be ascertained either before or even after the event? How has it been maintained in the past so far as it has? How far does this depend on free markets which no longer exist? The more I think about it, the more at sea I become.

"Finally, concerning the size of the cake. Suppose we managed our affairs as well as Austria. We decide in advance how much purchasing power to create. Suppose that at the end of the year someone says: We must have created too little because we have some human and material resources unemployed. Is this a valid argument? Surely not! Who can say that the resources if employed could have been competitively employed? Alternatively, if this argument is valid, is not the size of the cake a function (up to an uncertain point) of the purchasing power created earlier to enable the would-be participants to have bigger slices? How infinitely difficult your science is! To sum up:

1. I realize that inflation properly so called is confined to fluctuations of type 3 (right?)
2. I still think it worth while to remind people that there are also fluctuations of type 1 and 2 but I agree I haven't distinguished them clearly enough (though I do at one point distinguish them).
3. I think that even variations of type 1 will grow more important (mining thinner seams, using more expensive processes to make good shortages, etc.)
4. I am not clear whether variations of the OPEC type are to be classed in type 2 along with classic effects on price of variations in supply and demand.
5. If not, I am not clear how far variations of the OPEC sort are to be assimilated to type 3 (real inflation) or given a status of their own. I think they are bound to increase. No one knows how common they are already since classical competition ceased to control them.
6. I don't see how the control of the money supply (if it could be controlled) either to check inflation or to stimulate production, can be reconciled with the idea of a money supply which even in theory would be neither inflationary nor deflationary but objectively right.

"This book doesn't aim to be an amateur essay in economics. Its object is to explain, primarily to technologists, the instabilities of the world they live in and the extent to which technology does and/or might affect these for better or worse. In doing so it stresses the limitations of the technological fix but also takes account of the fact that, for better or worse, technologists are being roped in to model macro-economic systems on computers and are thus being drawn much more closely into the area of human governance. Two recurrent themes in the book are:

— that for more than two centuries Acts of God have been slipping into the category of governmental responsibility and control;
— that automatic controls, especially competition, have been losing prestige (a) because they have ceased to work very well and (b) because they involve losers as well as winners and in an egalitarian democracy no one expects to be a loser.

"The point you raise is partly semantic. The chapter is about 'Instabilities in the Human Milieu' and this section is about instability between wages and prices. I call it 'inflation' because I know no generally accepted word to cover all these instabilities. But I am concerned to point out that no playing around with money and credit can counteract the impoverishing effect of either a fall in the productivity of effort in real terms or a fall in its market value in money terms. Rigorous financial policy can, at least in theory, make us face economic facts, but it cannot alter them—except for its power to stimulate or damp potential economic activity which is being held up for lack of money supply.

"On OPEC, am I right in thinking that the effect of the price rise on non-OPEC countries was to give them the choice of inflating their currencies or accepting a greater degree of poverty? The OPEC countries themselves, on the other hand, must have had to increase their own money supply at least to the extent to which they brought their dollars home. Insofar as they invested them abroad, they shared of course in the depreciation which they had created. But surely they were still better off, weren't they?

"This enormous letter invites no reply of similar length, but your comments on my six sum-up points (and anything else I've got wrong) would be hugely welcome. I've a feeling that this letter is a better basis for the section on inflation than the one I sent you. But it is still probably foggier than it need be."

The following day he replies to Adolph's letter of 4 October, which had just arrived.

"I realize, of course, that economists use the word inflation only for the monetary phenomenon you describe, but is there not also an independent factor which I perhaps misleadingly call the relation between effort and reward which also affects prices? Our Civil Service pensions are said to be indexed against inflation, but what they are really indexed against is any change in the index of retail prices. If this goes up they go up, whether the cause be economic or financial.

"When OPEC prices rose, all the goods in shops rose by an amount at least equivalent to the increase in the element of energy which the price included. It may be that we were at the same time printing more money and granting more credit than we should have done, and that the total rise in price was further increased by this element. But nobody tried to distinguish between the two. In all arguments about wages and pensions the relativity to which people refer is the aggregate of these two relativities.

"I do not understand why you say that OPEC's attempt to increase its share of the cake by raising its export prices was futile. Did it not have precisely this effect? Admittedly, in that case the rise was due not to any real shortage of oil in the ground but to a cartel among the producers. But this need not always be so.

"The point I am trying to make is that throughout the colonial era the industrial West got a lot of raw materials, including energy, cheap from the underdeveloped countries, and in consequence had more to divide for the same effort than it has now. We now have to export more in order to import the same amount, quite apart from our monetary policy. Our oil exports are, I believe, now comparable in value to our oil imports and have followed the same price rise, so we are presumably no longer handicapped by this particular worsening in the terms of trade. But I imagine that the aggregate terms of trade have worsened and I am arguing that they are bound to do so increasingly as a result of the end of the colonial era.

"I think, if I remember, that this part of the argument about the colonial era is more heavily stressed in a chapter you have not seen and I hesitate to inflict it on you. But my main questions on this point of inflation are: am I not right that (1) an aggregate worsening in the terms of trade is bound to increase the price of goods in shops and is bound to lead to a demand for an increase in wages at least sufficient to offset this worsening? And (2) that this demand could not be met without introducing into the picture the quite separate but equally important element of monetary inflation?

"I am delighted that you like the chapter on unemployment. This is a particular reassurance because there are points in this, too, where I thought I might have gone wrong. I am evidently making some elementary mistake about GNP I realize that GNP means the sum of goods and services produced during a certain period. But if these are valued by the price at which they sell, and if this price is inflated by several billions of borrowed money, does it not follow that GNP includes the element of inflation? I thought it was this that distinguished it from GDP. I shall be most grateful if you will put me right on this.

"One of the 'services' produced by HMG is my old age pension. Does this appear in GNP? Or unemployment benefit? Or the 'service' of the national debt? Presumably all rates and taxes are included directly or indirectly, since they are all spent on providing services. If so, why not the surplus which is borrowed, insofar as it is all spent in providing goods and services?"

Monetary and financial policies

On October 20 he writes that, "since posting you my enormous letter, evoked by your comments on the section of my book headed Inflation, I have thought further about it and rewritten the whole section. I realize on reflection that in this section I am not talking only about inflation, but about the age-old threat of having to do more work for less return, and ultimately no return for any amount of work. It seems to me that this threat, though buried for the last few centuries, is returning again for various reasons, first to the disbelief and secondly to the horror of a generation which has come to depend absolutely on the opposite conclusion. This is one of the themes of the whole book.

"One early response to the threat is the demand to print more money and I realize that I have myself fallen into the common trap of assuming that, if indeed the perpetually up-and-up is being interrupted, it can only be because of mistaken financial policy. But one of the themes of the book is to contest this very assumption. I have therefore changed the title of the new section, and I have tried to include in the summary of this particular threat all the factors which make for it, including the monetary factor. I enclose a copy of the revised section, and I shall be very glad to know whether you think it is an improvement and what comments you may have on it.

"I have now, unbelievably, reached what appears to be the end of the book, and have even dictated a letter to the Open University, sending them copies of the second part which they have not previously seen. I do not know how long it will take them to decide whether they want to use the book for the course. If they do not I shall, of course, nonetheless offer it elsewhere; but that is for the future."

"Your letters of October 14-15 are a big step toward clarification and reconciliation of our views" says Adolph, replying by return mail October 22. "Now, you are dead right that there are two quite different sources for a price rise (or fall): events on the 'real' side and in the realm of money. For good reasons the profession confines the term 'inflation' to the latter events, because not only the 'illness' but the 'cure' are radically different.

"I would lump together—under modern conditions—your cases (1) and (2). Of course, discrepancies between supply and demand occur also as temporary distortions. But we are mainly interested in your chapter in long-term developments. And of course such long-term distortion may occur 'naturally'— Ricardo's main concern, of which more below—or 'artificially', of which OPEC is a striking example. The profession has not labelled what I will call case (1), but if you look for a label I would prefer: *effort and return*—this squares with Ricardo's concern about 'decreasing returns' of natural resources. In the course of history case (1) has been infinitely more important that case (2)—*inflation*. And you are quite right, in the long run worsening of terms of trade through 'natural' or manipulated 'OPEC' causes threatens the West with steadily falling returns per unit of effort.

"Now the 'pure' mechanism of case (1) has been described by Ricardo thus: population growth compels us to take worse and worse soil under the plough. This will raise the price of food. Labor, to maintain its standard of living, demands higher money wages—since he regards wages as being on the subsistence level such a rise is conditional for labor to survive, an argument that is not necessary. But, and there we come to an essential point, such rise in money wages cuts into profits. This is bound to curtail accumulation, and we approach a 'stationary' state with zero profits, wages at the subsistence level, population stagnant but—tremendous wealth of the landlords who earn ever more rent on intra-marginal land. Therefore he thought that free trade in corn, that imports from young countries (America) with surplus of good soil, is a condition for Britain to survive.

"There are in this temporary elements—wages on the subsistence level, little or no technical progress in agriculture—but also permanent ones. The permanent one is that, whenever 'returns per unit of effort' fall, a country gets poorer and no monetary tricks can change this fact. Thus, poverty indeed shows in rising prices if incomes in money terms remain constant with constant effort. So one monetary unit of purchasing power buys less and less in goods—the price rise is the mechanism through which the impoverishment is brought home to the consumer. Looking at the 'money supply', there is no need to increase it. The prevailing money supply is sufficient to transact a *smaller quantity* at higher prices. I condensed all this in a few sentences in the Inflation paper. Now obviously the 'remedy' can only be improvement in productivity—technical progress— which raises the return per unit of effort and thus overcomes poverty.

"So far I have confined my attention to the private sector. Now, the public sector can attain its aims only by diverting resources from the private sector, unless it is itself 'in business'. Some of the public aims are regarded as benefiting all members of the community—police, law enforcement, provision for health. These are 'accepted' by the electorate, even if their financing requires curtailing of private goods. But others—welfare provision and, sometimes, war (Vietnam) are not so regarded. 'Honest' financing, by making the public poorer, is resisted in a democracy. And so a fictitious manoeuver is substituted for open reduction of the public's consumption—unbalancing the budget, paying by increasing the money flow. It obviously cannot 'heal' the 'poverty' which public demand imposes on the public—it only redistributes the burden, from those who might have been taxed to those who cannot escape by raising the price of their services.

"Of course, in the last paragraph I have moved to my case (2)—inflation. Intentionally I have started with the government part because none of the great inflations, including our own, started in the private sector. In a small manner it did in the past in the boom periods of the cycle, when the banks overextended credit. But the subsequent depression quickly liquidated the inflationary effect. The inflationary spiral has always been a secondary reaction to the primary sin of governments—as an attempt, a fruitless one, to escape its consequences. But once initiated, this secondary force becomes (via expectations) a much stronger stimulus of case (2), perpetuating the process of rising prices long after budgets have been balanced. And of course, even without the sins of Vietnam, the cartel policy of OPEC would have led to genuine inflation if the Western public was not prepared to accept its impoverishment, expressed in higher oil prices, requiring either less consumption, or more exports than before for the old consumption, that is, curtailing the domestic market.

"But—this now is no 'impersonal mechanism'. Only with the connivance of the monetary authorities could the funds be made available to pay the higher wages etc. required seemingly to catch up with rising oil prices and its products. This is the element of truth in Friedman. To sum up: there are two quite different reasons for a rise in prices: poverty and monetary mismanagement. Though quite different, there is a connection: monetary mismanagement is a popular expedient to veil poverty, though what it does is shift the poverty burden to the socially weakest shoulders.

"Now, whether there is a money supply that is neither inflationary nor deflationary: ideally, this occurs when the supply of money is kept parallel with output. There again, Friedman is right. Only what is simple in theory is difficult in practice, considering the many causes of fluctuation of output. Keynes's idea of stimulating output through 'spending' has nothing to do with this. If you have idle resources all around (which includes also a partly frozen money stock), adding money as purchasing power acts as a lubricant, that is, by mobilizing what I called the frozen money stock, real resources are being put into employment again—if wages and prices remain unchanged. Otherwise the money stimulus is dispersed in wage-price rises instead of more employment. Again, the theory is good, but as we have learned, the 'fine tuning' required is very difficult.

"I hope that I have answered your questions; your list comes already very near to what I regard as the essence of the problem. So does your excellent postscript, except when you say that OPEC gave their buyers the choice between inflation or accepting a greater degree of poverty. Inflation only shifts the impact, does not reduce poverty. I must leave it at that." He adds a PS on GNP:

"1. Certainly, when GNP is measured at 'current' prices, the sum includes the effect of inflation. This is the reason why there is a second measure—certainly also used in Britain—in which the inflated total is deflated by a so-called 'price-deflator', some composite index. Naturally the result can only be approximate, but what is not so?

2. You have misunderstood the meaning of 'services'. It does not mean that government 'serves' you (pension or unemployment benefit) but the contribution to national provision by factors who do not produce 'goods' (police, teachers etc.) Whereas the output of goods is measured by sales price, services are measured by remuneration of the one who 'serves'.

3. Your pension, unemployment benefit, etc. are 'transfer payments', that is, they are taken away by taxes from one part of the public and given to another part. They are not counted specially, which would be double counting.

4. This may be clearer when you consider the concept of Gross National *Income*, which ideally must be equal to GNP. It consists of the wages, interest, rents, profits, that is all the items that appear in your tax declaration. Transfer payments raise the income of some at the expense of others, leaving the total unchanged. Or, if financed by inflation, they are taken care of, not too well, by the deflator."

"Certainly, any kind of 'spending' affects the *value* of GNP, expressed in money terms" he writes again November 2. "Whether it affects the *real value* of GNP depends on whether such spending mobilizes real resources that up to then were idle. This is the essence of 'Keynesianism' and his remedy for unemployment. (It works of course only if not only labor but also equipment is idle and can in this way be put back into production). If the additional government spending— not based on taxation—meets an economy with full use of resources (or with 'bottlenecks' that prevent the reintroduction of idle resources), the effect of such spending is inflationary. Does this make it clear?

"Perhaps I should add a word about the vague term 'government borrowing'. If the government borrows funds from the public which would otherwise have been spent by the public in consumption or investment, the spending of those funds by the government does not raise GNP above what it would have been anyhow. But this is a rare case of borrowing. Apart from the sheer printing of money, the funds borrowed by the government come from private *saving* that otherwise would not have been spent, and GNP rises—really or nominally—to that extent.

"I found the other day a paper of mine, published in *The Christian Newsletter*. Its main merit in retrospect is that it was edited by T.S. Eliot, whom I had to convince that, though we 'circle around', we 'center in on, etc.' but not 'around'! How great our hopes were then in spite of the immediate catastrophe of the war."

This crossed with Geoffrey's of November 3, which thanks Adolph for his of October 22: "You are the most lucid expositor ... only one question: it concerns the 'deflator' by which you tell me GNP is reduced in order to allow for inflation. I have never heard of this before. When I see references to GNP, as I constantly do, am I to assume that they are deflated or not deflated? I would have thought that it would have made a lot of difference."

Adolph tells him, November 10, that the USCouncil of Economic Advisers publishes monthly 'Economic Indicators'.

"There they offer two estimates of GNP, one in 'current dollars', one in '1972 dollars'. To arrive at the second figure they use a 'price deflator', that is, an index reflecting changes of the general price level. I do not know exactly how this index is composed—I think that it is a combination of producer and consumer price changes. Anyhow it tells us, e.g., that GNP in 1980 in current dollars amounted to *circa* $2,600 billion, whereas the 'deflated' figure is $1,480 billion. I do not know, but I assume that a similar procedure is applied in Britain either by the Treasury or the Bank of England. Any economist or City man should be able to tell you."

Geoffrey, November 25, continues to be puzzled on the question of GNP.

"The point arose, you remember, because I assumed that public borrowing was a straight addition to GNP, and you told me that this was not so. It seems to me that if a government raises funds by printing money (which I understand appears as a loan from the Central Bank) or by increasing the amount of credit, or by borrowing (at least borrowing from abroad), and spends the money which it so raises on providing the services of hospitals or schools or what not, this injection of spending power inflates GNP; and I do not see how it could be distinguished from other forms of spending which, as a measure of goods and services produced during the year, also appear in GNP. This leaves me in some doubt, I admit, about the distinction between GNP and GDP.

"The Open University held a meeting on my book nearly two weeks ago but I have not yet heard from them. I am doing a seminar tomorrow evening at a local college in a course on organizational behavior, and I take much longer preparing these things now than I used to do."

Looking back

Geoffrey's next letter is written in hospital, January 4 1982; it was to be his last letter to his old friend.

"I do hope you had Hanna[5] and the family with you over Christmas to make a private tent of peace and happiness and protect you from the spectres which haunt us on a larger scale.

"Not so I. I came into hospital three weeks ago and hope to home tomorrow or the next day. Since I have been unable to read (after day 2) or to write (until around day 20) I have had lots of time for reflection. I came in for two days of 'routine' blood transfusions (is any intervention with the human body so simple as to be called routine?) but began to bleed intestinally from what later proved to be two duodenal ulcers. The prof. held on for two more days but it didn't stop, so they operated and sewed up the ulcers. It was a relief to find I had stopped bleeding.

"I'm sure my blood was skilfully managed during the next few days. The totem pole blossomed with little bags of new colours. Then, better still, all my drips, drains and whatnots were removed. But there was some residual infection in the wound. This is being clobbered by antibiotics. It looks as if I were nearly out of that wood.

"I am more tormented than usual by the inhumanity of technology. Its selectivity is unbelievable. Why, when doing all this, neglect to humidify the bone dry air of wards kept at anything up to 80 degrees by a system neither mechanically controlled nor manually controllable, and treat the patients' coughing as a normal medical cost?

"In my reflection, my life seemed more coherent than I had realized. It divides sharply at Munich, when for the first time I became politically conscious—of a domestic rather than a foreign threat. I started a political movement in the City called The Association for Service and Reconstruction, and wrote two handbooks of its (mildly social democratic) policies. It gathered a lot of support, which embarrassed me because I did not know what to do with it. Its greatest value to me was to introduce me to Joe and so to you and the Moot.

"Phase 2 was the phony war and *The Christian Newsletter*. I wonder what coherence all those supplements would be found to have if read through now. I was startled the other day to be introduced to a seminar by the Chairman reading extensively from a book on English educational thought 1939-45, all anticipated in a CNL paper by Vickers.

"Phase 3, the war, back into the Army and my mission to British communities in South America. I've just re-read my report after 41 years. The message is confident and clear. Wonderful things are happening in beleaguered Britain. Britons abroad must be kept in touch or they will be as clueless as foreigners.

"Phase 4, a civil servant. Meetings, as the war moved to an end, about the role of Britain in Europe in the peace. No doubt anywhere that the only unoccupied Western European belligerent would have a leading part to play.

"Phase 5, the Attlee government, the Beveridge social legislation. What a change from the years after the first war. No sign visible to me that 'we' weren't as united and self-confident as during the Battle of Britain.

"Phase 6, me on the Coal Board, trying to help organize the most difficult of the nationalizations. Felt more at home with the national executive of the miners union than with my fellow board members. Fortified sense of social solidarity right across the industry. And at the same time, new theories of organization and planning, some seeming to me already misused though potentially useful. Some activity with academics, schools of management and so on.

"Phase 7, retirement and unexpected immersion as para-academic in the academic and professional world of North America, notably in organization, planning, medicine, health, management. Articulation of theories of social bonding increasingly remote from those I found there, and a growing sense of alienation from that world.

"Phase 8, 1970 onwards, sense of collapse of coherence in UK—the Wilson governments, Heath and the miners, Callaghan's failure to relate industrial and political goals of the trade union movement, 1979 winter of discontent, Thatcher. Sense of being in a country of strangers about whom no assumptions whatever can be made.

"When I list what seem to me to be the minimal constraints and commitments which need to be accepted by virtually all members of a society, if the society is to survive in tolerably stable form, it sounds like the dotings of an old man; which it is, but the more dotty when heard by those who cannot believe that any such society ever has existed or ever could exist. But it could and it did. I grew up taking it for granted.

"When I ask what has happened, why it has happened and what if anything can be done about it, I come up with the following answers:
1. It seems to me to be chiefly due to the rejection of all commitment and constraint based on occupation or political or social roles.
2. This in turn I find due (1) partly to the Enlightenment's concepts of freedom and equality and of reason as a resolver of differences in values, interests

and perceptions—all more than fully worked out now; (2) partly to the failure of all large foci of authority to do what people perhaps mistakenly have come to expect of them; (3) partly to the permeation of human thought by technological modes; and (4) partly by the dehumanization of life by ignoring the cultural dimension.

3.   I do not know what can be done about it but I expect that what will be done about it is social engineering and thought control on a very large scale.

"To understand this reversal of all my hopes I postulate a time lag built in to the succession of generations. Just as you in the 1930s could see a consensus hanging over from 1900, and I in 1945-55 could feel at home among trade unionists who came to consciousness in the 1930s, so I today find myself surrounded by, but lost in, a post-Hiroshima generation—and a generation which is post a lot of other things as well.

"Reverting to 1. above, I remember that up to 70 years ago it was commonplace for people to vow their loyalty to 'God, King and Country' and hugely to mistrust those who did not. And I ask myself whether these words do not have a meaning both wider and deeper than is—or was—commonly supposed.

"The word 'country' suggests to me a human historical-geographic system deeply rooted in space and time. Those who today accept membership of it accept duties towards it which may involve reform or revolution but which for the acceptor are inescapable and which indeed create and preserve the system by affirming it. The word 'king' is no longer convenient as a term covering all regulative and symbolic aspects of government, but we need such a word and we create such an entity whenever we acknowledge our relation to it.

"The word 'God' suggests to most people, I think, a source of the 'requiredness' involved in all responsibility. But it does not seem to me that a sense of requiredness necessarily implies one who requires, though a belief in such a one may well make the requirement stronger. (These ideas I pursue in some of the papers in that last collection, and also in the book just finished.)

"Loyalty to God, king and country may sound outmoded today, but I cannot conceive of a human society surviving after a sufficiency of its members had ceased to accord their commitment to the three systems which the words connote. Reification is a very present danger.

"I don't know why I have been moved to spell out these thoughts in a letter to you on this particular night. Perhaps it is just to mark my satisfaction at being able to express myself on paper again. Incidentally, I was told an hour ago that I may arrange to go home tomorrow."

He finishes the letter in Goring-on-Thames, January 7: "I am home again and have had a wonderful night and am revelling in being back in my own place." He adds the following postscript:

"*Summary*:

1.   All organization constrains as well as enables its parts.

2. Nearly all constraints are complementary, not mutual. We repay our debts not to the givers but to others (if at all).
3. Being good, i.e. meeting the constraints and commitments imposed by others, is far more important than being clever, and gets harder as complexity rises.
4. There is probably an optimum band for the density of the ultimate predator, man. If so, it has probably long been passed.
5. There will be room for individual heroism in the ultimate collapse, but not for collective adjustment.
6. Why not? Heroism is more valuable than adjustment."

Adolph's reply, January 19, assumes that this is yet another hurdle which Geoffrey will successfully surmount.

"At any rate, the experience seems to have strengthened your mind! How I share your resentment of what you call 'the inhumanity of technology'!

"But of course your main achievement has been the stocktaking about your past and the development it shows. I do not find it surprising that you write this to me. After all, how many of your contemporaries, with whom you are in close contact, are still alive? And you know that, by and large, in spite of our first 40 years having been spent in radically different surrounds, we are basically on the same wavelength.

"It is true, my political consciousness dates much further back, with traces even before the first war. I never told you that I accepted that war as a 'redemption' from the shallowness of the preceding period, as I felt it, and it took more than two years to wake me up to the realities. But then the breakdown of 1918 made me a political animal for the first five years of the Republic—with utopian hopes of contributing to building a 'good' society, as I understood it then. By the middle of the '20s disappointment set in, and with it the transition from a bureaucratic to an academic career.

"Well, you have read about this in that German interview I gave some years ago. Then came England and my awakening to the realities of a 'free' society. Though I never felt fully at home there—my anarchic German tradition rebelling against what, at the time, I realized as indispensable for democratic stability—this experience has stayed with me to this day, as you know. Still, I am with you that I cannot conceive of any 'solution' other than extensive 'social engineering', coupled with thought control. In fact, the latter 'institution' seems already firmly established, considering the activity of the media, together with the demise of more and more newspapers.

"Now where I have some doubt is the resurrection of God, King and Country. I know exactly what you have in mind, and agree with you that the absence of overarching loyalties is one root of the trouble. But remember what a 'dialectic' entity 'country' (nation) has become, how the most fundamental problems can be solved only supranationally, that is, by consensus of the main nations with the need to sacrifice major 'selfish' interests as nations. And king? Where else than in Britain, disregarding some small countries, is there still symbolic value in this? As far as God is concerned, you feel yourself the difficulty. This does not do away with the fundamental need for something that inspires loyalty. But I fear it can neither be resurrected nor 'invented'. I think that I can accept your handwritten summary—except your preference for heroism over 'adjustment'—it all depends who will adjust how to what ... I do hope that by receipt of this you will be fully restored."

Alas, Geoffrey was never to be fully restored. He displayed both adjustment and heroism in the face of his grave illness, trying to work until the week before he died. The blood transfusions became more and more frequent, until, in March, he was told that they would have to be daily to be of any use. He took the plunge, knowing he would lose mental clarity, and said he would have no more transfusions but would simply slip away. He returned home, where his daughter Pamela nursed and companioned him during his last few days. He died peacefully March 18, 1982, aged 87.

For Adolph, who celebrated his 89th birthday later that year, Geoffrey's death was a tremendous blow. He had lost the last of the friends with whom he had made the post-war intellectual journey, and a vital stimulant. He continued to be intellectually active and in fair physical shape with the help of a pacemaker. Soon after his wife died he left the United States in order to spend his last years near his daughter, Hanna, in Germany. Upon his return to his native country he was presented with the Grand Cross of the Order of Merit of the Federal Republic—the German equivalent of the knighthood bestowed upon Geoffrey at the end of World War II.

In 1988 he completed the proofreading of his new book *Has Freedom a Future?*[6], his update of *The Price of Liberty*. It was dedicated to Robert Heilbroner, who commented: "Adolph Lowe's book on freedom is a tract for our times, the wise testimony of one of the economists worthy of being called a worldly philosopher. It is a tough-minded analysis of the conditions needed for freedom in the modern age. I recommend it for everyone who is not afraid to wrestle with the future."

"One of the most eminent scholars of political economics alive today," says the book's blurb, "Adolph Lowe has written a broad, philosophical work examining freedom, its costs and the conditions—economic and political—under which it can be established and maintained. The culmination of a lifetime of teaching and thought, his book asserts that Western society is in the midst of a revolutionary transformation; without a new framework to replace traditional constraints, now rejected, this cultural upheaval will, he says, result in the breakdown of the order, stability and freedom which have been the foundation of modern Western society."

Notes

1 . Foreign "guest" workers.
2 . Vickers, G. 'Has Man Become a Cancer?', review of *North-South. A Programme for Survival*. Report of the Independent Commission on International Development Issues, under the Chairmanship of Willy Brandt, Pan Books 1980; and *World Conservation Strategy: Living Resource Conservation for Sustainable Development*. Report prepared by the International Union for Conservation of Nature and Natural Resources, Gland, Switzerland, 1980.
3 . Journal of Economic Issues, Vol. XIV No. 2, June 1980.
4 . Professor of Public Administration at George Washington University.
5 . Dr. Adolph Lowe's daughter.
6 . Lowe, Adolph. *Has Freedom a Future?* in The Convergence Series edited by Ruth Nanda Anshen, Praeger/Greenwood Press Inc., New York, 1988.

Epilogue

The editor of this correspondence has asked me to add a brief postscript to the body of the book. There is one reason why I welcome her request. It gives me an opportunity to give visible expression to my feelings of gratitude for what she has done, and I know that Geoffrey would join me enthusiastically. No reader can guess how heavy the labor of love has been in collecting, selecting and presenting the material that has gone into this book. Beyond this no further comments occur to me—except one. Any attentive reader may ask himself how it was at all possible that these letters were written. They portray two men whose origin, life history, national and social background, and even intellectual outlook, could hardly have been more different. The answer must be found, and I cannot stress this enough, in the fact that these letters display something more fundamental than wrestling with 'problems'. They mirror the bond of genuine friendship.

The story of how this friendship evolved, grew and persisted over four decades across the deep gulf indicated above is to me the essence of the book. At the same time, it is a challenging enigma. The nature of the mystery, though not its solution, can perhaps be best understood when we compare a friendship such as ours with love. There the erotic component explains why even radical differences in outlook and rational conviction can, at least periodically, be submerged by the flood of semi-biological energies.

Are we to conclude that genuine friendship is the strongest bond that binds two humans? Is it 'Freundschaft über alles'? I thank my friend the editor for having brought back to life those decades in which the mystery took shape.

ADOLPH LOWE
Wolfenbüttel, September 1990

Bibliography

Sir Geoffrey Vickers

1959: *The Undirected Society*, Toronto, University of Toronto Press.

1965: *The Art of Judgment*, London, Chapman & Hall; New York, Basic Books; Methuen University Paperbacks 1968; Harper & Row, 1983.

1967: *Towards a Sociology of Management*, London, Chapman & Hall; New York, Basic Books.

1968: *Value Systems and Social Process*, London, Tavistock Publications; New York, Basic Books. Paperback by Penguin Books, London 1970, and New York 1971.

1970: *Freedom in a Rocking Boat* (sub-title: *Changing Values in an Unstable Society*), London, Allen Lane, The Penguin Press. An original Pelican. US hard cover edition by Basic Books. Paperback by Penguin Books, London 1971, New York 1972.

1970: *Science and the Regulation of Society*. An occasional paper published and circulated by the Institute for the Study of Science in Human Affairs, University of Columbia.

1973: *Making Institutions Work*, London, Associated Business Programs Ltd.; New York, The Halstead Press.

1980: *Responsibility—its Sources and Limits*, Intersystems Publications, POB 624, Seaside, California 93955, USA.

1983: *Human Systems are Different*, London, Harper & Row.

1983: *Moods and Tenses* (sub-title: *Occasional Poems of an Old Man*). Published privately by Pamela Miller and Jeanne Vickers.

1984: *The Vickers Papers*, Open Systems Group (ed.), London, Harper & Row.

1987: *Policymaking, Communication and Social Learning*, edited by Adams, Forester and Catron. Transaction Publishers, New Brunswick (USA) and London (UK).

Dr. Adolph Lowe (in English)

1935: *Economics and Sociology* (sub-title: *A Plea for Cooperation in the Social Sciences)*, London; Tokyo 1953, Brazil 1956.

1937: *The Price of Liberty* (sub-title: *A German on Contemporary Britain)*, London.

1940: *The Universities in Transformation*, London.

1965: *On Economic Knowledge* (sub-title: *Toward a Science of Political Economics)*, Harper & Row, New York. German edition 1968, Frankfurt. Portuguese edition 1969, Rio de Janeiro. Japanese edition 1973, Tokyo. Second edition 1977 White Plains, USA.

1976: *The Path of Economic Growth*, Cambridge University Press, Cambridge, England.

1988: *Has Freedom a Future?* Praeger, New York and London.

Index

British Commonwealth, 28
    Constitution, 164
    Culture, 135
    Medical Research Council, 11, 36
    Operational Research Society, 107
Brown, George, 95
Brzezinski, Zbigniew, 104
Buber, Martin, 121
Buddhist monks, 187
burden of freedom, 186
Burke, 147
business monopolies, 159
Butler, Harold, 25

calamity, 174
Callaghan, Lord, 160, 171, 207, 210, 222
Cambridge economists, 173
Camus, Albert, 84, 99
    The Plague, 88-9
'Can Britain Survive?', 66
Carter, President Jimmy, 103-5, 162
Carthage, 143
Castle, Barbara, 95
catastrophes, 132, 134, 142, 145, 147, 171,
    191, 198
Catholic Church, 169
Cato, Dyonisius, 143
Catron, Bayard, 16, 98, 193, 195-7, 210
Center for Management Science, 79
Central European Federation, 28
Challenge, 153
Chamberlain, Nevile, 7, 173
changing ethics of distribution, 64, 72
Charlemagne, 161
Che Guevara, 85
checks and balances, 198
Chernobyl, 13
Cheshire cat, 209
China, 133, 169
Chinese ethics, 201
Christian Newsletter, The, 8, 9, 32, 220
Christianity and the Economic Order, 8
Chrysanthemums and the Sword, The, 201
Chrysler, 92
Churchill, 146, 173, 182, 200
Churchman, Dr. C. West, ix, 104
Cincinnatus, 146
City of Benares, 10
civil war, 172, 176
Clarke, Fred, 124
Club of Rome, 74
Coal Board, 222
coerced conformity, 171
coercion, 175
    and conflict, 70-1
collective bargaining, 61

collective relationships, 31
Colm, Gerhard, 6
COMECON, 207
command controls, 105
commitment, 4, 17
    and constraint, 130-2; see also 148,
    161-2, 222, 224
Committee on Economic Planning, 88
Common Market, 81-3
communication, 47, 78-9, 151, 158
    and control, 70
Communism, 27
    Communist countries, 158
competition, 207
compulsory arbitration, 150
computerization, 159
concept of liberty, 178
Conference on Church, Community and
    State, 8
conflict of values, 54
    of loyalty, 4
conformity, 132, 155, 210
Congress, 203
consensus, 143, 175
    focus of, 181
Conservative Party, 80-1, 147
constraints and commitments, 148, 161-2,
    222, 224; see also 130-2
consumer income, 211
containment of conflict, 65
contractual role, 91, 93
control of the controllers, 201
corporate power, 148
corporative state, 145
corruption, 165
Council of Economic Advisers, 106, 220
cowbells, 128-9
'Creating Alternative Futures', 174
Croix de Guerre, 5
Crosland, Anthony, 164
Cuba crisis, 162, 169
culture, 129, 131
    cultural consensus, 177
    cultural imperatives, 178
    cultural vacuum, 150, 152
    cultures as historical phenomena, 111
Cultural Contradictions of Capitalism, The
    (Bell), 113
cybernetics, 159
Czecho-Slovakia, 28

Dahrendorf, Rolf, 95-6
dairy cattle, 149
Darwin, 52
Davis, W. Jackson, 184
DeBrahe and Kepler, 45